ISLAM
Empire of Faith

ISLAM
Empire of Faith

Dr Suhail Saheed

MD Publications Pvt Ltd
New Delhi
www.mdppl.com

Published by :

MD Publications Pvt Ltd
"MD House", 11, Darya Ganj,
New Delhi - 110 002
Phone : +91-11-41563325 (Customer Service)
+91-11-41562846 (Editorial)
E-mail (orders): order@mdppl.com
Website: www.mdppl.com

ISBN: 978-81-7533-235-5

Published and Printed by Mr. Pranav Gupta on behalf of **MD Publications Pvt Ltd** at Mohit Enterprises, New Delhi.

PREFACE

Islam religion comes from an Arabic root word meaning "peace" and "submission." Islam teaches that one can only find peace in one's life by submitting to Almighty God (Allah) in heart, soul and deed. The same Arabic root word gives us "Salaam alaykum," ("Peace be with you"), the universal Muslim greeting.

Islam is a major world religion, with over 1 billion followers worldwide (1/5 of the world population). It is considered one of the Abrahamic, monotheistic faiths, along with Judaism and Christianity. Although usually associated with the Arabs of the Middle East, less than 10% of Muslims are in fact Arab. Muslims are found all over the world, of every nation, color and race.

Allah is the proper name for Almighty God, and is often translated merely as "God." Allah has other names that are used to describe His characteristics: the Creator, the Sustainer, the Merciful, the Compassionate, etc. Muslims believe that since Allah alone is the Creator, it is He alone that deserves our devout love and worship. Islam holds to a strict monotheism. Any worship and prayers directed at saints, prophets, other human beings or nature is considered idolatry.

The Qur'an teaches that God (Allah in Arabic), has sent prophets to other peoples, revealing the true religion of Islam. Muhammad, the last prophet (the seal of the prophets), has called them to return to the true faith. Those who reject his message will to be doomed to a fiery hell on the Day of Judgement. The Qur'an distinguishes between the monotheistic People of the Book (Jews, Christians and Sabeans), and polytheists or idolators on the other hand.

The central holy text of Islam is the Qur'an. Muslims believe that the words of the Qur'an were directly revealed by God, through the Prophet Muhammad. The Qur'an is a source of inspiration and guidance to Muslims, filled with reminders of God's mercy and blessings, warnings of punishment for wrongdoers, stories of ancient peoples and the lessons they learned, and instructions for daily living.

The basic beliefs of Muslims fall into six main categories, which are known as the "Articles of Faith" - i). Faith in the unity of God, ii). Faith in angels, iii). Faith in prophets, iv). Faith in books of revelation, v). Faith in an after life and vi). Faith in destiny/divine decree.

I am very grateful to Mr Pranav Gupta, Director of MD Publications Pvt Ltd, New Delhi for his kind cooperation and support for this book.

Dr Suhail Saheed

Contents

	Preface	*v*
1.	The Origins and Rise of Islam	1
2.	Education and Science in Building the Empire of Islam	37
3.	The Golden Age of Islam	75
4.	Empire of Faith and Obedience	145
5.	Faith in Prophets	207
6.	Moderate Islam and Faith	235
	Bibliography	283
	Index	287

1

The Origins and Rise of Islam

THE SPREAD OF ISLAM

The message of Islam went forth with electrifying speed from the oasis cities of Makkah and Madinah in the Arabian Desert. Within half a century of the Prophet's death, Islam had spread to three continents. Islam is not; as some imagine in the West, a religion of the sword or did it spread primarily by means of war. It was only within Arabia, where a crude form of idolatry was rampant, that Islam was propagated by warring against those tribes which did not accept the message of God—whereas Christians and Jews were not forced to convert. Outside of Arabia also the vast lands conquered by the Arab armies in a short period became Muslim not by force of the sword but by the appeal of the new religion. It was faith in One God and emphasis upon His Mercy that brought vast numbers of people into the fold of Islam. The new religion did not coerce people to convert. Many continued to remain Jews and Christians and to this day important communities of the followers of these faiths are found in Muslim lands.

Moreover, the spread of Islam was not limited to its miraculous early expansion outside of Arabia. During later centuries the Turks embraced Islam peacefully as did a large number of the people of the Indian subcontinent and the

Malay-speaking world. In Africa also, Islam has spread during the past two centuries even under the mighty power of European colonial rulers. Today Islam continues to grow not only in Africa but also in Europe and America where Muslims now comprise a notable minority. Islam was destined to become a world religion and to create a civilization which stretched from one end of the globe to the other. Already during the early Muslim caliphates, first the Arabs, then the Persians and later the Turks set about to create classical Islamic civilization. Later, in the 13th century, both Africa and India became great centers of Islamic civilization and soon thereafter Muslim kingdoms were established in the Malay-Indonesian world while Chinese Muslims flourished throughout China.

GLOBAL RELIGION

Islam is a religion for all people from whatever race or background they might be. That is why Islamic civilization is based on a unity which stands completely against any racial or ethnic discrimination. Such major racial and ethnic groups as the Arabs, Persians, Turks, Africans, Indians, Chinese and Malays in addition to numerous smaller units embraced Islam and contributed to the building of Islamic civilization. Moreover, Islam was not opposed to learning from the earlier civilizations and incorporating their science, learning, and culture into its own world view, as long as they did not oppose the principles of Islam. Each ethnic and racial group which embraced Islam made its contribution to the one Islamic civilization to which everyone belonged.

The sense of brotherhood and sisterhood was so much emphasized that it overcame all local attachments to a particular tribe, race, or language—all of which became subservient to the universal brotherhood and sisterhood of Islam. The global civilization thus created by Islam permitted people of diverse ethnic backgrounds to work together in cultivating various arts and sciences. Although the civilization was profoundly Islamic, even non-Muslim "people of the book" participated in the intellectual activity whose fruits belonged to everyone. The scientific climate was reminiscent of the present situation in America where scientists and men and women of learning from all over the world are active in the advancement of knowledge which belongs to everyone.

The global civilization created by Islam also succeeded in activating the mind and thought of the people who entered its fold. As a result of Islam, the nomadic Arabs became torch-bearers of science and learning. The Persians who had created a great civilization before the rise of Islam nevertheless produced much more science and learning in the Islamic period than before. The same can be said of the Turks and other peoples who embraced Islam. The religion of Islam was itself responsible not only for the creation of a world civilization in which people of many different ethnic backgrounds participated, but it played a central role in developing intellectual and cultural life on a scale not seen before. For some eight hundred years Arabic remained the major intellectual and scientific language of the world.

During the centuries following the rise of Islam, Muslim dynasties ruling in various parts of the Islamic world bore witness to the flowering of Islamic culture and thought. In fact this tradition of intellectual activity was eclipsed only at the beginning of modern times as a result of the weakening of faith among Muslims combined with external domination. And today this activity has begun anew in many parts of the Islamic world now that the Muslims have regained their political independence.

Rise of Islam

Muhammad, a prophet astute in statecraft and military strategy ýand an inspired statesman, changed the history and destiny of Arabia and of much of ýthe world. He was born about 570 to the Banu Hashim family, reputable merchants in the tribe of Quraysh in Mecca. According to tradition, he was a penniless orphan who married Khadija, the widow of a rich merchant, somewhat older than himself. He probably engaged in trade, and is said by some to have had responsibilities in connection with the Ka'aba stone. When he was about forty years old he began preaching a new religion, eventually meeting the opposition of Meccan oligarchy. Initially, Muhammad made few converts and many enemies. His first converts were Khadija, Ali (who became the husband of Fatima), and Abu-Bakr.

The Hijra

From about 620, Mecca became actively hostile, since much of its revenues depended on its pagan shrine, the Kaaba, under the protection of the Quraysh, and an attack on the existing Arab religion was an attack on the prosperity of Mecca. Following the death of Khadija in 621, Muham-mad married eleven other women. Tradition relates that he and his followers were invited to the town of Yathrib by Jewish and Christian tribes after they were no longer welcome in Mecca. In 622, the first year of the Muslim calendar, they set out on the Hijra, the emigration to Yathrib, later renamed Medina, meaning "the city" where Muhammad concluded a treaty with the tribes of Medina. A large number of Medinans, known as the Ansar (helpers), were attracted to Muhammad's cause. According to several sources, early versions of Islamic practice included Jewish practices such as the fast of Yom Kippur and prayer to Jerusalem, perhaps influenced by the Jews of Medina. These were eventually dropped, and the direction of prayer was turned to Mecca.

Battle of Badr

In 624 Muhammad learned of a war party of the Quraysh, who were setting out to Medina to avenge the apparently accidental death of one Hadrami, a relative of the leader of the Quraysh. Muhammad and his army, aided by the Ansar auxiliaries, rode out to meet them at Badr. This battle, related in the Quran, is often called the first battle of Islam, but in fact there had been several skirmishes before Badr. Despite the numerical superiority of the Qurayshites, the Battle of Badr was apparently a clear victory for Muhammad. The Quraysh lost about 70 warriors and leaders and 70 captured (these "round" numbers may be historical conventions) out of a fighting force of about a thousand.

Battle of Uhud

The Qurayshites prepared better for the battle of Uhud, fought in the following year. They gathered a force of some 3,000 men, including a strong cavalry contingent led by Khalid Ibn Walid, later a famous general of Islam. The battle was fought in the vally of Aqiq, north of Yathrib (Medina) in the shadow of Mount Uhud. Though the Muslims had the initial advantage, they fell to looting the camp of the Meccans and abandoned a good archery position in the high ground. This allowed Khalid ibn Walid to save the day for the Qurayshites and inflict heavy losses on the Muslims and the tradition relates that the Muslims lost 70 men in this battle. Uhud is often called the second battle of Islam, because it is the second battle referred to in the Quran, or perhaps because it was the second Ghazwa. A Ghazwa is a large scale raid that was led by Muhammad in person.

Battle of the Trench

Muhammad believed firmly in his position as last of the prophets and as successor of Jesus. Therefore, he seems at first to have expected that the Jews and Christians would welcome him and accept his revelations, but he was soon disappointed. Medina had a large Jewish population that controlled most of the wealth of the city, and a portion of them at least refused to give their new ruler any kind of religious allegiance. Muhammad, after a long quarrel, appropriated much of their property, and destroyed two Jewish tribes, the Banu Nadir and the Banu Quraizah.

Muhammad fought the Banu Nadir and expelled them from Meccah. According to tradition, in 627, remnants of the Banu Nadir instigated the formation of a large alliance (Ahzab) of tribes including the Quraysh, the Banu Quraiza and others and mounted an attack on Medina with a force of about 20,000.

Muhammad and his followers constructed a trench around Medina as a part of its fortification, purposely making one section narrower than the rest, so that the Meccan attackers would try to cross the trench at that point. This formed a convenient trap which resulted in the death of many Meccans. Unable to cross the trench, the Meccans besieged Medina. Medina was saved by a miracle reminiscent of the destruction of Senacharib before Jerusalem. After 27 days of siege, according to tradition, God sent a piercing blast of the cold east wind. The enemy's tents were torn up; their fires were put out, the sand and rain beat in their faces. Terrified by the portents, they broke camp and lifted the siege.

Treaty of Hudaybieh

In 628, Muhammad and his followers set out on a pilgrimage to Mecca, and met the Quraysh tribe at Hudaybiyeh, where the Quraysh had assembled to block the pilgrimage. Instead of fighting, the enemies concluded a treaty and the Muslims agreed not to make the pilgrimage that year. Instead, they turned on the Jews of the town of Khaybar, who were now no longer protected by the Quraysh, and attacked and subjugated the city.

Conquest of Mecca

By 630, Muhammad and the Muslims were strong enough to attack and conquer Mecca, despite the treaty, alleging that the Quraysh had violated the treaty first. The Meccans were forced to convert to Islam and the powerful Quraish and Umayya tribes were incorporated into the Islamic leadership by giving members of their leaders, especially Uthman, prominent positions in the military and government. By this time pagan Arabia had been converted, and the Prophet's missionaries, or legates, were active in the Eastern Empire, in Persia, and in Ethiopia.

The new religion evolved into a way of life and recipe for community organization, providing a religious and ideological framework for uniting the Arab tribes, and a social and organizational framework for regulating the unified action of the nomads. The separate tribes had been re-formed into a Muslim-Arab Umma (community). The Quran is, among other things, a handbook for rules of war, prescribing the laws of treaties and of booty and commanding the faithful to Jihad, (holy war) against any who interfere with the practice of Islam. In practice, Jihad was often carried out as aggressive war well beyond the borders of Islam. Muhammad had created powerful force that could now wrest control of much of the subcontinent. In 632, Muhammad died after a short illness.

Though he had been an astute statesman, he failed to make any arrangements for his succession. His successors were chosen one after the other from among the family and supporters of Muhammad. Abu Bakr, father-law of Muhammad, was his first successor. He was given command of the faithful as Khalifa (Caliph, deputy) of Muhammad. Several tribes living at some distance from Mecca refused to accept his rule, and a war of secession, the *Ridda,* was fought by Abu Bakr and his able general Khalid ibn al Walid to subjugate these tribes. Muslim successes in these wars and real or perceived threats from the neighboring Persian and Byzantine empires initiated a series of wars of conquest outside the Arabian Peninsula. Abu Bakr died in 634, and was replaced by Umar, who completed the initial expansion of Islam. The Byzantine and Persian empires had been greatly weakened by their struggles with each other and internal decay.

The Arabs had perfected a form of warfare suitable for the desert, and for those times and conditions. The swordsmen mounted on camels, and living by raids and foraging were self-sufficient and didn't concern themselves with supply lines. They could come out of the desert that bordered Persian and Byzantine domains and strike at will. If they failed in battle, they could quickly retreat into the desert, where it was difficult for enemies mounted on horseback to follow. The failing Byzantine and Persian empires could not organize field armies large enough to decisively defeat the Arabs, nor could they provide the manpower for proper stationary defensive fortifications. The Arabs quickly conquered Syria, Palestine, Iraq, Egypt and Persia. The Caliph Umar conquered Jerusalem in 640, and guaranteed the safety of the Christian holy places.

The Caliphate moved from Arabia

On the death of Umar (Omar) in 644, Uthman was chosen as Caliph. Uthman was murdered by mutinous soldiers in 656, provoking a civil war over the succession, and laying the foundation for an eventual split. In place of Uthma Ali, the son-in-law of Muhammad, who had married his daughter Fatima, became Caliph. Ali moved the capital from Media to Kufa, in what is now Iraq. The Arabian Peninsula, which had spawned Islam, remained an important religious center and the site of the holy pilgrimage to Mecca, but it was politically eclipsed and did not play an important part in the subsequent expansion of Islam. Ali fought a civil war against supporters of the party of Uthman and others. He defeated the widow of Muhammad and her supporters at Basra, in modern Iraq, in the battle of the Camel. Mu'awiya, who ruled the province of Syria from Damascus, claimed that he was the legitimate successor to the Caliphate, and challenged Ali indecisively in the battle of Sittin in 657.

The Kharjites (meaning "those who left") protested against the compromise outcome of the battle and formed a separate movement as adherents of Ali. They continued to be important until about the eleventh century and eventually evolved into Ibadi Islam. Ibadism is neither Sunni nor Shia, and exists mainly in Oman, East Africa, the Mzab valley in Algeria, the Nafus Mountains of Libya, and Jerba Island in Tunisia today. Ali was murdered in 661 and the Caliphate moved to Damascus under Mu'awiya, who founded the Umayyad dynasty. In the course of history, Islam diverged into numerous schools and sects with different approaches and philosophies ranging from fierce and puritanical schools such as the Wahhabi of Saudi Arabia to tolerant and spiritualistic Sufi practitioners. Four different Sufi schools (Tasawwuf) arose in different parts of the Islamic world: The Naqshbandiah, the Qadriah, the Chishtiah, and Suharwardiah. Sunni (meaning "orthodox") Sunni Islam includes four systems of law ((Madh'hab). One of these, the school of Malik ibn Anas (died in 796) which is observed today in much of Africa and Indonesia, originated with the scholars of Medina. The three other Sunni law schools (Hanafi, Shafii, and Hanbali) developed at about the same time, mostly based on Iraqi scholarship.

Rise of Shi'ism

Despite civil discord, Mu'awiya continued the rapid expansion of Islam throughout central and Eastern Asia, including Afghanistan. Mu'awiya also launched the first Muslim expeditions against Byzantine Constantinople, though he was unsuccessful. In 680, Mu'awiya died and was succeeded by Yazid. Yazid was challenged by Hussayn, the son of Ali, in the same year, and Hussayn and his followers were massacred in the battle of Karbala in Iraq. This event formed the impetus for the growth of the dissident Shi'ite movement, which had begun with the death of Ali in opposition to the Umayyads. The ranks of the Shi'ites were swelled by various discontented groups, notably by newly converted non-Arab Muslims, the *Mawali,* who demanded equal rights with Arabs. The Shi'a supported successors of Ali and family members of the Prophet as the only legitimate Caliphs. They spawned several related political and religious movements including the Isma'ili sect, the Carmathians and the Fatimid movement and dynasty. A central belief of the Shi'ites relates to the coming of a special leader, the *Mahdi,* the Muslim equivalent of the Jewish and Christian Messiah.

The majority of Shi'ites recognizes a line of twelve leaders, or Imams beginning with Ali and ending with Muhammad al Muntazar (Muhammad, the awaited one). These Shia, known as *"Twelvers,"* believe that the Twelfth Imam did not die but disappeared in 874, and that he will return as the "rightly guided leader," or *Mahdi,* and usher in a new, more perfect order. A second Shia group, the Ismailis, or the *"Seveners,"* follow a line of Imams that challenged the Seventh Imam and supported a younger brother, Ismail. The major Shi'a ritual is Ashura, the commemoration of the death of Husayn. Other practices include pilgrimages to shrines of Ali and his relatives. The Alawi of Syria and Lebanon are considered to be a branch of Ismaili Shi'ism, as is the Druze religion, which originated in Fatimid Egypt. Druze, Ismailis and Alawi share beliefs in emanations of God, in supernatural hierarchies, and in the transmigration of souls.

The Umayyads

In 683 Yazid died. A second civil war ensued, ending in Umayyad victory at the battle of Marj Rahit. The Caliph Marwan ruled for only a year, but arranged for the succession of his son Abd-al Malik. Abd-al Malik consolidated Arab gains and put down revolts by Kharjites and others with a heavy hand. His deputy Al-Hajjaj ibn Yussef was send to Iraq against its governor, the brother of Ibn al-Zubayr who was in rebellion, and after dealing with him, al-Hajjaj was sent to Mecca with Syrian troops under his command to subdue the rebellion of Ibn al-Zubayr and his followers. After a seven-month siege, Ibn al-Zubayr was killed and unity was restored to the Muslim empire. Al-Hajjaj's cruelty became a byword in Islam. He is said to have told the faithful at a mosque in Baghdad, "I have seen that some heads have ripened and are ready to be picked, I will be the one to pick them."

Abd-al Malik was succeeded in 705 by Walid, whose reign represented the height of Ummayad power. Walid resumed the expansion of the Muslim empire, conquering Sind in India and landing in Spain for the first time in 710. Walid was succeeded in 715 by Sulayman, who mounted a disastrous expedition against Constantinople that almost ruined the Arab state. In 717 he died, passing the Caliphate to Umar ibn Abdel Aziz, or Umar II. Umar II, a pious and able ruler, reconstructed and restored the Arabian empire. However, he reigned only 3 years, and was followed by Yazid and Hisham, and Marwan, the last Umayyad ruler in the East. In the West however, the Umayyads established an independent dynast in Spain, where Abd ar Rahman III became Caliph in 912. The last Umayyad Caliph of Spain was Hisham III, who ruled until 1032.

The Abbasids and the Climax of Arab Power

Disenfranchised and dissatisfied elements including Shi'ites united under the leadership of Abu Muslim in Persia, and raised a black flag of rebellion in Khurasan. These forces quickly gathered strength and swept away the resistance of the Arab tribes at the battle of the Great Zab, bringing to power Abu'l Abbas known as *al Saffah,* founder of the Abbasid caliphate. The rise of the Abbasid caliphate represented a true social revolution. Arabs been displaced by Persians and others. The distinctions of aristocracy disappeared. The distinction between Arab Muslims and converted Muslims was likewise wiped away and the basis was laid for the eclectic and tolerant Muslim society of the golden age of Islam. The Abbasid caliph Al-Mansour built a capital city on an island between the Tigris and the Euphrates rivers, in place of a small Persian village. He called his capital *Madinat as-Salam* - the city of peace, but it came to be known by most people by its older Persian name, Baghdad.

The Golden Age

The apogee of Abbasid power came under the famous caliph Haroun al-Rashid. The Arab/Muslim Empire had expanded from the Arabian Peninsula to cover all of North Africa, Mesopotamia and central Asia in a very brief period. Under Haroun Al Rashid (786-809) and his successors, Baghdad became the cultural center of the world, at a time when Europe was lost in the darkness of the early middle Ages. In particular, during the reign of Al-Ma'mun (819-833), Iraq and the Arabian empire catalyzed a remarkable cultural revolution, which included the generation of poetry and literature, compilations of folktales such as the famous tales of the 1001 Arabian nights, and translation of works of science and philosophy from other languages into Arabic, preserving and propagating the ancient classics. Baghdad was probably the richest city in the world. The caliph Al-Ma'mun collected texts, employed translators such as Hunayn ibn Ishaq, and established an academy in Baghdad, the Bayt al-Hikmah ("House of Wisdom"), with a large library and an observatory and research center, and private patrons encouraged science and the arts as well.

The contrast of the brilliance of Arab Islamic civilization with the benighted Frankish empire in Europe, ruled by illiterate monarchs such as Charlemagne, is striking. Muslim activity had a profound effect, not only on Muslim intellectual life, but also on the intellectual life of Western Europe. Much of the science and philosophy taught in universities in the Middle Ages was derived from Arabic translations, rendered into Latin in Spain in the 12th century. For the realm of Islam as well as for parts of Europe, the Muslim Arabs became the brokers of a cultural revolution, transmitting and integrating works of science, as well as technical advances from the far east, including the introduction of paper from China, and the introduction of the zero into mathematics from India, along with the "Arabic" numerals and system of reckoning that are used today throughout the world.

Further Spread of Islam

Though the caliphate splintered, Islam spread under various rulers to Sub-Saharan Africa and South East Asia, and into Indonesia. In Europe, in addition to Spain the Arabs began attacking Sicily as early as the reign of Mu'awiya. A serious effort was direct at Sicily by Ziyadatallah the Muslim ruler of Tunisia in 827, when aiding the dissident Byzantine admiral Euphemious. He sent a force of about a hundred ships, and with the fortuitous arrival of Spanish Muslims, was able to gain a foothold, occupying Palermo in 831. Muslim rule in Sicily and parts of southern Italy lasted until 1091 when they were finally expelled by the Normans under Roger I. Spain (Al-Andalus) was conquered by successive waves of Muslim invasions in the eighth century.

The Muslim advance into Europe was soon halted at the battle of Tours (also known as *the battle of Tours and Poitiers* and the *battle of Poitiers*) in 732. According to some accounts, this was an impressive and critical battle. Abd-er Rahman, governor of Spain led an army estimated to 60,000 to 400,000 soldiers across the Western Pyrenees and toward the Loire River, but they were met just outside the city of Tours by Charles Martel, (Charles the Hammer) and the Frankish Army, and defeated. According to other accounts the Muslim army was a small forward force. In any case, the Muslims persisted in Spain and solidified their hold there, Arabinizing the culture of Spain and enriching European culture. Spain soon became an independent Muslim country and parts of Spain remained in Muslim hands until it was conquered by Christians and the Muslims expelled or converted at the end of the 15th century. To this day, the expulsion from Spain is remembered with bitterness by Muslims, and Spain, known as *Al-Andalus* in Arabic, is considered territory lost from Dar al Islam (the realm of peace) to Dar al Harb (the realm of war).

Fall of the Abbasids and Decline of the Arabs

The Arab empire began to disintegrate soon after the Golden age, and a period of independent Caliphates and successive chaotic invasions followed. The Shi'ite Fatimids established an independent Caliphate in North Africa in

910, and conquered Egypt in 969, founding the city of Cairo. The Buwayhids occupied the throne of Persia in 932 and conquered Baghdad in 945. The Seljuk Turks in turn conquered Baghdad in 1055, and their rule spread to Syria and Palestine, where they displaced the Fatimids. The Fatimids, based in Egypt, briefly retook Jerusalem in 1098. In these centuries the Assassin sect arose, based mainly in Iran Iraq and derived from the Ismai'ilis. They were hired killers who services were offered to various Muslim rulers. It is frequently said that they used Hashish as a means of increasing their ferocity, but this may be a spurious tale.

The Crusades

The Muslims were challenged by the Crusaders who arrived in the Middle East in 1096 and captured Jerusalem in 1099. The Muslim world reacted slowly but surely to the unexpected and unwelcome intrusion of the "Franks." Salah Eddin, a Kurd, took control of Fatimid Egypt and declared an end to the Fatimid dynasty in 1171. He reconquered Jerusalem in 1187, having defeated the Crusaders at the battle of Hattin. The Crusaders lingered on in Syria and Palestine. The last fortress of the Crusaders, Acre, fell in 1291.

The Mongols

Despite the conquest of Baghdad by the Buwayhids and Seljuk Turks, the Abbasids still ruled nominally as Caliphs until 1258, when the Mongols under Hulagu (also Holagu, Huleku) sacked Baghdad, ending the temporal power of the Caliphate. The Mongols swept across the Middle East, reaching the Mediterranean and wreaking havoc in the already weakened remains of the Arab empire. The advance of Hulagu was finally stopped at the battle of Ayn Jalut near Nazereth in Palestine in 1260. The Mongols eventually converted to Islam and were integrated in the Muslim domains. However, the invasion of Hulagu was followed in the fourteenth and fifteen centuries by the invasion of Tamurlaine, who conquered Samarkand in central Asia and reached Syria about 1401.

The Mamluke Turks

The Mamlukes were a slave caste of warriors. About 1250 they took power in Egypt from the remains of the Ayubbid dynasty founded by Salah Eddin. It was they who defeated the Mongols at Ayn Jalut. Their rule was quickly extended over Palestine and Syria.

The Safavid Dynasty

In the confusion left by the retreating Mongols of Tamerlane, the Safavid dynasty took power in Persia in 1501, and established a strong independent state, though it eventually had to cede Baghdad and all of Iraq to the Ottoman Turks. Persians fought against western incursions, against the Uzbeks and against Sunni Muslims. In particular, the first Safavid Shah, Ismail I, pursued a policy of persecuting Muslims and interfering with Ottoman interests. This attracted the ire of the Turkish Sultans, who inflicted a decisive defeat on the Persians in 1514, causing the loss of northern Iraq and eastern Asia Minor. The Safavid's ruled until 1732.

The Ottoman Turks

While the Mamelukes were taking power in the southern part of the Middle East, the Ottoman Turks were gathering strength in the Asia Minor and spilling over into Europe. Their success was due to good organization and early exploitation of the power of fire arms, which was not realized by other Muslim antagonists. The Mamlukes had been Turkish slaves of the Arabs; the Ottomans in turn created a soldier caste of Janissaries (*Yeni Ceri,* meaning New Troops), who were Christians conscripted or captured at any early age and raised as fanatic Muslims. They originally served as the personal guard of the Sultan. After the 1380s Sultan Selim I recruited them by taxation in human form called *devshirmeh.* The sultan's men would conscript a number of non-Muslim, usually Christian, boys – at first at random, later by strict selection – and take them to be trained.

In Asia Minor, Osman I established the beginning of the Ottoman dynasty in 1293. Osman's successor Ohkran conquered most of western Asia Minor. By 1354 the Turks had a base at Gallipoli, a peninsula on the Mediterranean coast of Turkey. In 1351, Murad I took Adrianople. The Byzantine Empire was reduced to the city of Constantinople. In 1389, at the Battle of Kossovo, Murad I defeated Christian resistance and Ottoman power extended up to the Danube. Slowed for a time by the invasions of Tamerlane, the Ottomans maintained their power in their European possessions and in the 15th century their expansion resumed.

In 1443 or 1444, the forces of the Sultan Murad II defeated an army of Christian allies at the Bulgarian seaport of Varna. On May 29, 1453, Constantinople was conquered by the Sultan Mehmet the Conquerer (Mehmet the Ii). The Turks spread their rule progressively over practically the entire Middle East. In 1517 they defeated the Mamlukes, using canons and guns against the Mamkuke troops who were armed mostly with swords. The Hashemite Sharif of Mecca accepted Ottoman rule. In 1519 they extended their rule through most of North Africa, and later conquered and reconquered Iraq. In Europe, the Ottoman Turks conquered Wallachia, Transylvania Greece, Bulgaria, Serbia and Albania. As early as 1480, they had landed at Otranto in Italy, but their presence there proved to be short lived. By 1529 they were threatening Vienna, though their siege failed and they did not extend their empire beyond Hungary. The conquest of Constantinople made trade between Europe and the east more difficult.

The Europeans soon sought a sea route that would bring them to the spices of India without the intervention of Arab traders. Vasco Da Gama reached the Indies by sea in 1498, and opened the ocean trade between Europe and Asia. Thereafter, the overland trade routes of the Arabs and Turks declined in importance. The Ottoman Empire continued to flourish in the 16th and 17th centuries despite inherent weaknesses in the organization of the Sultanate. The first sign of weakness was the Turkish defeat in the sea battle of Lepanto (near Naupactus in Epirus, Western Greece) in 1571, by the anti-Ottoman alliance known as the Holy League. The Holy League was assembled by the influence of Pope Pious V and led by Don Juan of Austria. It consisted of the Papal States, Spain, Venice and Genoa. The decisive turning point in the Turkish struggle with Europe came with the second siege of Vienna in 1680.

The Turks were beaten back by a combined force of Germans and Austrians aided by 30,000 Poles under the Emperor Jan Sobieski. The Ottoman Empire declined in power and importance, but the fact of decline was not really grasped for another 120 years. Napoleon's rapid conquest of Egypt in 1798 clearly signaled to the Muslims that they had been left behind in the race for cultural development, and efforts were made to introduce Western arms, printing presses, music and dress. However, the Muslim world failed to industrialize and modernize, and the Turkish Empire continued to retreat before the advances of the Russians and to disintegrate due to internal causes. Throughout the nineteenth century, they were partly saved by the British and French who were interested in maintaining Turkey as a means of stopping Russian expansion, and in protecting their growing interests in Turkey, which was considerably indebted to them. All the powers, including Russia, pursued a policy of keeping the Sultan in power and maintaining the integrity of the Turkish Empire.

At the same time, the Western powers encouraged or took advantage of the dissolution of certain parts of the Empire. Greece was taken from Turkey in 1830 following an internal revolt, and Serbia became autonomous in 1829 following the Russo-Turkish War. Lebanon became autonomous in 1861. Egypt remained independent after the withdrawal of Napoleon, though it was forced to give up conquests in Syria and Palestine. Turkey lost further territories, especially in the

Balkans, after the Crimean war in 1856 and after the Balkan crisis of 1878. In 1908 the government of Turkey was seized by the Young Turks, a group of college students and dissident soldiers who had focused the discontent of many with the despotism and inefficiency of the regime, and the nationalist hopes of Arabs and others. In 1908, the Young Turks forced Sultan Abdülhamid II to reinstitute the 1876 constitution and recall the legislature. In 1914, Turkey entered WW I under on the side of the Central Powers. Britain decided that it was time to dismantle the Ottoman Empire.

A British officer, T.E. Lawrence (Lawrence of Arabia) aided a Muslim revolt by the Hashemite family, rulers of Mecca and the Hijaz. The British, Australians and French carried out a long and bloody battle in the Gallipoli peninsula, and finally were forced to withdraw, suffering about 250,000 casualties. However, General Allenby conquered Palestine and Syria, and the Turks retreated before the British and the rebellious Arabs, as well as the Russians pressing from the north. Turkey was forced to sign an ignominious peace at Sevres in 1919, but Kemal Ataturk, who seized the government from Young Turks, refused to honor it and negotiated better terms at Lausanne in 1922 after defeating the invading Greeks. Ataturk abolished the Caliphate formally in the same year and began the modernization of Turkey.

The Ottoman Empire, the last empire of the Muslims, was at an end, and the Middle East was carved up by Britain and France into nation states, mandates and protectorates, all of which eventually became independent following World War II. In Saudi Arabia, the Wahhabi Saud family, based in the Eastern Najd areas took power, displacing the Hashe-mites who ruled the Hijaz. The Hashemites had been promised an Arabian kingdom by the British in return for their support of the British and the revolt against the Ottoman Turks. The British compensated the Hashemites for the loss of the Hijaz by giving them the Kingdoms of Transjordan and Iraq.

Arabic Identity, Nationalism and Islam

The spread of Islam necessarily spread Arabic culture, language and customs. The Quran is written in Arabic and may not be translated for religious practice, so that knowledge of Arabic is important for all Muslims. As the empire spread, the Arabic language became the medium of local pre-existing cultures. In particular, early Arab culture and poetry owes a great debt to Persian. The term "Arab" became associated with speakers of Arabic rather than being confined only to the original inhabitants of the Arabian Peninsula, though today it is sometimes used with reference to the Bedouin of Arabia and at other times used to refer to all Arab-speaking peoples. The Arab empire was in many ways dependent on foreigners, who were integrated into it to varying degrees. The Arabs employed a Turkish slave-caste, the Mamelukes, as soldiers. Christians and Jews served as merchants and administrators, especially in Egypt, and later under the Ottoman Turks. All of these different people were integrated, with varying degrees of completeness and varying enthusiasm, under the rubric of "Arabs."

The historical development of Islam, the Arab state and its successor states, was different from that of the West. Some claim that because of this development, there is no real national feeling in the Arab world, but this is not necessarily the case. An Arab is part of the Arabic *Umma* (roughly translated as "community" - it is sometimes translated as 'nation') and a Muslim Arab is also a member of the Islamic *Umma*. An Arab may also have a particular "national" identity, as a member of a *"Sha'ab"* such as the Palestinian *Sha'ab.* In modern times, the rise of nationalism has also caused a reassertion of particularism, and of the separate identities of different ethnic and religious groups such as the Egyptians, the Bedouin and Peninsular Arabs, the Maronite Christians and the Amazigh people of North Africa. Islam and Arab culture developed a model of toleration and coexistence long before these were practiced in the West.

The model was different however, from the cultural pluralism or melting pot models of modern Western society. Pluralism and separateness was recognized and regulated. Middle Eastern societies tend to be segmented, so that for example, Armenians, Jews, Greeks and others live in separate quarters, go to separate schools, have different occupations from each other, and each have a separate and recognized place in society. Christians and Jews were classified as people of the book and allowed rights as *dhimmi,* a second class citizenship that was a handicap of varying degrees of discomfort in different ages and in different Muslim countries, and might involve restrictions on worship, special dress, exclusion from administrative posts and other strictures.

Land conquered by Muslims was awarded on leasehold to Muslims. Conversion of Jews and Christians was usually not forced. Though for a period in the 12th century, Spain and North Africa came under the rule of a fanatic sect, the Mu'ahaddin, who forced conversion of Jews and Christians to Islam. Conversion to Islam was made particularly attractive because it resulted in reduction of taxes, freedom from slavery for captive and the possibility of advancement. Captive women forced to marry Muslims do not have to change their religion, but their children must be raised as Muslims. The persecution of Hindus under some of the Muslim Moghul emperor Auranzeb was notorious. Nonetheless, for the most part, both Arab and subsequent Ottoman Muslim empires exhibited toleration of Jewish and Christian faiths, and even of pagan worship that was unknown in Europe. After the Jews were expelled from Spain, the Sultan Bayezid II welcomed them to Ottoman Turkey, and the Ottoman Empire allowed Jews exiled from Spain to settle in Palestine, where they formed communities in Tiberias and Hebron.

The Arab-Israel Conflict

Arabs remained bitter that the British did not immediately fulfill their promise for an independent Arab empire that included Syria, and for the granting of Palestine as a homeland for the Jews. The Sykes-Picot Agreement of 1916 called for part of Palestine to be under British rule, part to be placed under a joint Allied government, and for Syria and Lebanon to be given to the France. However, Britain also offered to back Arab demands for postwar independence from the Ottomans in return for Arab support for the Allies and seems to have promised the same territories to the Arabs. November 1917, before it had conquered Jerusalem and the area to be known as Palestine, Britain issued the Balfour Declaration, stating Britain's support for the creation of a Jewish national home in Palestine, and leading to the League of Nations mandate for Palestine. The mandate, and subsequent creation of the State of Israel, led to the Arab Israel conflict, which has resulted in several wars.

Pan-Arabism

Frustrated Arab nationalist ambitions and socialist and fascist ideologies gave rise to several movements and political parties. In particular, the Ba'ath party was founded in Syria in 1928 by Michel Aflaq and Salah al-Din Bitar with a Pan-Arab nationalist program and elements of both Marxism and fascism. Aflak and Bitar were influenced by Arab nationalist trends that had begun in time of the Turks, inspired in part by the Islamic and Arab reform ideologies of Jamal al-Din al-Afghani (1839-1897), his student Muhammad Abduh (1849-1905), and Abduh's student, Muhammad Rashid Rida (1865-1935). These thinkers called for a renewal of Islam, with limited borrowing of concepts from the West. Abduh in particular was active in promoting Arab autonomy within Ottoman Turkey, and had placed great hopes in the Young Turks. Rida grew increasingly anti-Western with time, and was a great influence on Hassan al-Banna, who founded the Muslim Brotherhood. While Aflak was a Greek Orthodox Christian, Ba'ath ideology adopted an affinity for Islam, and Pan-Arabists saw one of their goals as asserting the primacy of the Arabs in the Muslim world.

As World War II drew to a close, Arab national ambitions and the desire to prevent creation of a Jewish homeland in Palestine led to the creation of the Arab League and soon after, to the rise of Arab national sentiment. Gamal Abdel Nasser, president of Egypt, took advantage of the anti-imperialist feeling to become the leader of a Pan-Arab ideology, which tried to unite Arabs beyond the confines of the nation states, and to encourage a program of modernization and secularization. This program met opposition from Muslim traditionalists. Pan-Arabism declined after Nasser instigated the Six-Day War with Israel, which resulted in a disastrous Arab defeat. Other contenders eventually took Nasser's place as leaders of Pan-Arabism, notably Saddam Hussein of Iraq. However, the rise of Islamist fundamentalism or Islamism, offered an ideology that largely displaced pan-Arabism. Pan-Arabism was also challenged by nationalist particularism, especially in Egypt itself, where people have a profound sense of their identity as Egyptians, as distinct from "Arabs."

ISLAMISM

Islamism is a general name for all forms of Islamic fundamentalism, and includes several different and sometimes competing political and religious movements, notably the Shi'ite followers of the late Ayatollah Khomeini, extremist Wahhabi Muslims in Saudi Arabia (not necessarily all Wahhabi Muslims), some of the Deobandi sect in India, the Afghani Taliban, the Muslim Brotherhood, the Palestinian Hamas, the Hizbulla, Islamic Jihad and Jama'at Islamia in several countries, as well as and followers of Osama Bin Laden and the infamous Al-Qaeda, a network of Sunni Islamists. Islamic parties like the Turkish AKP are sometimes called "Islamist," though they may not share the radical program of Islamists, and may be more akin to the Christian Democrat parties of Europe. Their philosophy should not be confused with radical Islamism. Radical Islamism has common ideological roots with Pan Arabism, in the ideas of Jamal al-Din al-Afghani (1839-1897), his student Muhammad Abduh (1849-1905), and Abduh's student, Muhammad Rashid Rida (1865-1935).

Another ideological father of Islamism was probably Sayed Abul Ala Maududi (or Mawdoodi), who lived in what is now Pakistan, and who was influenced by Deobandi ideology as well as by Al-Banna. He called for an Islamic state governed by Sha'aria (Sha'ria -Islamic law) and tried to reconcile Islam with modern science. Maududi founded the Jamaat-e-Islami in 1941 and headed the movement until 1972. His key work was, "Towards Understanding Islam" (*Risalah Diniyat*). Afghani and Abduh were liberals, but Rida develo-ped Abduh's philosophy into a xenophobic and racist anti-colonialism, which had as its goal re-establishment of the Caliphate and imposition of Sharia law. The radical Islamists have in common the convictions that Islam must dictate the political organization of the state as well as religious life, intolerance of the West and hatred for Jews as such.

This preceded hatred for Israel, but formed a basis for it. Jews are despised as agents of Western democracy and human rights. Israel is hated because it is considered a foreign implant in the Islamic Middle East. They also have an ideology or theology of liberation, in which the poor nations of the south play the part of the oppressed proletariat. This last was possibly amplified by Marxist Islamic thinkers of Central Asia, and figures prominently in Shi'a Islamist ideology, including that of the Hizbullah. However, it is quite explicit in the ideas of Hassan al-Banna and Sayyid Qutb, Egyptian Islamists, whose ideas developed independently of Marxist influence and who were more influenced by German Fascism. Islamists attribute the decline of Islamic civilization to laxity in religious observance, and demand a return to strict observance of the Quran. Most Islamist groups advocate re-establishment of the Caliphate and Jihad (holy war) against the West and believe that Islam, which requires the rule of God, is inherently opposed to democracy, which is the rule of man.

The Arab and Muslim world has suffered several frustrating disappointments. National ambitions were partially frustrated by the Western take over of the Middle East after World War I, which, in the Arab view, prevented the realization of the aims of Arab nationalism that had begun to crystallize during the last years of the Ottoman Empire, and humiliated the Muslim Umma. In particular, the rise of Israel is a sore point and a focus for anti-Western resentment. Much of the Arab and Muslim world, burdened by high population growth and lack of a middle class, has failed to industrialize and lags far behind the west in standard of living, quality of life and democratic institutions. Literacy rates are low and infant mortality is high relative to the West. The introduction of modern medicine has produced a population explosion that hampers economic growth.

Muslims blame oil-greedy western countries for repressive regimes that they claim have stifled growth, even in the oil rich Arabian Peninsula and Persian Gulf area. Islamists have leveraged on this discontent and frustration to build populist movements that often have an extremely destructive and reactionary philosophy. They are opposed both by moderate Muslims who favor western style democratic reform and by conservative Salafi fundament-alists who are uninterested in innovation and social reform. Islamist doctrine is not a passive philosophy, but a program for action. One of their favorite "military" tools is the suicide attack on civilians. Persons who die in such attacks are considered to be holy martyrs (*Shahid*). Islamists were responsible for suicide attacks on the US forces in Lebanon in the '80s. They have been involved in plots to assassinate Arab leaders in different countries, and they instigated and carried out the attack on the United States on September 11, 2001. Shi'a Islamists came to power in Iran in 1979 and formed an Islamic Republic.

The Muslim Brotherhood

The Muslim Brotherhood (Ikhwan) in Egypt has been a longstanding threat to the regime. Founded in 1928 by

Hassan al-Banna, their popularity grew rapidly in the 30s and 40s despite vigorous repression. They combined strict Islamic practice, Fascist ideology and pro-Axis politics. In 1948, following their efforts in mobilizing volunteers to fight in the war against "the Zionists" in Palestine to prevent establishment of a Jewish state, they were ready to launch a coup against the Egyptian monarchy. However, On December 8, 1948, Prime Minister Nuqrashi Pasha disbanded the Ikwhan in Egypt. Less than three weeks later, the Ikhwan assassinated Nuqrashi Pasha; Hassan al-Banna was assassi-nated by government agents on February 12, 1949. The Ikhwan had organized extensively in Gaza, and remnants of the Ikhwan eventually founded Palestinian groups including the Hamas.

In Egypt, leadership of the movement was taken over by Sayyid Qutb. Qutb had been more or less exiled or sent to the USA in 1948 and studied there. He returned with a profound hatred for the United States and the West, including Western materialism and sexual permissiveness, which he viewed as depravity. He wrote extensively against democracy and characterized western society as "Jahil" - that is, benighted in the same way as the pre-Islamic Jahiliyah period in Arabia. He called for Jihad against these infidels. Gamal Abdel Nasser banned the Muslim brotherhood after they were involved in plots to assassinate him, and Qutb was executed in 1965. Eventually, Islamic Jihad did assassinate Anwar Sadat after he signed a peace treaty with Israel. Recently (2004), the Muslim Brothers in Egypt announced that they were modifying their philosophy to a more moderate stance which abjured violence and supported democracy.

A Muslim Brother revolt that planned to overthrow the Syrian government and assassinate Syrian president Hafez el-Assad was suppressed by gassing tens of thousands of people in El-Hama in 1982. In Iran, Shi'a Islamists led by Ayatollah Khomeini came to power in 1979. The Iranians support the Hizbulla guerilla group in Lebanon and the Islamic Jihad Palestinian terrorist group. The initially ferocious Iranian regime has mellowed with time, and some democratic reforms have been established. Likewise the Hizbollah in Lebanon claim that they want to come to power democratically. However, it is now clear that the conservative clerics in Iran who hold the real power will not give it up in favor of the democratically elected president and his reform-minded supporters. A recent election in Iran was rigged by eliminating candidates who were judged to be insufficiently "Islamic." Osama Bin-Laden gained power by organizing Islamic resistance to the Soviet-supported regime in Afghanistan, with the aid of the United States. Following the partial eclipse of Saddam Hussein after operation Desert Storm, Bin Laden and his Al-Qaeda Mujaheddin may have assumed increased importance as the symbols of successful resistance to the West and the infidels.

On September 11, 2001, Osama Bin Laden's Al-Qaeda movement carried out suicide attacks against the World Trade Center in New York and the Pentagon in Washington DC. According to Bin Laden, the attacks were aimed at punishing the United States for the presence of its soldiers in Saudi Arabia, which is supposed to be off limits to non-Muslims, and for its support of Israel. Bin-Laden and Al-Qaeda may actually be aiming at the much more limited goal of taking power in oil-rich Saudi Arabia. Despite the removal of the Taliban regime from Afghanistan by allied military intervention, forcing Osama Bin Laden into hiding, Al Qaeda has since been responsible for terror attacks aimed at moderate regimes throughout the Muslim world, especially in Saudi Arabia and Turkey. The US invasion of Iraq and the swiftness of the American victory have taken the Arab and Muslim worlds by surprise, despite the well known superiority of Western arms. The effects of this upheaval have not been completely assimilated in the Middle East, and probably will not be totally evident until the success or failure of the Americans in their war aims becomes apparent. There are signs that it has produced both stirrings of democratization and a desire to appease the USA, and a counter-reaction of resentment and growing discontent.

THE RIGHTLY GUIDED CALIPHS

Upon the death of the Prophet, Abu Bakr, the friend of the Prophet and the first adult male to embrace Islam, became caliph. Abu Bakr ruled for two years to be succeeded by 'Umar who was caliph for a decade and during whose rule Islam spread extensively east and west conquering the Persian empire, Syria and Egypt. It was 'Umar who marched on foot at the end of the Muslim army into Jerusalem and ordered the protection of Christian sites. 'Umar also established the first public treasury and a sophisticated financial administration. He established many of the basic practices of Islamic government.

'Umar was succeeded by 'Uthman who ruled for some twelve years during which time the Islamic expansion continued. He is also known as the caliph who had the definitive text of the Noble Quran copied and sent to the four corners of the Islamic world. He was in turn succeeded by 'Ali who is known to this day for his eloquent sermons and letters, and also for his bravery. With his death the rule of the "rightly guided" caliphs, who hold a special place of respect in the hearts of Muslims, came to an end.

THE CALIPHATE

Umayyad

The Umayyad caliphate established in 661 was to last for about a century. During this time Damascus became the capital of an Islamic world which stretched from the western borders of China to southern France. Not only did the Islamic conquests continue during this period through North Africa to Spain and France in the West and to Sind, Central Asia and Transoxiana in the East, but the basic social and legal institutions of the newly founded Islamic world were established.

Abbasids

The Abbasids, who succeeded the Umayyads, shifted the capital to Baghdad which soon developed into an incomparable center of learning and culture as well as the administrative and political heart of a vast world. They ruled for over 500 years but gradually their power waned and they remained only symbolic rulers bestowing legitimacy upon various sultans and princes who wielded actual military power. The Abbasid caliphate was finally abolished when Hulagu, the Mongol ruler, captured Baghdad in 1258, destroying much of the city including its incomparable libraries.

While the Abbasids ruled in Baghdad, a number of powerful dynasties such as the Fatimids, Ayyubids and Mamluks held power in Egypt, Syria and Palestine. The most important event in this area as far as the relation between Islam and the Western world was concerned was the series of Crusades declared by the Pope and espoused by various European kings. The purpose, although political, was outwardly to recapture the Holy Land and especially Jerusa-lem for Christianity. Although there was at the beginning some success and local European rule was set up in parts of Syria and Palestine, Muslims finally prevailed and in 1187 Saladin, the great Muslim leader, recaptured Jerusalem and defeated the Crusaders.

North Africa and Spain

When the Abbasids captured Damascus, one of the Umayyad princes escaped and made the long journey from there to Spain to found Umayyad rule there, thus beginning the golden age of Islam in Spain. Cordoba was established as the capital and soon became Europe's greatest city not only in population but from the point of view of its cultural and intellectual life. The Umayyads ruled over two centuries until they weakened and were replaced by local rulers. Meanwhile in North Africa, various local dynasties held sway until two powerful Berber dynasties succeeded in uniting much of North Africa and also Spain in the 12th and 13th centuries. After them this area was ruled once again by local dynasties such as the Sharifids of Morocco who still rule in that country. As for Spain itself, Muslim power continued to wane until the last Muslim dynasty was defeated in Granada in 1492 thus bringing nearly eight hundred years of Muslim rule in Spain to an end.

AFTER THE MONGOL INVASION

The Mongols devastated the eastern lands of Islam and ruled from the Sinai Desert to India for a century. But they soon converted to Islam and became known as the Il-Khanids. They were in turn succeeded by Timur and his descendents who made Samarqand their capital and ruled from 1369 to 1500. The sudden rise of Timur delayed the formation and expansion of the Ottoman Empire but soon the Ottomans became the dominant power in the Islamic world.

Ottoman Empire

From humble origins the Turks rose to dominate over the whole of Anatolia and even parts of Europe. In 1453 Mehmet the Conqueror captured Constantinople and put an end to the Byzantine Empire. The Ottomans conquered much of eastern Europe and nearly the whole of the Arab world, only Morocco and Mauritania in the West and Yemen, Hadramaut and parts of the Arabian Peninsula remaining beyond their control. They reached their zenith of power with Suleyman the Magnificent whose armies reached Hungary and Austria. From the 17th century onward with the rise of Western European powers and later Russia, the power of the Ottomans began to wane. But they nevertheless remained a force to be reckoned with until the First World War when they were defeated by the Western nations. Soon thereafter Kamal Ataturk gained power in Turkey and abolished the six centuries of rule of the Ottomans in 1924.

Persia

While the Ottomans were concerned mostly with the western front of their empire, to the east in Persia a new dynasty called the Safavids came to power in 1502. The Safavids established a powerful state of their own which flourished for over two centuries and became known for the flowering of the arts. Their capital, Isfahan, became one of the most beautiful cities with its blue tiled mosques and exquisite houses. The Afghan invasion of 1736 put an end to Safavid rule and prepared the independence of Afghanistan which occurred formally in the 19th century. Persia itself fell into turmoil until Nader Shah, the last Oriental conqueror, reunited the country and even conquered India. But the rule of the dynasty established by him was short-lived. The Zand dynasty soon took over to be overthrown by the Qajars in 1779 that made Tehran their capital and ruled until 1921 when they were in turn replaced by the Pahlavis.

India

As for India, Islam entered into the land east of the Indus River peacefully. Gradually Muslims gained political power beginning in the early 13th century. But this period which marked the expansion of both Islam and Islamic culture came to an end with the conquest of much of India in 1526 by Babur, one of the Timurid princes. He established the powerful Mogul empire which produced such famous rulers as Akbar, Jahangir, and Shah Jahan and which lasted, despite the gradual rise of British power in India, until 1857 when it was officially abolished.

Malaysia and Indonesia

Farther east in the Malay world, Islam began to spread in the 12th century in northern Sumatra and soon Muslim kingdoms were established in Java, Sumatra and mainland Malaysia. Despite the colonization of the Malay world, Islam spread in that area covering present day Indonesia, Malaysia, the southern Philippines and southern Thailand, and is still continuing in islands farther east.

Africa

As far as Africa is concerned, Islam entered into East Africa at the very beginning of the Islamic period but remained confined to the coast for some time, only the Sudan and Somaliland becoming gradually both Arabized and Islamized. West Africa felt the presence of Islam through North African traders who travelled with their camel caravans south of the Sahara. By the 14th century there were already Muslim sultanates in such areas as Mali, and Timbuctu in West Africa and Harar in East Africa had become seats of Islamic learning. Gradually Islam penetrated both inland and southward. There also appeared major charismatic figures that inspired intense resistance against European domination. The process of the Islamization of Africa did not cease during the colonial period and continues even today with the result that most Africans are now Muslims carrying on a tradition which has had practically as long a history in certain areas of sub-Saharan Africa as Islam itself.

Islam in the United States

It is almost impossible to generalize about American Muslims: converts, immigrants, factory workers, doctors; all are making their own contribution to America's future. This complex community is unified by a common faith, underpinned by a countrywide network of a thousand mosques. Muslims were early arrivals in North America. By the eighteenth century there were many thousands of them, working as slaves on plantations. These early communities cut off from their heritage and families, inevitably lost their Islamic identity as time went by. Today many Afro-American Muslims play an important role in the Islamic community.

The nineteenth century, however, saw the beginnings of an influx of Arab Muslims, most of them settled in the major industrial centers where they worshipped in hired rooms. The early twentieth century witnessed the arrival of several hundred thousand Muslims from Eastern Europe:

the first Albanian mosque was opened in Maine in 1915; others soon followed, and a group of Polish Muslims opened a mosque in Brooklyn in 1928. In 1947 the Washington Islamic Center was founded during the term of President Truman, and several nationwide organizations were set up in the fifties. The same period saw the establishment of other communities whose lives were in many ways modelled after Islam. More recently, numerous members of these groups have entered the fold of Muslim orthodoxy. Today there are about five million Muslims in America.

AFTERMATH OF THE COLONIAL PERIOD

At the height of European colonial expansion in the 19th century, most of the Islamic world was under colonial rule with the exception of a few regions such as the heart of the Ottoman Empire, Persia, Afghanistan, Yemen and certain parts of Arabia. But even these areas were under foreign influence or, in the case of the Ottomans, under constant threat. After the First World War with the breakup of the Ottoman Empire, a number of Arab states such as Iraq became independent, others like Jordan were created as a new entity and yet others like Palestine, Syria and Lebanon were either mandated or turned into French colonies.

As for Arabia, it was at this time that Saudi Arabia became finally consolidated. As for other parts of the Islamic world, Egypt which had been ruled by the descendents of Muhammad Ali since the 19th century became more independent as a result of the fall of the Ottomans, Turkey was turned into a secular republic by Ataturk, and the Pahlavi dynasty began a new chapter in Persia where its name reverted to its eastern traditional form of Iran. But most of the rest of the Islamic world remained under colonial rule.

Arab

It was only after the Second World War and the dismemberment of the British, French, Dutch and Spanish empires that the rest of the Islamic world gained its independence. In the Arab world, Syria and Lebanon became independent at the end of the war as did Libya and the sheikdoms around the Gulf and the Arabian Sea by the 1960's. The North African countries of Tunisia, Morocco and Algeria had to fight a difficult and, in the case of Algeria, long and protracted war to gain their freedom which did not come until a decade later for Tunisia and Morocco and two decades later for Algeria. Only Palestine did not become independent but was partitioned in 1948 with the establishment of the state of Israel.

India

In India Muslims participated in the freedom movement against British rule along with Hindus and when independence finally came in 1947, they were able to create their own homeland, Pakistan, which came into being for the sake of Islam and became the most populated Muslim state although many Muslims remained in India. In 1971, however, the two parts of the state broke up, East Pakistan becoming Bangladesh.

Far East

Farther east still, the Indonesians finally gained their independence from the Dutch and the Malays theirs from Britain. At first Singapore was part of Malaysia but it separated in 1963 to become an independent state? Small colonies still persisted in the area and continued to seek their independence, the kingdom of Brunei becoming independent as recently as 1984.

Africa

In Africa also major countries with large or majority Muslim populations such as Nigeria, Senegal and Tanzania began to gain their independence in the 1950's and 1960's with the result that by the end of the decade of the 60's most parts of the Islamic world were formed into independent national states. There were, however, exceptions. The Muslim states in the Soviet Union failed to gain their autonomy or independence. The same holds true for Sinkiang (called Eastern Turkistan by Muslim geographers) while in Eritrea and the southern Philippines Muslim independence movements still continue.

National States

While the world of Islam has entered into the modern world in the form of national states, continuous attempts are made to create closer cooperation within the Islamic world as a whole and to bring about greater unity. This is seen not only in the meetings of the Muslim heads of state and the establishment of the OIC (Organization of Islamic Countries) with its own secretariat, but also in the creation of institutions dealing with the whole of the Islamic world. Among the most important of these is the Muslim World League (Rabitat al-alam al-Islami) with its headquarters in Makkah. Saudi Arabia has in fact played a pivotal role in the creation and maintenance of such organizations.

Revival and Re-assertation of Islam

Muslims did not wish to gain only their political independence. They also wished to assert their own religious and cultural identity. From the 18th century onward Muslim reformers appeared upon the scene who sought to reassert the teachings of Islam and to reform society on the basis of Islamic teachings. One of the first among this group was Muhammad ibn 'Abd al-Wahhab, who hailed from the Arabian Peninsula and died there in 1792. This reformer was supported by Muhammad ibn al-Sa'ud, the founder of the first Saudi state. With this support Muhammad ibn 'Abd al-Wahhab was able to spread his teachings not only in Arabia but even beyond its borders to other Islamic lands where his reforms continue to wield influence to this day.

In the 19th century Islamic assertion took several different forms ranging from the Mahdi movement of the

Sudan and the Sanusiyyah in North Africa which fought wars against European colonizers, to educational movements such as that of Aligarh in India aiming to reeducate Muslims. In Egypt which, because of al-Azhar University, remains to this day central to Islamic learning, a number of reformers appear, each addressing some aspect of Islamic thought. Some were concerned more with law, others economics, and yet others the challenges posed by Western civilization with its powerful science and technology.

These included Jamal al-Din al-Afghani who hailed originally from Persia but settled in Cairo and who was the great champion of Pan-Islamism that is the movement to unite the Islamic world politically as well as religiously. His student, Muhammad 'Abduh, who became the rector of al-Azhar was also very influential in Islamic theology and thought. Also of considerable influence was his Syrian student, Rashid Rida, who held a position closer to that of 'Abd al-Wahhab and stood for the strict application of the Shari'ah. Among the most famous of these thinkers is Muhammad Iqbal, the outstanding poet and philosopher who is considered as the father of Pakistan.

Reform Organizations

Moreover, as Western influence began to penetrate more deeply into the fiber of Islamic society, organizations gradually grew up whose goal was to reform society in practice along Islamic lines and prevent its secularization. These included the Muslim Brotherhood (Ikhwan al-muslimin) founded in Egypt and with branches in many Muslim countries, and the Jama'at-i Islami of Pakistan founded by the influential Mawlana Mawdudi. These organizations have been usually peaceful and have sought to reestablish an Islamic order through education. During the last two decades, however, as a result of the frustration of many Muslims in the face of pressures coming from a secularized outside world, some have sought to reject the negative aspects of Western thought and culture and to return to an Islamic society based completely on the application of the Shari 'ah.

Today in every Muslim country there are strong movements to preserve and propagate Islamic teachings. In countries such as Saudi Arabia Islamic Law is already being applied and in fact is the reason for the prosperity, development and stability of the country. In other countries where Islamic Law is not being applied, however, most of the effort of Islamic movements is spent in making possible the full application of the Shari'ah so that the nation can enjoy prosperity along with the fulfillment of the faith of its people. In any case the widespread desire for Muslims to have the religious law of Islam applied and to reassert their religious values and their own identity must not be equated with exceptional violent eruptions which do exist but which are usually treated sensationally and taken out of proportion by the mass media in the West.

2

Education and Science in Building the Empire of Islam

In seeking to live successfully in the modern world, in independence and according to Islamic principles, Muslim countries have been emphasizing a great deal the significance of the role of education and the importance of mastering Western science and technology. Already in the 19th century, certain Muslim countries such as Egypt, Ottoman Turkey and Persia established institutions of higher learning where the modem sciences and especially medicine were taught. During this century educational institutions at all levels have proliferated throughout the Islamic world. Nearly every science ranging from mathematics to biology as well as various fields of modern technology are taught in these institutions and some notable scientists have been produced by the Islamic world, men and women who have often combined education in these institutions with training in the West.

In various parts of the Islamic world there is, however, a sense that educational institutions must be expanded and also have their standards improved to the level of the best institutions in the world in various fields of learning especially science and technology. At the same time there is an awareness that the educational system must be based totally on Islamic principles and the influence of alien cultural and ethical values and norms, to the extent that they are negative, be diminished. To remedy this problem a number of international Islamic educational conferences have been held, the first one in Makkah in 1977, and the foremost thinkers of the Islamic world have been brought together to study and ponder over the question of the relation between Islam and modern science. This is an ongoing process which is at the center of attention in many parts of the Islamic world and which indicates the significance of educational questions in the Islamic world today.

ISLAMIC SCIENCE AND LEARNING UPON THE WEST

The oldest university in the world which is still functioning is the eleven hundred-year-old Islamic university of Fez, Morocco, known as the Qarawiyyin. This old tradition of Islamic learning influenced the West greatly through Spain. In this land where Muslims, Christians and Jews lived for the most part peacefully for many centuries, translations began to be made in the 11th century mostly in Toledo of Islamic works into Latin often through the intermediary of Jewish scholars most of whom knew Arabic and often wrote in Arabic. As a result of these translations, Islamic thought and through it much of Greek thought became known to the West and Western schools of learning began to flourish.

Even the Islamic educational system was emulated in Europe and to this day the term chair in a university reflects the Arabic kursi (literally seat) upon which a teacher would sit to teach his students in the madrasah (school of higher learning). As European civilization grew and reached the high middle Ages, there was hardly a field of learning or form of art, whether it was literature or architecture, where there was not some influence of Islam present. Islamic learning became in this way part and parcel of Western civilization even if with the advent of the Renaissance, the West not only turned against its own medieval past but also sought to forget the long relation it had with the Islamic world, one which was based on intellectual respect despite religious opposition. The Islamic world remains today a vast land stretching from the Atlantic to the Pacific, with an important presence in Europe and America, animated by the teachings of Islam and seeking to assert its own identity.

Despite the presence of nationalism and various secular ideologies in their midst, Muslims wish to live in the modern world but without simply imitating blindly the ways followed by the West. The Islamic world wishes to live at peace with the West as well as the East but at the same time not to be dominated by them. It wishes to devote its resources and energies to building a better life for its people on the basis of the teachings of Islam and not to squander its resources in either internal or external conflicts. It seeks finally to create better understanding with the West and to be better understood by the West. The destinies of the Islamic world and the West cannot be totally separated and therefore it only in understands each other better that they can serve their own people more successfully and also contribute to a better life for the whole of humanity.

Formal protections for Islam and other non-Orthodox faiths came only under Catherine II, who introduced a new paradigm of toleration designed to make religious discipline useful to the empire and to project imperial power on its frontiers. But this mode of toleration did not mean official indifference or neutrality toward non-Orthodox religious affairs. In the tradition of the "well-ordered police state" (*Polizeistaat*), the regime became directly involved in the regulation of central aspects of religious life in nearly every community.

For Catherine and her successors, the treatment of each faith depended on its utility to the state; its contribution to the maintenance of empire defined the scope of toleration. The tsars increasingly relied on Orthodoxy as a symbol of the national character of the monarchy, and some bureaucrats shared the church's view that conversion to the tsar's religion represented a testament of loyalty to the state. But in the wake of revolutionary events in Europe, the regime looked to compulsory submission to state-regulated religious institutions, even in non-Orthodox forms, as a safeguard against revolution in Russia, viewing religious conformity as the cornerstone of morality and public order and as a measure of its subjects' political attitudes.

Unlike elsewhere in Europe, tsarist law never permitted its subjects to renounce confessional allegiance and declare themselves "without a confession" (*konfessionslos*). Obligatory enrollment in a religious community brought nearly all subjects under the bureaucratic supervision of an official hierarchy. The policing of morality thus remained the responsibility both of officially recognized ecclesiastical authorities and of the state. As Mikhail Speranskii, the influential adviser to Alexander I, noted in 1803, in ancient Rome, and "everywhere in well-ordered states," "preventive police" concerned themselves with censorship, public decorum, the suppression of "rumors and interpretations harmful to the government," and "the safeguarding of the rites of religion and the curbing of schisms."

Under Nicholas I, new legal codes declared Orthodox Christianity the "preeminent and predominant" faith of the empire but also systematically backed other religions on the premise that "all peoples inhabiting Russia praise Almighty God in different languages according to the creed and confession of their forefathers, blessing the reign of the Russian Monarchs, and praying to the Creator of the universe for the increase of the prosperity and strengthening of the power of the Empire." Court records, petitions, and denunciations reveal how, in largely secret proceedings, the state became deeply enmeshed in intra-confessional disputes as the guardian and patron of religious "orthodoxy" for the tolerated faiths of Islam, Catholicism, Protestantism, Judaism, Buddhism, and both branches of Armenian Christianity.

As Laura Engelstein has shown, Nicholas's government here acted as "the defender of absolute values in a world of revolutionary change." Like the regime's new efforts aimed at "disciplining the boundaries of true belief" among the Orthodox, its adoption of regulatory measures to ensure conformity in other communities made up another dimension of the tsarist "project of administrative modernization." Officials endorsed other faiths' capacity to order the family, instill morality, and guarantee the overlap of religious and worldly sanction for transgressions against temporal authority. Confessional communities that subjected followers to divine as well as monarchical judgment provided useful forms of social discipline to complement the will of the sovereign.

Despite rebellion in 1830–1831 in Poland, for example, F. F. Berg, the governor-general of the Kingdom of Poland and a Protestant, continued to regard Catholicism as "sometimes very useful for the government, because it helps it keep the people in check." The *Digest of Laws* made this connection between religious orthodoxy and political loyalty clear in its instruction to rabbis "to explain to Jews their law... and make them understand ... [its] true meaning" and to "direct Jews to observe moral obligations [and] to obey the general state laws and established authorities." Moreover, the state appointed mullahs, priests, pastors, and rabbis to attend to the spiritual needs (and obligations) of non-Orthodox soldiers, sailors, and prisoners.

In extending toleration, Russian bureaucrats nonetheless retained the authority to intervene in areas that they claimed in the name of the state, including questions of dogma, ritual, and ecclesiastical organization. *Polizeistaat* toleration supported religion only in its canonical and, where appropriate, "enlightened" forms. The law excluded sectarians, atheists, and "free-thinkers," as well as those who exceeded the boundaries of "moderation" in their piety. The architects of the first Islamic hierarchy assigned it the task of monitoring the "Muhammadan law" so that "superstition and other abuses, which cannot be tolerated, do not creep into" its affairs. The criminal code protected official non-Orthodox rites from interference, but religion that strayed beyond clerical direction and the approved canon of texts, prayers, and songs threatened the moral and social order.

Who determined the content of "orthodoxy" within each tradition and who figured as a "heretic" became a matter of critical importance for imperial officials, religious authorities, and lay people? Such policies of toleration figure prominently in analyses that attempt to account for the durability and relative strength of the empire. Andreas Kappeler argues that, from the Muscovite period well into the nineteenth century, the tsars maintained a pragmatic regard for the status quo by co-opting indigenous elites into the ruling apparatus and accommodating local customs, beliefs, and laws. Kappeler's influential view of the accommodationist imperial ethos reflects accurately the intentions of Russian authorities. But the perspective of the communities themselves suggests that the institutional and legal architecture for toleration did not simply confer and maintain the autonomy of established elites.

Officials sought out for cooptation individuals whom they took to be the leaders of these communities; however, the search for cooperative elites embroiled them in questions of dogmatic, ritual, and legal interpretation. The prospect of support for particular positions initiated intense competition for patronage within these divided communities. Indigenous mediators between community and state who earned official backing often lacked legitimacy within their own communities. The state did not confirm religious notables in traditional roles as much as it created new elites. State backing confirmed some customary prerogatives, but many of the "traditional" rights for which clerics sought support were, in fact, novel. Patronage enabled Muhammadzhan Husainov, the first mufti, Stanislaus Siestrzewcewicz, the Catholic metropolitan, and Iraklii Lisovskii and Joseph Semashko, metropolitans of the Uniate Church, as well as the Armenian primates Ep-rem and Hovhannes to claim an unprecedented degree of power over their rivals and competing interpretations of their faiths.

Confronted with the opposition of other clerics, lay-people, and superiors in Rome, Jerusalem, and elsewhere, the authority of these new elites rested less on clerical or lay consensus than on police power. The regime conferred new privileges on each confessional elite while subjecting it to more formal supervision. Following the consistorial model established in Napoleonic France, Russian officials sought to maximize the contribution of religion to morality and respect for authority by incorporating its leadership directly into the state. In 1810, Alexander I created the Main Administration of the Religious Affairs of Foreign Confessions. This office (later a department in the Ministry of the Interior) took on the arbitration of controversies within "foreign" faith communities and bolstered the authority of state-approved clerics as the guardians of morality, the presumed foundation of public order.

To this end, many members of these new "clergies" received exemption from corporal punishment. The state imposed financial obligations on them but also created new positions of power and cultural control, such as the censorship of religious literature. It enlisted Jewish communal government, the *kahal,* in the enforcement of laws against the contraband, even permitting the imposition of the rabbinic ban (the *herem,* formally prohibited in 1804) against smugglers. In 1827, the government capitalized on religious and communal bonds by making the *kahal* responsible for the selection of recruits because, as Eli Lederhendler observes, the authorities assumed that Jews "could be expected to heed their own rabbis and leaders even when they disregarded the laws of the Christian state." Like the Orthodox clergy, these clerics acted as adjuncts of state authority, discharging bureaucratic duties and performing the "useful" task of preaching submission to Russian law.

Under Nicholas I, the state consolidated multiconfessional elite that shared significant resources and ambitious plans for amplifying the powers of central authorities to discipline religious life through bureaucratic and police controls. The regime acquiesced to the mufti's claim that his judicial opinions (*fatwas*) bound all Muslims. When the state empowered Jewish lay and rabbinic elites to implement the conscription of Jews, many used their new power to advance the cause of piety, targeting vagrants, poor families, as well as violators of Jewish law for the draft. State-sponsored reorganization tended toward the centralization of ecclesiastical authority, religious opinion, and wealth, paralleling the institutional transformation under way in the Russian Orthodox establishment and in other churches throughout Europe.

The state benefited from internal contests for religious authority and local initiatives for state patronage against rivals. The regime found Catholics willing to reorganize the church to resemble the French and Habsburg churches, which enjoyed significant independence from the Holy See. Rival-ries for supremacy within the Armenian Church involved clerics in Russia, the Ottoman Empire, India, and Iran. In supporting candidates to the office of the patriarchate at Etchmiadzin, tsarist diplomats saw an opportunity not only to cultivate notables with pro-Russian sympathies but also to create an institution with authority over Armenians in neighboring states. St. Petersburg backed local claims to represent "the entire Armenian nation" against skeptical subordinates in Russia and competitors in Jerusalem and Istanbul.

Similarly, the regime assembled the varied Protestant churches in the empire under an "Evangelical Church," although it favored the Lutheranism of the Baltic German nobles. The statute of 1832 created a general consistorial regime but only intensified local doctrinal and social conflicts. Its endorsement of Lutheran dogma sparked controversy in mixed Lutheran and Reformed communities on the Volga and in southern Russia, dividing congregations over the form of altars, crosses, and the singing of prayers. Against this consistorial system and the standardizing texts and liturgy of the 1832 statute, charismatic preachers inspired movements that broke away in anticipation of Christ's imminent second coming and the end of the world. To counter these "separatists" and "superstitious sects," Nicholas backed the Protestant "orthodoxy" defined by the general consistory.

And while the state supported Orthodox missions to dissenters, Muslims, and "pagans" from the late 1820s, conversionary efforts principally targeted apostates from Orthodoxy. Buddhists, Muslims, and Jews who engaged in religious disputes with their co-religionists continued to seek—and receive—support for their views within the bureaucracy. In the case of Buddhism, alliances between officials searching for loyal authorities approximating a "church" and monastic elites seeking state backing transformed local hierarchies. In 1853, Nicholas I approved a centralized apparatus in Eastern Siberia to oversee these temples and their "clergy." The implications of such measures proved most dramatic for traditions that did not depend on an internally established hierarchical organization.

For the Ministry of the Interior, determining what constituted "orthodox" opinion proved even more difficult when its officials could not look to an institution resembling a church structure. Judaism and Islam presented the state with very similar dilemmas. Officials scrutinized Jewish affairs with an eye to cultivating a form of Judaism that would be "useful" to both the Jews and the state. The Nicholaevan regime thus took steps to educate and institute an enlightened rabbinate. Reared in state institutions, "learned Jews" (*uchenye evrei*) and crown rabbis would supply officials with authoritative knowledge about Jewish law and perform some of the same disciplinary tasks as Muslim clerics. A Rabbinical Commission established in 1848 acted, like the Orenburg Assembly, as the highest authority on the religious law.

In Muslim communities, legislation inspired by Orthodox ecclesiology set apart ecclesiastical elite from lay society and extended the power of the former over the latter. In each "parish" (*prikhod*), the regime aimed at consolidating a formal "Muhammadan clergy" (*dukhovenstvo*) from among a group of men previously distinguished only by their learning and their standing in the eyes of local communities. The state assigned monopolies over the performance of marriage and divorce, the rites of burial, and the administration of oaths for state service, legal transactions, and witness testimony. Prohibitions against involvement in trade and other activities formalized and professionalized the clerical status of mullahs and rabbis. Some of these newly appointed clerics evaded attempts to limit their livelihoods, while others welcomed assistance against laypeople (and lower clerics) who performed marriages, burials, or other duties outside of their legal purview.

Non-Orthodox clerics likewise fulfilled a wide range of bureaucratic and social functions that complemented state undertakings in the realm of charity, welfare, and education, overseeing poorhouses, soup kitchens, orphanages, and hospitals. Confessional schools and religious courts played a pivotal role in the imperial educational and judicial systems. Like Islamic courts, the Jewish *beth-din* dealt with marriage, divorce, inheritance, commerce, and contracts. Such institutions administered oaths to soldiers, witnesses, and litigants, demonstrating that the Orthodox creed was not the only pledge of political loyalty recognized by the state. For criminal offenses, subjects answered to both state and ecclesiastical officials; they were subject not only to secular punishment but to "penitence," "admonition," and other sanctions administered by religious personnel.

The non-Orthodox faiths played a critical role in

disciplining the family. Just as the Orthodox Church regulated marriage to ensure domestic tranquility as a foundation of the political order, the Ministry of the Interior expected non-Orthodox leaders to exert similar controls. Endowed with unprecedented police powers, the new clergies monitored compliance with statutes establishing minimum ages for marriage, as well as questions of legitimacy, fidelity, incest, and the submission of children to parents. Far from autonomous actors, these authorities remained vulnerable to challenges from both the state and the laity. Officials intervened in marriage disputes at the request of dissatisfied litigants and overturned the rulings of these authorities. Through these new instruments and the appellate mechanisms that linked them to central judicial organs, religious and secular authorities expanded their power to regulate family life.

At the same time, this mediating role increased their knowledge about, and access to, local communities, enabling them to police many contacts between confessional groups and proscribe most kinds of intermarriage. While the administration provided new mechanisms of social control, the law reinforced clerical dependence on secular power by prohibiting existing mechanisms for compelling conformity, such as the rabbinic resort to punishment "by fines, curses, and expulsion from the community." Similarly, the state denied Muslim clerics the use of corporal punishment, abrogating a range of Quranic punishments for theft, adultery, alcohol, and other offenses against religion. Thus a basic tension marked sponsorship of non-Orthodox hierarchies and their disciplinary powers: the law forged interdependence between clerics and state officials by expanding clerical authority in some areas and limiting it in others.

While Russian officials thus sought to establish a clear chain of command running from St. Petersburg into the local parish, mosque, or synagogue community, they also remained responsive to challenges from below. Officials looked to lay initiative to keep clerical abuses in check. They proved sympathetic to lay reformers who admonished mullahs who drank wine or priests who seduced parishioners. Charges of "false teaching" and the exercise of miraculous powers suggested subversion and prompted police investigations. Despite the many shortcomings of the tsarist legal system and threats from co-religionists ranging from social ostracism to murder, laypeople continued to look to the tsar's justice to overturn religious judgments. Clerical sanction alone remained insufficient to maintain the absolute power of informal religious courts, which relied on state authorities to implement controversial rulings.

Successful overtures to Russian officials depended on the litigants' ability to translate internal disputes into tsarist political categories. In constructing their complaints and denunciations, contestants confronted the challenge of casting their opponents' views and actions as "heresy"—and thus beyond the scope of official toleration. Heresy in any community constituted a political issue in tsarist Russia: to the police, religious dissent and heterodoxy almost invariably involved a broader challenge to the existing order. When a new "rationalist" hymnal appeared among reformist Protestants in 1819, the tsar condemned the book, vowing to "protect" the Evangelical Church from "rules deviating from Christian morality."

In 1823, the Ministry of the Interior acquiesced to the Catholic hierarchy's request to suppress the champions of heterodox doctrine such as Ignace Lindl (who rejected the pope, the cult of the saints, and the Virgin Mary) by expelling the German mystic. Jews, too, looked to tsarist police to aid them against opponents and often represented religious differences as political crimes. From the late eighteenth century, the Talmudic elite in Lithuania drew Russian police into conflicts between them and the *Hasidim,* adherents of a new pietistic movement. Based on Jewish denunciations, police arrested some prominent Hasidic leaders and placed others under surveillance. *Hasidim* such as the Jews of

Rogachev of Mogilev province responded by warning the minister of the interior that their antagonists, such as the "learned Jew" Moisei Berlin, "not only did not come up to the goals and expectations of the government, but served as an example of depravity and the slackening of the fulfillment of God's law and the dogma of our religion for youth."

Concern for policing orthodoxy was not limited to the Ministry of the Interior or even to clerical elites. Laypeople also calculated that heresy left unchecked would undermine the community from within. Spokesmen for the Jewish Enlightenment (Haskalah) turned to the regime, seeking patronage for their vision of a religion compatible with "civic responsibilities to the tsar and motherland" as well as "respectable and useful labor in all branches of the crafts, commerce, and agriculture." Like the *Hasidim* and their foes, proponents and critics of the Haskalah did not shy away from denouncing their opponents. For Jews and Muslims, toleration circumscribed religious autonomy while linking confessional disputes to state patronage and policing. Despite the conservative aims of officials, support for novel forms of bureaucratic organization and doctrinal emphasis brought change to every community.

Ceremonies and liturgies integrated tsar and fatherland, while the rites of marriage, divorce, and death became the business of new hierarchies as well as of the Ministry of the Interior. Religious authorities adopted statistics, archives, examinations, and inspections as measures of internal social control. The recording of marriages, births, divorces, and deaths facilitated a more systematic and uniform application of canon law in Christian confessions, aided in establishing religious norms to govern the inner life of the family and community in others, and assisted the government in the levying of taxes and recruits.

Police intervention became a dynamic agent of communal transformation, suppressing particular interpretations of the faith and advancing others. However, this kind of intervention did not emerge as a result of a concerted policy of "divide and rule" or a grand integrative strategy from above. Legislation and institutions governing the non-Orthodox often took shape as ad hoc responses to initiatives from members of these groups. Muslims, Jews, and others themselves shaped this process by initiating and placing limits on contacts with tsarist authorities. A closer examination of the expansion of the state into the lives of Muslim men and women on the southeastern frontier reveals how the interdependence of Muslim communities and the regime grew out of the practice of *Polizeistaat* toleration and the collective pursuit of religious orthodoxy. From the fifteenth century, when Russia first acquired Muslim populated lands, Muscovite rulers accommodated Muslims informally.

In the next century, Russian expansion into the Volga and Urals regions put an end to local Muslim dynasties. Islamic institutions continued to exist beyond the purview of the state but remained subject to periodic assault at the hands of Orthodox militants, who leveled mosques and schools. As in other Muslim societies, learned men and women assumed positions of religious leadership outside the auspices of formal hierarchies. No single authority either defined or enforced a particular interpretation of Islamic orthodoxy, and Muslims engaged in debate largely without recourse to enforcement beyond the pressures of local, close-knit communal life. However, in the late eighteenth and early nineteenth centuries, the regime transformed the foundations of Islamic culture in the empire by extending its patronage to Islamic institutions, including generous state subsidies for mosques, the printing of the Quran and other religious texts, and, most important, the creation of a centralized hierarchy.

The Orenburg Assembly used its regulatory and investigative authority to oversee religious life in each mosque community by administering clerical examinations, licenses, visitations, and the archival recording of judicial decisions. Through these new instruments, state-appointed Islamic authorities advanced novel understandings of the *shari'a,* which encompassed the norms, obligations, and rights enjoined by God's will for all the faithful. While following the directives of St. Petersburg, the mufti and judges (*kadis*) of the assembly capitalized on official support to pursue their own agenda. They relied on the police to secure the uniform application of a narrower and, in their view, more "orthodox" range of opinions of the Hanafi School of law (one of the four established Sunni legal traditions) and Naqshbandi Sufi order.

Under Mufti Abdulvakhid Suleimanov, for example, the assembly utilized the Saratov provincial administration to pursue a disputed issue within Sufism about the legality of performing the rite of remembrance of the name of God (*zikr*) silently or vocally. In 1862, it ordered Muslims in the village of Tatarskie Kanadi to desist from "pronouncing prayers aloud," declaring that those who did not refrain from vocal *zikr* would be barred from the mosque as "apostates from the *sharia*" (*otstupniki ot Sharigata*). Armed with the tools of a modernizing regime, they combated similar departures from Naqshbandi positions and other regional variations in Islamic legal interpretation arising from the varied customs and social conditions of local communities, broad clerical discretion, and the circulation of diverse texts with a plurality of accepted opinions on particular issues.

In sponsoring the mufti, the state gained a voice who recognized the empire as the "House of Islam" (*dar al-Islam*), a territory where Muslims could fulfill their religious duties. Muslim authorities represented such a potentially valuable resource for the government because they claimed guardianship of an array of legal matters that European jurisprudence would elsewhere break up into "civil," "criminal," "ecclesiastical," or "commercial" law. In determining the religious legality of personal behavior, the men of learning and piety (ulama) interpreted a vast body of sources, including the Quran, the sayings and acts of the

Prophet, and various legal commentaries. The ulama claimed textual authority in the name of protecting the community against error and irreligion.

Prayer-leaders exhorted villagers and townspeople who neglected communal prayer. They reconciled quarreling husbands and wives, educated the youth, and guided Muslims to live pious lives according to the *shari'a*. At the same time, the muftis cooperated with provincial officials who requested *fatwas* defining the instructions of secular officials as sacred obligations. *Fatwas* penned by the second mufti, Abdusalam Abdrakhimov, directed Muslims to send their children to Kazan University for medical training in 1831 and, wielding citations from the Quran and other sources, exhorted peasants in 1832 to labor diligently in the fields, sowing and harvesting at the appropriate times, as a defense against poverty and the pleasures of sin.

Recognized by the tsar with the award of a gold medal, Abdrakhimov demonstrated his value again in 1836 when he reminded his charges that "each orthodox Muslim is obliged to obey the authorities and the laws" and to avoid sin, which invokes "God's anger and punishment." In sermons, treatises, oaths, and prayers for the imperial family, official ulama enjoined obedience, loyalty, and patriotism. They aided the state in carrying out conscription and other administrative functions and preached the submission of children to their parents—and of Muslims to the regime. Although officials expected the ulama to assist the insertion of the political order into each locale, these Muslim scholars did not necessarily enjoy unbounded authority in their own communities. Even after the introduction of the official hierarchy, their powers still depended on the opinion of the local lay community who elected them and could later petition the state for their removal.

Contemporary biographical literature compiled by Muslim scholars celebrated the exemplary lives of those whose reputations for learning and piety empowered them to correct the religion of the people. Notable scholars gained renown for study in cosmopolitan centers of Islamic scholarship such as Bukhara, Kabul, Baghdad, Cairo, and Istanbul, or, closer to home, in the village of Tatarskaia Kargala on the steppe frontier of Orenburg province, and many imams earned (or inherited from their fathers) a name for being "gentle and gracious" in their relations with members of the mosque community. Still others were remembered for their acerbic wit. Gabbas b. Gabderräshid äl-Küshäri once confronted the prayer-leader of the village of Shashï, who had placed the niche marking the direction for prayer on the wrong side of the mosque. When the prayer-leader defended his mistake by citing a text of foreign origin (*A Collection of Signs*) pointing to Mecca in the West, Küshäri retorted, "Hey, stupid, was *A Collection of Signs* written in your Shashï?"

Clerics like the unfortunate imam of Shashï became increasingly exposed in the nineteenth century to ridicule and other challenges from scholars and laypeople who could now turn to state institutions to "correct" what they held to be unorthodox practices. In turn, the fragile position of Muslim clerics forced them to seek out closer association with officials to back their authority. Village prayer-leaders combating debauchery, the refusal to attend prayers, the celebration of "un-Islamic" holidays, and competition from unlicensed rivals frequently had to resort to denouncing their parishi-oners not only to the Islamic hierarchy but to local police. As the imam Mukhamet'zhan Kuziakhmetov warned his flock in 1871, "for insubordination and non-fulfillment" of the *shari'a,* "[you] may be punished by God and the civil court."

The instruments of the modern state became essential to "orthodox" claims about the fulfillment of God's will. Recent research has pointed to the intense debates among Muslim scholars in Russia about interpretation of the *shari'a,* or divine law. By tracing the contours of these conflicts among Muslim elites, these studies challenge the image of a monolithic and timeless Islam. But the dynamism of these conflicts owed much to the fact that the contest for religious authority extended beyond the elites. Reformist Muslim scholars such as Rizaeddin Fahreddinev wrote numerous treatises defending clerical authority over lay Muslims and the power of men over women who stood to receive a "terrible punishment" in the afterlife for disobeying their husbands. But the licensed keepers of Islamic knowledge were not the only ones committed to correcting those who had ostensibly strayed from the true path.

Lay and clerical opponents of the interpretive monopoly of elites relied on a tradition in which interpretation of the *shari'a* potentially produced multiple solutions to a wide array of specific problems, ranging from divorce to commercial transactions. Until the modern era of nation-states and legal codification, Islamic law did not reside in a single text or authority. Indeed, most Muslim scholars regarded *fatwas* as mere opinions—not binding rulings, except where temporal authorities backed their writ. In a legal tradition that relied on numerous authoritative sources and entertained the possibility of varied outcomes depending on the local social context, determining a *single*, uniform "orthodoxy" for police enforcement unleashed intense conflicts. Official endorsement of orthodoxy meant that, in practice, the police became responsible for enforcing Islamic judicial decisions.

In an influential study of Islamic law, Lawrence Rosen has highlighted the role of the Islamic judge as a mediator, a facilitator of "social bargaining," whose aim "is to put people back in the position of being able to negotiate their own permissible relationships without predetermining just what the outcome of those negotiations ought to be." Under the Orenburg Assembly, prayer-leaders and judges assumed this role in formal legal proceedings and informally outside the mosque courtyard. Many of their decisions fitted with "the cultural concepts and social relations to which they were inextricably tied." But, equally important, parties to disputes often eschewed mediation and opted for direct state intervention instead. When litigants turned to the police, debates over the *shari'a* shifted from the local social environment, where neighbors and spouses might bargain and reconcile, toward coercive settlement of intractable differences under state control.

Police involvement in returning wives who had fled their husbands, removing children from divorced spouses, or restraining controversial preachers did not facilitate negotiation but brought a bureaucratic finality to contested cases. Lay Muslims thus looked to the institutions of the empire to insist on their own interpretations of God's law. Armed with knowledge acquired in a vast network of Quranic schools as well as through poetry, pilgrimage, sermons, and the circulation of printed and manuscript tracts, men and women pointed out the errors of clerics, relatives, and neighbours who avoided the mosque, drank wine, sang prayers, beat their wives, or committed adultery. They even attacked prayer-leaders who failed to perform the rites, such as communal prayer, burial of the dead, and the celebration of holidays, that dramatized the bonds of community. Mediated by translators, scribes, and bilingual informants, calls for state involvement made explicit references to imperial statutes and decrees.

Muslims developed novel rhetorical strategies to press their cases, integrating tsarist law codes, decrees, and procedure alongside appeals to the tsar and imperial family, the Quran, the sayings and acts of the Prophet, and other Islamic legal literature. Denunciations that translated local conflicts over spiritual authority and theological interpretation into the vocabulary of tsarist law and the Orthodox Church proved most successful in launching police investigations. The criminal code became a valuable tool in the hands of Muslims who learned to cast their opponents as self-styled "saints," "pretenders," and "schismatics" (*raskol'niki*) or to connect them with inciting conversion to Islam.

For the seekers of true religion, like the villagers of Bazitamak in Orenburg province who denounced their imam to Tsar Nicholas in 1849, intervention became a catalyst for strengthening the community and a guarantor of Islamic orthodoxy. They argued that the state, too, benefited from true religion and suffered from its neglect; in the absence of prayers led by the imam, "the Muhammadan people [had] almost begun to forget its faith," and youth strayed toward criminality "without reproach from the imam about fear of God." In Kazan, Muslims tried to solicit police intervention "in accordance with both the *shari'a* and the civil law" against Muslim women who appeared in public with "open faces" and engaged in prostitution. When Muslim peasants in Orenburg province addressed a petition to Nicholas I in 1833 to seek his help in ridding the village of their prayer-leader, they were motivated not by feelings of ethnic solidarity but by the conviction that the state would serve the cause of piety by punishing their imam, Sharafutdin Rakhimov.

For these peasants, the conflict with Rakhimov represented a struggle to live according to God's law and to remove the polluting influence of an imam who refused to lead the community in worship, tormented the souls of the dead by neglecting their burial, and even beat one of his denouncers to a state of "great ill-health." Acting on their denunciation, the local police removed the imam from his position for "deeds carried out not only against the Muhammadan religion and its rules but also imperial statutes" and thereby affirmed these petitioners' vision of the regime as the disciplinary instrument of a community governed by the sacred law. Similarly, in February 1832, peasants in the district of Kazan gathered to condemn their mullah for provoking God's punishment, but they did not confine themselves to the rough justice of the village.

The men of the community turned against Mullah Lupman Fatkullin to the township administration, seeking his removal and expulsion from the village. They informed local authorities that Fatkullin violated the *shari'a* by ignoring the five daily prayers, disregarding his obligation to instruct the children, and subjecting especially pious men—and even women—to "foul insults." The villagers echoed many Muslims who complained that the failings of their prayer-leaders had led to the decline of morals and the corruption of youth. Their denunciations drew on established anti-clerical tropes about greedy and self-interested mullahs. But pious concern for the collective obligations of the divine law may also have reflected local adaptation of new forms of Sufi thought transmitted orally by scholars and in manuscripts that circulated throughout the empire.

By appealing to authorities outside of their own village, and beyond the Muslim community, these locals effectively challenged the licensed ulama; they looked to the regime to restore "collective prayer" and spare the community from "the shudder of divine punishment," which the villagers saw in "the recent [outbreak of] the dangerous disease of cholera near our village." Notwithstanding the ambiguous status of appeal in the Islamic tradition, Muslims embraced the practice in Russia as a means to challenge the outcome of Islamic law court cases and safeguard the rights and obligations that they understood as essential components of the *shari'a*. Laypeople challenged prayer-leaders and judges by looking beyond the village or town mosque community to the police, the Orenburg Assembly, and the minister of the interior, whom a petition from mullahs in Orenburg province in 1863 styled the "Minister of Interior and Muslim Religious Affairs [*sic*]."

Similar appellate mechanisms appeared in other empires, but tsarist officials defended "orthodox" interpretation of the *shari'a* more consistently than their British or French counterparts. Where European judges incorporated considerations of "equity" and Roman legal principles, Russians looked almost exclusively to authoritative interpretation of the Islamic tradition. In the tsarist setting, Muslims had access to two interrelated modes of appeal. In the first, aggrieved parties, as individuals or as kin groups, contested the resolution of divorce, inheritance, and other disputes by asking the Orenburg Assembly to review the case. In the second, litigants petitioned Russian officials ranging from the local bailiff to the emperor to overturn the rulings of local ulama, to compel husbands to refrain from beating their wives, or otherwise commit themselves to live "in accordance with the *shari'a.*"

In both types of appeal, the process began with the composition of a petition or complaint (usually on the basis of oral testimony) at the offices of the local police; the police investigated claims about the violation of the *shari'a,* gathered evidence, and then oversaw the execution of the final judgment. Litigants might simultaneously pursue both strategies or, after exhausting the first option, turn to the tsar with confidence that the laws of the empire supported God's law. Both state archival records and Muslim historical sources show how contests over religious authority quietly transformed these small, face-to-face communities and their relationship to the state, as men and women adopted the practice of soliciting intervention to contest the outcomes of divorce, inheritance, and other cases involving the *shari'a.*

In 1820, Bibi Kiz Bike petitioned the mufti to secure maintenance (*nafaqa*) from her husband. In the same year, a villager named Sayyid from the Volga province of Simbirsk abrogated a marriage contract with his future son-in-law, Mecid, by refusing to permit his daughter Bibi Habibe to marry her fiancé. Mecid charged Sayyid with violating an agreement sanctioned by the *shari'a* and turned to the district police chief, who organized an investigation and gathered testimony from the villagers. After consulting the Orenburg Assembly, the police instructed local mullahs to assist in determining the legality of the contract on the basis of Islamic law. The mullahs apparently tried to reconcile the families of the betrothed, but, when mediation failed, the mufti Husainov put an end to the case by ruling that Sayyid was obliged to turn his daughter over to Mecid—a judgment to be delivered to the litigants and carried out jointly by the mullahs and the police.

By the second quarter of the century, Muslims in over a dozen provinces had learned to act on the social and religious obligation to discipline co-religionists by turning to the regime and its Islamic institutions to restore the communal religious standards and the purity of the faith commanded by God's law. While recourse to tsarist law became an essential tool in the hands of Muslims whose competing visions of the *shari'a* animated clerical rivalries and village feuds, men and women also looked to the state to compel their spouses to live "according to the *shari'a*." As in other Muslim societies, women emerged as particularly active litigants. Often assisted by guardians and kin, they utilized courts and appeals to restrain abusive husbands, defend their honor, and even initiate divorce based on the claim that the *shari'a* accorded them these rights.

Women such as Khamida Salikhova, from the village of Novoe-Baltachevo in Orenburg province, turned to Nicholas I to protest the brutality of their husbands, asserting in petitions that physical abuse justified the awarding of a divorce "in accordance with the Muhammadan faith." Invoking the protection of imperial law and officials, appeals from disgruntled wives, disappointed husbands, and frustrated prayer-leaders seeking justice and fulfillment of the divine will made the tsarist police arbiters of the most intimate of religious and familial disputes.

LESSONS FROM THE OTTOMAN *EMPIRE*

The Ottoman Empire was an Islamic polity that originated in early-fourteenth-century Anatolia. Islam had been established in Anatolia before the emergence of the empire, but between the fourteenth and sixteenth centuries the religion spread with Ottoman conquest to the Balkan Peninsula and central Hungary. This does not mean that the population was uniformly Muslim. In many parts of the

Ottoman Empire, most notably in the Balkan Peninsula, Christians formed a majority of the population, and even in areas where Muslims formed a majority there was usually also a minority of non-Muslim inhabitants. Unlike some of the rulers of western Europe, the Ottoman sultans never attempted to impose religious uniformity. Islam was, however, the dominant religion, and the political structure of the empire reflected this fact. The dynasty itself was Muslim and, before the reforms of the nineteenth century, with rare exceptions, non-Muslims could not hold regular political office or military command.

Christians and Jews were able to participate in the maintenance of the empire by serving as tax farmers or contractors supplying, for example, cloth for Janissary uniforms or materials to the naval arsenals, but they could not serve as viziers, provincial governors, or army commanders. In the fourteenth and fifteenth centuries a few Christian fief holders in the Balkans retained their positions in the years immediately after the Ottoman conquest but, as their descendants converted to Islam, this phenomenon disappeared within a generation. In the Balkans, too, some Christian groups served as military auxiliaries into the sixteenth century. More important in the day-to-day lives of the sultan's subjects, the system of law courts also reflected the dominant position of Islam.

The Christian and Jewish communities maintained their own courts for regulating intra-communal affairs, but only the network of Muslim courts covered the entire empire, and only Muslim courts were open to all the sultan's subjects, irrespective of religion. Any cases involving Muslims or a Muslim and a non-Muslim had to be heard in the Muslim court and, in principle, a non-Muslim could not testify against a Muslim. The exclusion, therefore, of non-Muslims from political office and the supremacy of Islamic law guaranteed the hegemonic position of Islam within the Ottoman Empire. At the same time, the imposition of *jizya*, a poll tax on adult non-Muslim males, and the occasional short-lived imposition of dress restrictions on non-Muslims, symbolized the inferior position of Christians and Jews.

By the time of the emergence of the Ottoman Empire in the fourteenth century, Islam was fully formed as a system of belief with its associated intellectual, legal, and cultural attributes. The central concept of the religion was "knowledge," or *'ilm*, meaning specifically the knowledge of God through revelation. God had revealed himself to mankind through the missions of the prophets, among whom Abraham (Ibrahim), the monotheistic founder of the Ka'ba at Mecca, Moses (Musa), and Jesus (Isa) held especially revered positions. The recognition of Abraham, Moses, and Jesus as prophets before the final revelation of Islam justified the tolerated but subordinate positions of Jews and Christians within the Ottoman Empire and other Islamic polities. God's final and most perfect revelation was through the prophet Muhammad, "the Seal of the Prophets."

The primary text of revelation is the Koran. This is regarded by Muslims as the literal word of God transmitted to mankind through the medium of the Prophet. The record of the sayings and actions—the hadith—of the Prophet, as an exemplar to mankind, form the second text of the revelation. It is through the Koran and hadith, therefore, that man can know God and, in principle, these form the foundation of knowledge, or *'ilm.* A seeker after knowledge had first to study Arabic, the language of revelation and the language of science, which acquired a role in the Ottoman Empire and in the Islamic world as the universal language of religion, somewhat similar to the role of Latin in western Christendom.

The study of the sacred texts and the sciences in general also required grounding in logic and rhetoric. With these tools at his disposal, a scholar could embark on any of the specialized branches of *ilm,* which developed as discrete, though interrelated genres: the interpretation of the Koran *(tafsir)*, the study of hadith, theology *(kalam)*, dogma *(aqaid)* or law *(fiqh)*. These were the sciences through which one acquired knowledge of God, and which therefore formed the central curriculum of Ottoman and other Islamic colleges. Subsidiary sciences—for example, the life of the Prophet *(sira)*, history *(tarikh)*, the vitae of saints or scholars by generation *(tabaqat)*—served to strengthen sectarian or dynastic identity, and all came to form genres of Ottoman literature. Of the sciences, it was the study of law *(fiqh)* that enjoyed the greatest prestige and made the greatest impact on communal and individual lives.

It represented not exactly God's commands to mankind, as these are ultimately unknowable, but the best that humankind can achieve in its efforts to discover God's law. It regulated not only secular affairs, notably in the sphere of family law, but also rituals such as ablution, prayer, fasting, and forbidden foods. The basics of the law, popularized as the "five pillars of Islam"—the profession of faith, prayer five times daily, charity, fasting during Ramadan, and the pilgrimage to Mecca—are something that every Muslim must know. In many respects, therefore, it was the adoption of Islamic law—the *shar* or *sharia*—that gave Ottoman, and other Islamic societies, their distinctive form. A person who had studied *ilm* was an *alim* ('one who knows [God]') and enjoyed great prestige. The plural of *alim* is *ulama*, and the ulema came to form a respected class within all Muslim societies, often, as in the Ottoman Empire, wielding political as well as legal and spiritual power.

Ilm was not, however, the only route to knowing God. Already in the early centuries of Islam some claimed to know God through direct revelation, a condition exemplified by the saying of al-Sarraj (d. 988): "There is no *ilm* that is known and nothing that is understood except what exists in the Book of God, or is transmitted from the Messenger of God, or in what is revealed in the hearts of saints." In order to distinguish the knowledge of God acquired by direct revelation "in the hearts of saints," its adepts, the Sufis, referred to it not as *alm,* but as *urf or marifa,* both words having the sense of "knowledge." This doctrine had revolutionary potential, since a person claiming knowledge via direct divine inspiration could claim to be above the divine law as professed by the ulema. Indeed some Sufis, notably al-Hallaj (d. 909), who reputedly suffered death for declaring "I am God," did emerge, in the Ottoman Empire and elsewhere, as opponents of the religious and political order. What is more remarkable, however, is how *tasawwuf,* the faith of the Sufis—radically different from the religion of the ulema—came to form a branch of orthodox Islam.

In principle, *ilm* and *urf* are antagonistic in their fundamental beliefs. In orthodox belief, God created the world ex nihilo; he revealed himself through his prophets; the world will end with the Resurrection and the Judgment, where individuals will be judged and assigned in eternity to Heaven or Hell. In Sufi belief, all creation was originally one with God. God created mankind and the universe because "He was a hidden treasure and wished that He should be known." Since this separation from the Creator, all Creation has yearned to return to its Maker. The Sufi therefore yearns to be reunited with God, as the lover yearns for union with the beloved. In orthodox Islam, knowledge of God comes through written revelation whose interpretation is the preserve of the ulema. In Sufi belief, knowledge of God is acquired through direct experience, or "taste" of God.

There has at all times been antagonism between some of the orthodox ulema and the Sufis. For example, in the Ottoman Empire of the mid-sixteenth century, the jurist Ibrahim of Aleppo (d. 1549) and the Ottoman chief mufti, Çivizade Mehmed (d. 1542), adopted anti-Sufi positions, while the Sufis for their part conducted a literary polemic against these orthodox opponents. The poet Khayali (d. 1556/57) compared the orthodox ulema that could not recognize that God was in the world around them to "fish who are in the sea, but do not know what the sea is."

Nonetheless, opponents of the Sufis remained a minority and *tasawwuf* in practice became an important strand of mainstream Islam in the Ottoman Empire. *Tasawwuf* grew in importance through doctrinal development. In the developed Sufi theory of knowledge, the first rule that a Sufi must follow is obedience to the *sharia.* This precept brought *tasawwuf* within the bounds of orthodoxy. Second, the spiri-tual goal of most Sufis was not to declare "I am God," but to seek "annihilation of the self in God": the Sufi's soul became like "a drop of wine in the ocean of God's love." In other words, *tasawwuf* became quietist rather than activist. At the same time, *tasawwuf* became institutionalized.

Different orders of Sufis formed around the memories of Sufi saints, and these organizations acquired properties and endowments, to preserve which they had to remain acceptable to orthodox Islamic regimes. Finally, the favorable opinions of al-Ghazali (d. 1111), perhaps the most influential Islamic thinker made *tasawwuf* acceptable to most orthodox opinion. Some orders, it is true, remained unacceptable. In the Ottoman Empire, an offshoot of the Bayrami order of Sufis, which formed after 1450, adopted the activist belief that God is manifest in the human form, thus putting men—or at least their members—above the dictates of the *sharia.* These Sufis constituted an underground and ineffective, though persecuted, opposition to orthodox Islam and the Ottoman sultanate.

Although *tasawwuf* may have been the strongest influence on the beliefs of many, if not most, Ottoman Muslims and permeated Ottoman literature, music, and visual art, it was the Islam of the ulema that was significant in determining the structures of the empire. A few surviving literary fragments suggest that in the fourteenth century, the level of Islamic learning in the Ottoman Empire was very low. Persons wishing for an advanced Islamic education at this period traveled to the old Islamic world, especially to Damascus or Cairo, and it was largely these returning scholars who transferred Islamic doctrine and law to the Ottoman realms and trained the early generations of Ottoman ulema. By the mid-fifteenth century, with the establishment of a system of colleges within the empire and the formation of a learned class, there was no further need for such learning journeys.

The religious colleges (madrasas) attached to mosques throughout the empire, established on the model of the madrasas in the old Islamic world, were the institutions that trained the ulema. The most prestigious colleges were royal foundations, with the Eight Colleges of Mehmed II (1451–1481) and the colleges attached to the mosque of Suleiman I (1520–1566), completed in 1557, enjoying the highest rank, and the foundations of senior statesmen occupying the second tier. Each college was an independent institution with a separate endowment. In the sixteenth century, however, Suleiman I and later Mehmed III (1595–1603) made efforts to formalize the hierarchy of colleges and, to a degree, to control the curriculum, which remained firmly based on the medieval Islamic classics.

By the seventeenth century there seems to have been a well-recognized hierarchy, based on the wealth of the endowment and the level of the curriculum. From the late seventeenth century, when the empire began to lose territories, some colleges suffered as the lands that provided their endowments passed into foreign hands. It was the colleges that maintained the level of Islamic learning in the empire. A graduate might find a position as imam in an important mosque; he might stay in the system as a teacher *(mudarris)*; or he might choose a career as a judge *(qadi)*. However, if he opted for a legal career immediately on graduating, he would, at least between the sixteenth and eighteenth centuries, find his career confined to the judgeships of small towns. Judgeships of the great cities, especially of Istanbul, Edirne, and Bursa, were reserved for *mudarris*es from the Eight Colleges or other high-ranking madrasas.

Furthermore, between the sixteenth and the eighteenth centuries, a few ulema families monopolized these prestigious teaching positions and judgeships. It was also from the judges of the great cities that the sultan chose the two military judges *(kadiaskers)*, the senior judges of the empire, who sat on the Imperial Council. Below the level of the great cities, however, most of the judges and religious officials tended to be local men, who from the sixteenth century would normally have received part of their education in Istanbul. The judges, at all levels, administered Islamic law, and in continuing to exercise this function at all times, including times of crisis, they played the major role in ensuring the stability and continuity of Ottoman government. Of the four schools of law within Sunni Islam—the Shafii, Maliki, Hanbali, and Hanafi—the Ottomans adopted the Hanafi school, presumably because this is the school that was already established in pre-Ottoman Anatolia.

As the Hanafi jurists typically offer more than one acceptable solution to each legal problem, the Hanafi was perhaps the most flexible of the schools and, for this reason, the most suitable to form the basis of a working legal system. After their formative period in the early Islamic centuries, the four schools remained mutually exclusive. According to Hanafi theorists, for example, a person could have recourse to a Shafii judge only in the two cases for which the Hanafi School offered no solution: the dissolution of an oath or when a deserted wife seeks dissolution of marriage. The Ottomans endorsed this exclusivity, although among the general population in the Arab lands there was some movement between schools.

Judges in the Ottoman Empire as elsewhere put the law into effect by virtue of the delegation to them of sultanic power and above the judges stood the muftis. A mufti is a religious authority with the competence to issue *fatwas*, authoritative opinions on any religious-legal problems that questioners may ask. A *fatwa* is not an executive command:

it requires a judge's or sovereign's decree to put it into effect. It also differs from a judge's decree, in that the judge's decree is valid only for the case in hand, while the *fatwa* has a universal validity. Ottoman *fatwa*s reflect this understanding by reformulating each question so as to conceal the identity of the questioner, even if the questioner was the sultan himself, to remove specific details of the case such as time, locality, or personal identities, and to eliminate details not relevant to the case in question.

Between the sixteenth and eighteenth centuries, Ottoman *fatwa*s in their content, format, and anonymity came increasingly to resemble the classical juristic texts which were the source of their authority. The mufti in theory remained above and apart from the secular power, a concept embodied from the sixteenth century in Ottoman ceremonial, where the sultan stands in the presence of the chief mufti. His authority derived from his role as interpreter of the Holy Law in its application to mundane realities, including the realities of political power. In much of the Islamic world, muftis acquired their role through public recognition rather than official appointment, and really did stand apart from the secular power. In the Ottoman Empire, however, the muftis were effectively part of the government.

The chief mufti, or *sheikh al-islam* as he came to be known by the seventeenth century, was the senior figure in the religious-legal establishment, and usually achieved the position by serving first as a senior judge and then as a military judge; like these offices, the chief mufti ship after the mid-sixteenth century came to be the preserve of a very few ulema families. The chief mufti owed his exalted position partly to the Islamic view that accorded greater dignity to muftis than to judges, but also to the prestige of two sixteenth-century holders of the office, Kemal Pashazade (1525–1534) and Ebus-suud Mehmed (1545–1574). Ebus-suud in particular systematized the chief mufti's major function of issuing *fatwa*s, ensuring that his office was able to undertake a great volume of work to a high standard. The system that he established remained in its essentials intact until the end of the empire. The chief mufti came to have an important, if informal, role in the Ottoman government. Outside the capital, muftis were sometimes official appointees, but did not enjoy high status of the chief mufti, and their function could often be fulfilled by the *mudarris* of a local college.

By the time of the establishment of the Ottoman Empire, *tasawwuf* was well established in the Islamic world and accepted, within limits, as a form of orthodox Islam. Groups of Sufis had established and continued to establish their own orders *(tariqas)* throughout the Islamic world, each with its own saints and distinctive beliefs and rituals. Many of the orders that originated outside the empire found disciples in Ottoman territories. For example, the Khalveti order, named after the eponymous saint Umar al-Khalwati, originated in late-fourteenth-century Azerbaijan. During the fifteenth century the disciples of the Khalveti sheikh Yahya al-Shirvani (d. c. 1463) brought the order to Anatolia. When he was governor of Amasya, the future sultan Bayezid II (1480–1512) was initiated as a Khalveti and established the order in Istanbul after he became sultan. Later, Murad III (1574–1595) was also initiated. Other orders originated within the Ottoman Empire itself. For example, the Bayrami order was the creation of Hajji Bayram (d. 1429/30), who established the fraternity originally among the craftsmen of Ankara. His successor Ak Shemseddin (d. 1459) became a spiritual mentor to Mehmed II.

Once established, Sufi orders sometimes split into smaller groups, the Khalvetis, for example, giving birth to ten or more subgroups during the sixteenth and seventeenth centuries. The Bayramis, too, split into two groups after 1450, the orthodox group following Ak Shemseddin, the "heretical" group, the Melamis, coming under the leadership of Ömer the Cutler (d. 1475/6). This group became particularly active in Bosnia. By the late seventeenth century, however, the Melamis had reemerged as an orthodox order, although distinct from the original Bayramis. Conversely, different groups could merge. The Bektashi order, which took its name from a fourteenth century saint, Hajji Bektash, formed as a coherent order under the leadership of Balim Sultan about 1500, and absorbed and syncretized a wide range of Sufi and other popular beliefs. The Bektashis became particularly well established in Albania.

Many Muslims in the Ottoman Empire belonged to a Sufi order, giving these an essential role not only in disseminating popular faith but also in establishing networks and social solidarity among members. In some orders membership included women giving them a role not available in orthodox Islam. The orders could also acquire charitable functions, the rural lodges of the Bektashis, for example, providing accommodation for travelers. Above all, they influenced the cultural life of the empire. Each order had its own liturgy and ceremonies, usually involving music, recitation, singing, and sometimes dancing, and to preserve their traditions the orders had to train adepts in these arts, many of whom acquired fame beyond the confines of the organization.

The Mevlevi order—the so-called whirling dervishes—had a particular educational role. The sacred text of the order, the lengthy mystical poem known as the Mesnevi, by its eponymous saint, Mevlana Celaleddin Rumi (d. 1273), is written in Persian, a language that Mevlevis therefore had to learn. Since Persian was not taught in Ottoman madrasas, it was above all the Mevlevi lodges that provided instruction and were instrumental in maintaining the enormous prestige of Persian culture in the Ottoman Empire. They also acted as musical and literary academies. The most celebrated Ottoman composers and many Ottoman poets from the seventeenth to the nineteenth century were Mevlevis. While the Mevlevi order was a repository of Ottoman high culture, the Bektashis played a similar role in transmitting popular culture, for example in preserving and adding to the corpus of Turkish religious poetry attributed to the semi-mythical Sufi of the thirteenth or fourteenth century, Yunus Emre.

Although *tasawwuf* had an intellectual tradition and a structure of "knowledge" that imitated *ilm,* its primary appeal was aesthetic rather than intellectual. The liturgies of the orders, which aimed to produce a state of ecstasy in participants as they "became drunk with the wine of God's love," offered a religious and theatrical experience that was not available in the impressive but austere ceremonies in the mosques. What was equally important is that the orders, and particularly those with a popular following, institutionalized popular piety, with its appetite for saints and miracles. The hagiographies of Sufi saints, such as Enisi's early sixteenth-century vita of the Bayrami Ak Shemseddin, formed a branch of popular literature that provided entertainment, edification, and a focal point for people's loyalties as adherents to a particular Sufi order. At the same time the shrines of saints, whether or not they had an association with a particular order, became sites of pilgrimage, offering cures for diseases or other of life's problems.

It was at this level that beliefs of Ottoman Muslims and Christians often became indistinguishable, with formerly Christian shrines, such as the Sufi lodge at Seyyid Gazi in Anatolia, becoming sites of Muslim veneration. Other sites attracted both Muslim and Christian pilgrims. An example of this was the shrine of St. George on the island of Levitha near Patmos, which became a site of Greek Orthodox, Catholic, and Muslim pilgrimages, St. George also acquiring the Turkish name Koc Baba. Popular practices, notably visiting saints' tombs and the liturgical use of music and dancing, always aroused the opposition of a section of the ulema. Hostility to these practices became particularly intense in mid-seventeenth-century Istanbul, when Mehmed Kadizade (d. 1635) and his followers, disciples of the fundamentalist scholar Mehmed of Birgi (d. 1575), preached against them in public, attacking in particular the rituals of the Khalvetis.

Such attacks, however, never had a lasting effect, and most of the many *fatwas* issued on the subject of the Sufi orders are in fact tolerant of their practices, the higher ulema on the whole espousing a latitudinarian understanding of Islam. The affiliation of several sultans and many members of the political elite with the orders ensured that, in general, they enjoyed political protection. Furthermore, popular belief was ineradicable, and permeated even the sultan's palace. As examples of this, the sultans provided employment for makers of talismans, and in 1640, the advice writer Kochi Bey urged the new sultan Ibrahim I (1640–1648) to carefully preserve a loaf of bread whose grain revealed the name Allah. Nonetheless, despite the latitude of tolerated belief and practice, an official definition of heresy did emerge and became a matter of concern especially during the sixteenth century.

This development was closely linked to the claims of the Ottoman dynasty, which drew on Islamic themes to legiti-mize its rule. Until about 1500, these legitimizing elements came primarily from folk religion. Through dreams, God had promised sovereignty to the first sultan Osman and his father; the dynasty had gained a spiritual descent from Osman's marriage to the daughter of a saint; saints led the sultan's warriors in battle. In the sixteenth century, however, the dynasty came to derive its legitimacy from orthodox Islamic tradition. This was partly a consequence of the increasing influence of classically trained ulem a in the empire, but partly also a consequence of external events. In 1516/17, the conquest of the Mamluk empire made Selim I (1512–1520) and his successors lords of Mecca and Medina, the holy cities of Islam.

This gave the Ottoman sultan the prestigious title of "Servitor of the Two Holy Places," and also the responsibility for the safety of the pilgrimage routes to Mecca. He could now, as the upholder of the religion, claim primacy among

Islamic sovereigns. At the same time, the rise to power in Iran of the Safavid dynasty, which claimed spiritual power as leaders of the Safavid Sufi order, and whose Shiism contrasted with the Sunnism of the Ottomans, presented a religious and political threat to the Ottoman Empire, especially since the Safavids found many adherents to their order among the sultan's subjects in Anatolia.

The Ottomans countered Safavid propaganda by declaring the Safavids and their followers to be worse than infidels, and by presenting the Ottoman dynasty as the only defenders of Sunni Islam against this mortal danger. By the mid-century, Suleiman I was declaring himself to be "the one who makes smooth the path for the precepts of the *sharia*" and the one "who makes manifest the Exalted Word of God" and who "expounds the signs of the luminous *sharia*." He was also the first Ottoman sultan to assume the title of caliph, implying the leadership of the entire Islamic world. With these developments the dynasty identified itself so closely with orthodox Sunni Islam that disloyalty to one implied disloyalty to the other. It was particularly during Suleiman's reign, and partly as a result of his claim to be the defender of the faith, that heresy acquired a clear definition.

In identifying heresy, the ulema were not concerned with a person's inner belief or private actions. These are matters between the individual and God. Their concern was with stated belief, certain tenets of the Holy Law or Sunni dogma providing the test. If, for example, a Sufi declared that the ceremonies of his order constituted an act of worship *(ibada)*, a term which in the *sharia* refers only to the obligatory purification, prayer, fasting, and alms-giving, then he was a heretic, because in claiming the ceremonies to be "obligatory" he was claiming an authority in prescribing ritual that only the *sharia* possessed. It was this test that the sultan used to execute the Melami Oðlan Þeyh and his followers in 1528. Provided, however, the Sufi did not declare his practices to be an act of worship, he remained within the bounds of orthodoxy. Since the *sharia* forbids Muslims to drink wine, if a Muslim declares wine to be licit, he has abjured the *sharia*, and become liable to death.

If, however, he drinks wine without believing it to be licit he is not a heretic. In Ottoman religious "trials" the key to identifying heresy was the accused's statements on what is canonically forbidden, permitted, and obligatory. A heretic was someone who stated beliefs did not conform with the *sharia*. However, in the more merciless pursuit of Safavid sympathizers within the Ottoman realms a key indicator was whether or not the accused cursed the Orthodox caliphs, the denunciation of the first three successors to the prophet Muhammad being a tenet in Shiite belief. Public behavior could also indicate heresy. It was for this reason that Suleiman I decreed in 1537 that the authorities should build mosques in all villages that lacked one and note who failed to attend the obligatory congregational prayers.

In this way the sultan not only enforced Sunni ritual, in his capacity as protector of the faith, but could also, by their refusal to perform obligatory prayers, identify heretics. Since by this time the sultan identified his own legitimacy with Sunni orthodoxy, disavowal of the commands of the *sharia* was also identified as an act of rebellion against the dynasty. In practice, therefore, the definition of heresy served to identify political opponents of the dynasty, and with changing political circumstances certain heretical beliefs became more acceptable. The persecution of Ottoman Shiites, for example, seems to have stopped when, from the mid-seventeenth century, the Safavids of Iran no longer presented a political and ideological danger. Furthermore, since the Ottoman government demanded of Muslims no more than verbal adherence to certain tenets of the *sharia* and the outward performance of its obligatory rituals, and did not examine inward faith, a huge variety of beliefs and practices were able to flourish unmolested within Ottoman Islam.

3

The Golden Age of Islam

The Islamic Golden Age, also sometimes known as the Islamic Renaissance, was traditionally dated from the 700 A.D. to 1200 A.D.C.E., but has been extended to the 15th and 16th centuries by some scholars. During this period, artists, engineers, scholars, poets, philosophers, geographers and traders in the Islamic world contributed to the arts, agriculture, economics, industry, law, literature, navigation, philosophy, sciences, sociology, and technology, both by preserving and building upon earlier traditions and by adding inventions and innovations of their own. Howard R. Turner writes: "Muslim artists and scientists, princes and laborers together made a unique culture that has directly and indirectly influenced societies on every continent."

During the Muslim conquests of the 7th and early 8th centuries, Rashidun armies established the Islamic Empire, which was one of the ten largest empires in history. The Islamic Golden Age was soon inaugurated by the middle of the 8th century by the ascension of the Abbasid Caliphate and the transfer of the capital from Damascus to the Persian city of Baghdad illustrating the strong Persian presence in the Abbasid Caliphate. The Abbassids were influenced by the Quranic injunctions and hadith such as "The ink of the scholar is more holy than the blood of martyrs" stressing the value of knowledge. During this period the Muslim world became the unrivalled intellectual centre for science, philosophy, medicine and education as the Abbasids championed the cause of knowledge and established the "House of Wisdom" in Baghdad; where both Muslim and non-Muslim scholars sought to translate and gather all the world's knowledge into Arabic.

Many classic works of antiquity that would otherwise have been forgotten were translated into Arabic and later in turn translated into Turkish, Persian, Hebrew and Latin. During this period the Muslim world was a cauldron of cultures which collected, synthesized and significantly advanced the knowledge gained from the ancient Iraqi, Roman, Chinese, Indian, Persian, Egyptian, North African, Greek and Byzantine civilizations. Rival Muslim dynasties such as the Fatimids of Egypt and the Umayyads of al-Andalus were also major intellectual centres with cities such as Cairo and Córdoba rivaling Baghdad.

A major innovation of this period was paper - originally a secret tightly guarded by the Chinese. The art of paper-making was obtained from prisoners taken at the Battle of Talas (751), resulting in paper mills being built in the Persian cities of Samarkand and Baghdad. The Arabs improved upon the Chinese techniques of using mulberry bark by using starch to account for the Muslim preference for pens vs. the Chinese for brushes. By AD 900 there were hundreds of shops employing scribes and binders for books in Baghdad and even public libraries began to become established, including the first lending libraries. From here paper-making spread west to Fez and then to al-Andalus and from there to Europe in the 13th century.

Much of this learning and development can be linked to topography. Even prior to Islam's presence, the city of Mecca served as a center of trade in Arabia. The tradition of the pilgrimage to Mecca became a center for exchanging ideas and goods. The influence held by Muslim merchants over African-Arabian and Arabian-Asian trade routes was tremendous. As a result, Islamic civilization grew and expanded on the basis of its merchant economy, in contrast to their Christian, Indian and Chinese peers who built societies from agricultural landholding nobility. Merchants brought goods and their faith to China, India (the Indian subcontinent now has over 450 million followers), South-east Asia (which now has over 230 million followers), and the kingdoms of Western Africa and returned with new inventions. Merchants used their wealth to invest in textiles and plantations. Aside from traders, Sufi missionaries also played a large role in the spread of Islam, by bringing their message to various regions around the world. The principal locations included: Persia, Ancient Mesopotamia, Central Asia and North Africa. Although, the mystics also had a significant influence in parts of Eastern Africa, Ancient Anatolia (Turkey), South Asia, East Asia and South-east Asia.

ETHICS

Many medieval Muslim thinkers pursued humanistic, rational and scientific discourses in their search for knowledge, meaning and values. A wide range of Islamic writings on love, poetry, history and philosophical theology show that medieval Islamic thought was open to the humanistic ideas of individualism, occasional secularism, skepticism and liberalism. Religious freedom, though society was still controlled under Islamic values, helped create cross-cultural networks by attracting Muslim, Christian and Jewish intellectuals and thereby helped spawn the greatest period of philosophical creativity in the middle Ages from the 8th to 13th centuries. Another reason the Islamic world flourished during this period was an early emphasis on freedom of speech, as summarized by al-Hashimi (a cousin of Caliph al-Ma'mun) in the following letter to one of the religious opponents he was attempting to convert through reason:

"Bring forward all the arguments you wish and say whatever you please and speak your mind freely. Now that you are safe and free to say whatever you please appoint some arbitrator who will impartially judge between us and lean only towards the truth and be free from the empary of passion, and that arbitrator shall be Reason, whereby God makes us responsible for our own rewards and punishments. Herein I have dealt justly with you and have given you full security and am ready to accept whatever decision Reason may give for me or against me. For "There is no compulsion in religion" (Quran 2:256) and I have only invited you to accept our faith willingly and of your own accord and have pointed out the hideousness of your present belief. Peace be upon you and the blessings of God!"

The earliest known treatises dealing with environmentalism and environmental science, especially pollution, were Arabic treatises written by al-Kindi, al-Razi, Ibn Al-Jazzar, al-Tamimi, al-Masihi, Avicenna, Ali ibn Ridwan, Abd-el-latif, and Ibn al-Nafis. Their works covered a number of subjects related to pollution such as air pollution, water pollution, soil contamination, municipal solid waste mishandling, and environmental impact assessments of certain localities. Cordoba, al-Andalus also had the first waste containers and waste disposal facilities for litter collection.

Institutions

A number of important educational and scientific institutions previously unknown in the ancient world have their origins in the early Islamic world, with the most notable examples being: the public hospital (which replaced healing temples and sleep temples) and psychiatric hospital, the public library and lending library, the academic degree-granting university, and the astronomical observatory as a research institute (as opposed to a private observation post as was the case in ancient times).

The first universities which issued diplomas were the Bimaristan medical university-hospitals of the medieval Islamic world, where medical diplomas were issued to students of Islamic medicine who were qualified to be practicing doctors of medicine from the 9th century. The Guinness Book of World Records recognizes the University of Al Karaouine in Fez, Morocco as the oldest degree-granting university in the world with its founding in 859 CE. Al-Azhar University, founded in Cairo, Egypt in the 975 CE, offered a variety of academic degrees, including postgraduate degrees, and is often considered the first full-fledged university. The origins of the doctorate also dates back to the *ijazat attadris wa 'l-ifttd* ("license to teach and issue legal opinions") in the medieval Madrasahs which taught Islamic law.

By the 10th century, Cordoba had 700 mosques, 60,000 palaces, and 70 libraries, the largest of which had 600,000 books. In the whole al-Andalus, 60,000 treatises, poems, polemics and compilations were published each year. The library of Cairo had two million books, while the library of Tripoli is said to have had as many as three million books before it was destroyed by Crusaders. The number of important and original medieval Arabic works on the mathematical sciences far exceeds the combined total of medieval Latin and Greek works of comparable significance, although only a small fraction of the surviving Arabic scientific works have been studied in modern times. A number of distinct features of the modern library were introduced in the Islamic world, where libraries not only served as a collection of manuscripts as was the case in ancient libraries, but also as a public library and lending library, a centre for the instruction and spread of sciences and ideas, a place for meetings and discussions, and sometimes as a lodging for scholars or boarding school for pupils.

The concept of the library catalogue was also introduced in medieval Islamic libraries, where books were organized into specific genres and categories. Several fundamental common law institutions may have been adapted from similar legal institutions in Islamic law and jurisprudence, and introduced to England by the Normans after the Norman Conquest of England and the Emirate of Sicily, and by Crusaders during the Crusades. In particular, the "royal English contract protected by the action of debt is identified with the Islamic *Aqd,* the English assize of novel disseisin is identified with the Islamic *Istihqaq,* and the English jury is identified with the Islamic *Lafif.*"

Other legal institutions introduced in Islamic law include the trust and charitable trust (Waqf), and the agency and aval (Hawala), and the lawsuit and medical peer review. Other English legal institutions such as "the scholastic method, the license to teach," the "law schools known as Inns of Court in England and *Madrasas* in Islam" and the "European commenda" (Islamic *Qirad*) may have also originated from Islamic law. These influences have led some scholars to suggest that Islamic law may have laid the foundations for "the common law as an integrated whole".

Polymaths

Another common feature during the Islamic Golden Age was the large number of Muslim polymath scholars, who were known as "Hakeems", each of whom contributed to a variety of different fields of both religious and secular learning, comparable to the later "Renaissance Men" (such as Leonardo da Vinci) of the European Renaissance period. During the Islamic Golden Age, polymath scholars with a wide breadth of knowledge in different fields were more common than scholars who specialized in any single field of learning. Notable medieval Muslim polymaths included al-Biruni, al-Jahiz, al-Kindi, Avicenna, al-Idrisi, Ibn Bajjah, Ibn Zuhr, Ibn Tufail, Averroes, al-Suyuti, Geber, Abbas Ibn Firnas, Alhacen, Ibn al-Nafis, Ibn Khaldun, al-Khwarizmi, al-Masudi, al-Muqaddasi, and Nasîr al-Dîn al-Tûsî, among others.

ECONOMY

Age of Discovery

The Islamic Empire significantly contributed to globalization during the Islamic Golden Age, when the knowledge, trade and economies from many previously isolated regions and civilizations began integrating due to contacts with Muslim explorers, sailors, scholars, traders, and travelers. Some have called this period the "Pax Islamica" or "Afro-Asiatic age of discovery", in reference to the Jewish (known as Radhanites), Sogdian and Muslim South-west Asian and North African traders and explorers who travelled most of the Old World, and established an early global economy across most of Asia and Africa and much of Europe, with their trade networks extending from the Atlantic Ocean and Mediterranean Sea in the west to the Indian Ocean and China Sea in the east.

This helped establish the Islamic Empire (including the Rashidun, Umayyad, Abbasid and Fatimid caliphates) as the world's leading extensive economic power throughout the 7th-13th centuries. Several contemporary medieval Arabic reports also suggest that Muslim explorers from al-Andalus and the Maghreb may have travelled in expeditions across the Atlantic Ocean between the 9th and 14th centuries.

Agricultural Revolution

The Islamic Golden Age witnessed a fundamental transformation in agriculture known as the "Muslim Agricultural Revolution" or "Arab Agricultural Revolution". Due to the global economy established by Muslim traders across the Old World, this enabled the diffusion of many plants and farming techniques between different parts of the Islamic world, as well as the adaptation of plants and techniques from beyond the Islamic world. Crops from Africa such as sorghum, crops from China such as citrus fruits, and numerous crops from India such as mangos, rice, and especially cotton and sugar cane, were distributed throughout Islamic lands which normally would not be able to grow these crops.

Some have referred to the diffusion of numerous crops during this period as the "Globalisation of Crops", which, along with an increased mechanization of agriculture, led to major changes in economy, population distribution, vegetation cover, agricultural production and income, population levels, urban growth, the distribution of the labour force, linked industries, cooking and diet, clothing, and numerous other aspects of life in the Islamic world. During the Muslim Agricultural Revolution, sugar production was refined and transformed into a large-scale industry by the Arabs, who built the first sugar refineries and sugar plantations. The Arabs and Berbers diffused sugar throughout the Islamic Empire from the 8th century.

Muslims introduced cash cropping and the modern crop rotation system where land was cropped four or more times in a two-year period. Winter crops were followed by summer ones. In areas where plants of shorter growing season were used, such as spinach and eggplants, the land could be cropped three or more times a year. In parts of Yemen, wheat yielded two harvests a year on the same land, as did rice in Iraq. Muslims developed a scientific approach to agriculture based on three major elements; sophisticated systems of crop rotation, highly developed irrigation techniques, and the introduction of a large variety of crops which were studied and catalogued according to the season, type of land and amount of water they require. Numerous encyclopaedias on farming and botany were produced, containing accurate, precise detail.

Market Economy

Early forms of proto-capitalism and free markets were present in the Caliphate, where an early market economy and early form of merchant capitalism was developed between the 8th-12th centuries, which some refer to as "Islamic capitalism". A vigorous monetary economy was created on the basis of the expanding levels of circulation of a stable high-value currency (the *dinar*) and the integration of monetary areas that were previously independent. Innovative new business techniques and forms of business organisation were introduced by economists, merchants and traders during this time.

Such innovations included early trading companies, credit cards, big businesses, contracts, bills of exchange, long-distance international trade, early forms of partnership (*mufawada*) such as limited partnerships (*mudaraba*), and early forms of credit, debt, profit, loss, capital (*al-mal*), capital accumulation (*nama al-mal*), circulating capital, capital expenditure, revenue, cheques, promissory notes, trusts (*waqf*), startup companies, savings accounts, transactional accounts, pawning, loaning, exchange rates, bankers, money changers, ledgers, deposits, assignments, the double-entry bookkeeping system, and lawsuits. Organizational enterprises similar to corporation's independent from the state also existed in the medieval Islamic world. Many of these early proto-capitalist concepts were adopted and further advanced in medieval Europe from the 13th century onwards.

The systems of contract relied upon by merchants was very effective. Merchants would buy and sell on commission, with money loaned to them by wealthy investors, or a joint investment of several merchants, who were often Muslim, Christian and Jewish. Recently, a collection of documents was found in an Egyptian synagogue shedding a very detailed and human light on the life of medieval Middle Eastern merchants. Business partnerships would be made for many commercial ventures, and bonds of kinship enabled trade networks to form over huge distances. Networks developed during this time enabled a world in which money could be promised by a bank in Baghdad and cashed in Spain, creating the cheque system of today.

Each time items passed through the cities along this extraordinary network, the city imposed a tax, resulting in high prices once reaching the final destination. These innovations made by Muslims and Jews laid the foundations for the modern economic system. Though medieval Islamic economics appears to have been closer to proto-capitalism, some scholars have also found a number of parallels between Islamic economic jurisprudence and communism, including the Islamic ideas of zakat and riba.

Industrial Growth

Muslim engineers in the Islamic world made a number of innovative industrial uses of hydropower, and early industrial uses of tidal power, wind power, steam power, fossil fuels such as petroleum, and early large factory complexes (*tiraz* in Arabic). The industrial uses of watermills in the Islamic world date back to the 7th century, while horizontal-wheeled and vertical-wheeled water mills were both in widespread use since at least the 9th century. A variety of industrial mills were being employed in the Islamic world, including early fulling mills, gristmills, hullers, paper mills, sawmills, shipmills, stamp mills, steel mills, sugar mills, tide mills and windmills. By the 11th century, every province throughout the Islamic world had these industrial mills in operation, from al-Andalus and North Africa to the Middle East and Central Asia.

Muslim engineers also invented crankshafts and water turbines, employed gears in mills and water-raising machines, and pioneered the use of dams as a source of water power, used to provide additional power to watermills and water-raising machines. Such advances made it possible for many industrial tasks that were previously driven by manual labour in ancient times to be mechanized and driven by machinery instead in the medieval Islamic world. The transfer of these technologies to medieval Europe had an influence on the Industrial Revolution. A number of industries were generated due to the Muslim Agricultural Revolution, including early industries for agribusiness, astronomical instruments, ceramics, chemicals, distillation technologies, clocks, glass, mechanical hydro powered and wind powered machinery, matting, mosaics, pulp and paper, perfumery, petroleum, pharmaceuticals, rope-making, shipping, shipbuilding, silk, sugar, textiles, water, weapons, and the mining of minerals such as sulphur, ammonia, lead and iron.

Early large factory complexes (*tiraz*) were built for many of these industries and knowledge of these industries were later transmitted to medieval Europe, especially during the Latin translations of the 12th century, as well as before and after. For example, the first glass factories in Europe were founded in the 11th century by Egyptian craftsmen in Greece. The agricultural and handicraft industries also experienced high levels of growth during this period.

Labour

The labour force in the Caliphate was employed from diverse ethnic and religious backgrounds, while both men and women were involved in diverse occupations and economic activities. Women were employed in a wide range of commercial activities and diverse occupations in the primary sector (as farmers for example), secondary sector (as construction workers, dyers, spinners, etc.) and tertiary sector (as investors, doctors, nurses, presidents of guilds, brokers, peddlers, lenders, scholars, etc.). Muslim women also had a monopoly over certain branches of the textile industry.

Slaves were purchased on the frontiers of the Islamic world and then imported to the major centers, where there were slave markets from which they were widely distributed. Slaves occupied an important place in the economic life of Islamic world. Large numbers of slaves were exported from eastern Africa to work in salt mines and labour-intensive plantations; the best evidence for this is the magnitude of the Zanj revolt in Iraq in the 9th century. Slaves were also used for domestic work, military service, bought for the harems, and civil administration. Central and east European slaves were generally known as Saqaliba (i.e., Slavs).

Technology

A significant number of inventions were produced by medieval Muslim engineers and inventors, such as Abbas Ibn Firnas, the Banû Mûsâ, Taqi al-Din, and most notably al-Jazari. Some of the inventions believed to have come from the Islamic Golden Age include the camera obscura, coffee, soap bar, shampoo, pure distillation, liquefaction, crystallization, purification, oxidisation, evaporation, filtration, distilled alcohol, uric acid, nitric acid, alembic, crankshaft, valve, reciprocating suction piston pump, mechanical clocks driven by water and weights, combination lock, quilting, pointed arch, scalpel, bone saw, forceps, surgical catgut, windmill, inoculation, smallpox vaccine, fountain pen, cryptanalysis, frequency analysis, three-course meal, stained glass and quartz glass, Persian carpet, celestial globe.

Urbanization

As urbanization increased, Muslim cities grew unregulated, resulting in narrow winding city streets and neighbourhoods separated by different ethnic backgrounds and religious affiliations. These qualities proved efficient for transporting goods to and from major commercial centres while preserving the privacy valued by Islamic family life. Suburbs lay just outside the walled city, from wealthy residential communities, to working class semi-slums. City garbage dumps were located far from the city, as were clearly defined cemeteries which were often homes for criminals. A place of prayer was found just near one of the main gates, for religious festivals and public executions. Similarly, Military Training grounds were found near a main gate.

Muslim cities also had advanced domestic water systems with sewers, public baths, drinking fountains, piped drinking water supplies, and widespread private and public toilet and bathing facilities. By the 10th century, Cordoba had 700 mosques, 60,000 palaces, and 70 libraries.

Sciences

The traditional view of Islamic science was that it was chiefly a preserver and transmitter of ancient knowledge. For example, Donald Lach argues that modern science originated in Europe as an amalgam of medieval technology and Greek learning. These views have been disputed in recent times, with some scholars suggesting that Muslim scientists laid the foundations for modern science, for their development of early scientific methods and an empirical, experimental and quantitative approach to scientific inquiry. Some scholars have referred to this period as a "Muslim scientific revolution", a term which expresses the view that Islam was the driving force behind the Muslim scientific achievements, and should not to be confused with the early modern European Scientific Revolution leading to the rise of modern science. Edward Grant argues that modern science was due to the cumulative efforts of the Hellenic, Islamic and Latin civilizations.

Scientific Method

Early scientific methods were developed in the Islamic world, where significant progress in methodology was made, especially in the works of Ibn al-Haytham (Alhazen) in the 11th century, who is considered the pioneer of experimental physics. The most important development of the scientific method was the use of experimentation and quantification to distinguish between competing scientific theories set within a generally empirical orientation. Ibn al-Haytham (Alhazen) wrote the *Book of Optics*, in which he significantly reformed the field of optics, empirically proved that vision occurred because of light rays entering the eye, and invented the camera obscura to demonstrate the physical nature of light rays.

Ibn al-Haytham has also been described as the "first scientist" for his introduction of the scientific method, and his pioneering work on the psychology of visual perception is considered a precursor to psychophysics and experimental psychology.

Peer review

The earliest medical peer review, a process by which a committee of physicians investigates the medical care rendered in order to determine whether accepted standards of care have been met, is found in the *Ethics of the Physician* written by Ishaq bin Ali al-Rahwi (854–931) of al-Raha in

Syria. His work, as well as later Arabic medical manuals, state that a visiting physician must always make duplicate notes of a patient's condition on every visit. When the patient was cured or had died, the notes of the physician were examined by a local medical council of other physicians, who would review the practising physician's notes to decide whether his/her performance have met the required standards of medical care.

If their reviews were negative, the practicing physician could face a lawsuit from a maltreated patient. The first scientific peer review, the evaluation of research findings for competence, significance and originality by qualified experts, was described later in the *Medical Essays and Observations* published by the Royal Society of Edinburgh in 1731. The present-day scientific peer review system evolved from this 18th century process.

Astronomy

Some have referred to the achievements of the Maragha School and their predecessors and successors in astronomy as a "Maragha Revolution", "Maragha School Revolution" or "Scientific Revolution before the Renaissance". Advances in astronomy by the Maragha school and their predecessors and successors include the construction of the first observatory in Baghdad during the reign of Caliph al-Ma'mun, the collection and correction of previous astronomical data, resolving significant problems in the Ptolemaic model, the development of universal astrolabes, the invention of numerous other astronomical instruments, the beginning of astrophysics and celestial mechanics after Ja'far Muhammad ibn Mûsâ ibn Shâkir discovered that the heavenly bodies and celestial spheres were subject to the same physical laws as Earth, the first elaborate experiments related to astronomical phenomena and the first semantic distinction between astronomy and astrology by Abû al-Rayhân al-Bîrûnî, the use of exacting empirical observations and experimental techniques, the discovery that the celestial spheres are not solid and that the heavens are less dense than the air by Ibn al-Haytham, the separation of natural philosophy from astronomy by Ibn al-Haytham and Ibn al-Shatir, the first non-Ptolemaic models by Ibn al-Haytham and Mo' ayyeduddin Urdi, the rejection of the Ptolemaic model on empirical rather than philosophical grounds by Ibn al-Shatir, the first empirical observational evidence of the Earth's rotation by Nasîr al-Dîn al-Tûsî and Ali al-Qushji, and al-Birjandi's early hypothesis on "circular inertia."

Several Muslim astronomers also considered the possibility of the Earth's rotation on its axis and perhaps a heliocentric solar system. It is known that the Copernican heliocentric model in Nicolaus Copernicus' *De revolutionibus* was adapted from the geocentric model of Ibn al-Shatir and the Maragha school (including the Tusi-couple) in a heliocentric context, and that his arguments for the Earth's rotation were similar to those of Nasîr al-Dîn al-Tûsî and Ali al-Qushji.

Chemistry

Geber (Jabir ibn Hayyan) is considered a pioneer of chemistry, as he was responsible for introducing an early experimental scientific method within the field, as well as the alembic, still, retort, and the chemical processes of pure distillation, filtration, sublimation, liquefaction, crystallisation, purification, oxidisation and evaporation. The study of traditional alchemy and the theory of the transmutation of metals were first refuted by al-Kindi, followed by Abû Rayhân al-Bîrûnî, Avicenna, and Ibn Khaldun. In his *Doubts about Galen*, al-Razi was the first to prove both Aristotle's theory of classical elements and Galen's theory of humorism false using an experimental method. Nasîr al-Dîn al-Tûsî stated an early version of the law of conservation of mass, noting that a body of matter is able to change, but is not able to disappear. Alexander von Humboldt and Will Durant consider medieval Muslim chemists to be founders of chemistry.

Mathematics

Among the achievements of Muslim mathematicians during this period include the development of algebra and algorithms by the Persian and Islamic mathematician Muhammad ibn Mûsâ al-Khwârizmî, the invention of spherical trigonometry, the addition of the decimal point notation to the Arabic numerals, the discovery of all the trigonometric functions besides sine, al-Kindi's introduction of cryptanalysis and frequency analysis, al-Karaji's introduction of algebraic calculus and proof by mathematical induction, the development of analytic geometry and the earliest general formula for infinitesimal and integral calculus by Ibn al-Haytham, the beginning of algebraic geometry by Omar Khayyam, the first refutations of Euclidean geometry and the parallel postulate by Nasîr al-Dîn al-Tûsî, the first attempt at a non-Euclidean geometry by Sadr al-Din, the development of symbolic algebra by Abû al-Hasan ibn Alî al-Qalasâdî, and numerous other advances in algebra, arithmetic, calculus, cryptography, geometry, number theory and trigonometry.

Medicine

Islamic medicine was a genre of medical writing that was influenced by several different medical systems. The works of ancient Greek and Roman physicians Hippocrates, Dioscorides, Soranus, Celsus and Galen had a lasting impact on Islamic medicine. Muslim physicians made many significant contributions to medicine, including anatomy, experimental medicine, ophthalmology, pathology, the pharmaceutical sciences, physiology, surgery, etc. They also set up some of the earliest dedicated hospitals, including the first medical schools and psychiatric hospitals. Al-Kindi wrote the *De Gradibus*, in which he first demonstrated the application of quantification and mathematics to medicine and pharmacology, such as a mathematical scale to quantify the strength of drugs and the determination in advance of the most critical days of a patient's illness. Al-Razi (Rhazes) discovered measles and smallpox, and in his *Doubts about Galen*, proved Galen's humorism false.

Abu al-Qasim (Abulcasis) helped lay the foudations for modern surgery, with his *Kitab al-Tasrif*, in which he invented numerous surgical instruments, including the first instruments unique to women, as well as the surgical uses of catgut and forceps, the ligature, surgical needle, scalpel, curette, retractor, surgical spoon, sound, surgical hook, surgical rod, and specula, and bone saw. Ibn al-Haytham (Alhacen) made important advances in eye surgery, as he correctly explained the process of sight and visual perception for the first time in his *Book of Optics*.

Ibn Sina (Avicenna) helped lay the foundations for modern medicine, with *The Canon of Medicine*, which was responsible for introducing systematic experimentation and quantification in physiology, the discovery of contagious disease, introduction of quarantine to limit their spread, introduction of experimental medicine, evidence-based medicine, clinical trials, randomized controlled trials, efficacy tests, and clinical pharmacology, the first descriptions on bacteria and viral organisms, distinction of mediastinitis from pleurisy, contagious nature of tuberculosis, distribution of diseases by water and soil, skin troubles, sexually transmitted diseases, perversions, nervous ailments, use of ice to treat fevers, and separation of medicine from pharmacology.

Ibn Zuhr (Avenzoar) was the earliest known experimental surgeon. In the 12th century, he was responsible for introducing the experimental method into surgery, as he was the first to employ animal testing in order to experiment with surgical procedures before applying them to human patients. He also performed the first dissections and postmortem autopsies on humans as well as animals. Ibn al-Nafis laid the foundations for circulatory physiology, as he was the first to describe the pulmonary circulation and coronary circulation, which form the basis of the circulatory system, for which he is considered "the greatest physiologist of the Middle Ages." He also described the earliest concept of metabolism, and developed new systems of physiology and psychology to replace the Avicennian and Galenic systems, while discrediting many of their erroneous theories on humorism, pulsation, bones, muscles, intestines, sensory organs, bilious canals, esophagus, stomach, etc.

Ibn al-Lubudi rejected the theory of humorism, and discovered that the body and its preservation depend exclusively upon blood, women cannot produce sperm, the movement of arteries are not dependent upon the movement of the heart, the heart is the first organ to form in a fetus' body, and the bones forming the skull can grow into tumors. Ibn Khatima and Ibn al-Khatib discovered that infectious diseases are caused by microorganisms which enter the human body. Mansur ibn Ilyas drew comprehensive diagrams of the body's structural, nervous and circulatory systems.

Physics

The study of experimental physics began with Ibn al-Haytham, a pioneer of modern optics, who introduced the experimental scientific method and used it to drastically transform the understanding of light and vision in his *Book of Optics*, which has been ranked alongside Isaac Newton's *Philosophiae Naturalis Principia Mathematica* as one of the most influential books in the history of physics, for initiating a scientific revolution in optics and visual perception. The experimental scientific method was soon introduced into mechanics by Biruni, and early precursors to Newton's laws of motion were discovered by several Muslim scientists. The law of inertia, known as Newton's first law of motion, and the concept of momentum were discovered by Ibn al-Haytham (Alhacen) and Avicenna.

The proportionality between force and acceleration, considered "the fundamental law of classical mechanics" and foreshadowing Newton's second law of motion, was discovered by Hibat Allah Abu'l-Barakat al-Baghdaadi, while the concept of reaction, foreshadowing Newton's third law of motion, was discovered by Ibn Bajjah (Avempace). Theories foreshadowing Newton's law of universal gravitation were developed by Ja'far Muhammad ibn Mûsâ ibn Shâkir, Ibn al-Haytham, and al-Khazini. Galileo Galilei's mathematical treatment of acceleration and his concept of impetus were enriched by the commentaries of Avicenna and Ibn Bajjah to Aristotle's *Physics* as well as the Neoplatonist tradition of Alexandria, represented by John Philoponus.

Other Sciences

Many other advances were made by Muslim scientists in biology (anatomy, botany, evolution, physiology and zoology), the earth sciences (anthropology, cartography, geodesy, geography and geology), psychology (experimental psychology, psychiatry, psychophysics and psychotherapy), and the social sciences (demography, economics, sociology, history and historiography). Other famous Muslim scientists during the Islamic Golden Age include al-Farabi (a polymath), Biruni (a polymath who was one of the earliest anthropologists and a pioneer of geodesy), Nasîr al-Dîn al-Tûsî (a polymath), and Ibn Khaldun (considered to be a pioneer of several social sciences such as demography, economics, cultural history, historiography and sociology), among others.

OTHER ACHIEVEMENTS

Architecture

The Great Mosque of Xi'an in China was completed *circa* 740, and the Great Mosque of Samarra in Iraq was completed in 847. The Great Mosque of Samarra combined the hypostyle architecture of rows of columns supporting a flat base above which a huge spiraling minaret was constructed. The Spanish Muslims began construction of the Great Mosque at Cordoba in 785 marking the beginning of Islamic architecture in Spain and Northern Africa. The mosque is noted for its striking interior arches. Moorish architecture reached its peak with the construction of the Alhambra, the magnificent palace/fortress of Granada, with its open and breezy interior spaces adorned in red, blue, and gold. The walls are decorated with stylized foliage motifs, Arabic inscriptions, and arabesque design work, with walls covered in glazed tiles.

Another distinctive sub-style is the architecture of the Mughal Empire in India in the 15-17th centuries. Blending Islamic and Hindu elements, the emperor Akbar constructed the royal city of Fatehpur Sikri, located 26 miles (42 km) west of Agra, in the late 1500s and his grandson Shah Jahan had constructed the mausoleum of Taj Mahal for Mumtaz Mahal in the 1650s, though this time period is well after the Islamic Golden Age. In the Sunni Muslim Ottoman Empire massive mosques with ornate tiles and calligraphy were constructed by a series of sultans including the Süleymaniye Mosque, Sultanahmet Mosque, Selimiye Mosque, and Bayezid II Mosque.

Arts

The golden age of Islamic (and/or Muslim) art lasted from 750 to the 16th century, when ceramics, glass, metalwork, textiles, illuminated manuscripts, and woodwork flourished. Lustrous glazing was an Islamic contribution to ceramics. Islamic luster-painted ceramics were imitated by Italian potters during the Renaissance. Manuscript illumination developed into an important and greatly respected art, and portrait miniature painting flourished in Persia. Calligraphy, an essential aspect of written Arabic, developed in manuscripts and architectural decoration.

Literature

The most well known fiction from the Islamic world was *The Book of One Thousand and One Nights* (*Arabian Nights*), which was a compilation of many earlier folk tales told by the Persian Queen Scheherazade. The epic took form in the 10th century and reached its final form by the 14th century; the number and type of tales have varied from one manuscript to another. All Arabian fantasy tales were often called "Arabian Nights" when translated into English, regardless of whether they appeared in *The Book of One Thousand and One Nights*, in any version, and a number of tales are known in Europe as "Arabian Nights" despite existing in no Arabic manuscript.

This epic has been influential in the West since it was translated in the 18th century, first by Antoine Galland. Many imitations were written, especially in France. Various characters from this epic have themselves become cultural icons in Western culture, such as Aladdin, Sinbad and Ali Baba. However, no medieval Arabic source has been traced for Aladdin, which was incorporated into *The Book of One Thousand and One Nights* by its French translator, Antoine Galland, who heard it from an Arab Syrian Christian story-teller from Aleppo. Part of its popularity may have sprung from the increasing historical and geographical knowledge, so that places of which little was known and so marvels were plausible had to be set further "long ago" or farther "far away"; this is a process that continues, and finally culminate in the fantasy world having little connection, if any, to actual times and places.

A number of elements from Arabian mythology and Persian mythology are now common in modern fantasy, such as genies, bahamuts, magic carpets, magic lamps, etc. When L. Frank Baum proposed writing a modern fairy tale that banished stereotypical elements, he included the genie as well as the dwarf and the fairy as stereotypes to go. Ferdowsi's *Shahnameh*, the national epic of Iran, is a mythical and heroic retelling of Persian history. *Amir Arsalan* was also a popular mythical Persian story, which has influenced some modern works of fantasy fiction, such as *The Heroic Legend of Arslan*. A famous example of Arabic poetry and Persian poetry on romance (love) is *Layla and Majnun*, dating back to the Umayyad era in the 7th century. It is a tragic story of undying love much like the later *Romeo and Juliet*, which was itself said to have been inspired by a Latin version of *Layli and Majnun* to an extent.

Ibn Tufail (Abubacer) and Ibn al-Nafis were pioneers of the philosophical novel. Ibn Tufail wrote the first fictional Arabic novel *Hayy ibn Yaqdhan* (*Philosophus Autodidactus*) as a response to al-Ghazali's *The Incoherence of the Philosophers*, and then Ibn al-Nafis also wrote a fictional novel *Theologus Autodidactus* as a response to Ibn Tufail's *Philosophus Autodidactus*. Both of these narratives had protagonists (Hayy in *Philosophus Autodidactus* and Kamil in *Theologus Autodidactus*) who were autodidactic feral children living in seclusion on a desert island, both being the earliest examples of a desert island story. However, while Hayy lives alone with animals on the desert island for the rest of the story in *Philosophus Autodidactus*, the story of Kamil extends beyond the desert island setting in *Theologus Autodidactus*, developing into the earliest known coming of age plot and eventually becoming the first example of a science fiction novel.

Theologus Autodidactus, written by the Arabian polymath Ibn al-Nafis (1213-1288), is the first example of a science fiction novel. It deals with various science fiction elements such as spontaneous generation, futurology, the end of the world and doomsday, resurrection, and the afterlife. Rather than giving supernatural or mythological explainations for these events, Ibn al-Nafis attempted to explain these plot elements using the scientific knowledge of biology, astronomy, cosmology and geology known in his time. His main purpose behind this science fiction work was to explain Islamic religious teachings in terms of science and philosophy through the use of fiction. A Latin translation of Ibn Tufail's work, *Philosophus Autodidactus*, first appeared in 1671, prepared by Edward Pococke the Younger, followed by an English translation by Simon Ockley in 1708, as well as German and Dutch translations.

These translations later inspired Daniel Defoe to write *Robinson Crusoe,* regarded as the first novel in English. *Philosophus Autodidactus* also inspired Robert Boyle to write his own philosophical novel set on an island, *The Aspiring Naturalist*. The story also anticipated Rousseau's *Emile: or, On Education* in some ways, and is also similar to Mowgli's story in Rudyard Kipling's *The Jungle Book* as well as Tarzan's story, in that a baby is abandoned but taken care of and fed by a mother wolf. Dante Alighieri's *Divine Comedy,* considered the greatest epic of Italian literature, derived many features of and episodes about the hereafter directly or indirectly from Arabic works on Islamic eschatology: the *Hadith* and the *Kitab al-Miraj* (translated into Latin in 1264 or shortly before as *Liber Scale Machometi,* "The Book of Muhammad's Ladder") concerning Muhammad's ascension to Heaven, and the spiritual writings of Ibn Arabi.

The Moors also had a noticeable influence on the works of George Peele and William Shakespeare. Some of their works featured Moorish characters, such as Peele's *The Battle of Alcazar* and Shakespeare's *The Merchant of Venice, Titus Andronicus* and *Othello,* which featured a Moorish Othello as its title character. These works are said to have been inspired by several Moorish delegations from Morocco to Elizabethan England at the beginning of the 17th century.

Music

A number of musical instruments used in Western music are believed to have been derived from Arabic musical instruments: the lute was derived from the *al'ud,* the rebec (ancestor of violin) from the *rebab,* the guitar from *qitara,* naker from *naqareh,* adufe from *al-duff,* alboka from *al-buq,* anafil from *al-nafir,* exabeba from *al-shabbaba* (flute), atabal (bass drum) from *al-tabl,* atambal from *al-tinbal,* the balaban, the castanet from *kasatan,* sonajas de azófar from *sunuj al-sufr,* the conical bore wind instruments, the xelami from the *sulami* or *fistula* (flute or musical pipe), the shawm and dulzaina from the reed instruments *zamr* and *al-zurna,* the gaita from the *ghaita,* rackett from *iraqya* or *iraqiyya,* the harp and zither from the *qanun,* canon from *qanun,* geige (violin) from *ghichak,* and the theorbo from the *tarab.*

A theory on the origins of the Western Solfège musical notation suggests that it may have also had Arabic origins. It has been argued that the Solfège syllables (*do, re, mi, fa, sol, la, ti*) may have been derived from the syllables of the Arabic solmization system *Durr-i-Mufassal* ("Separated Pearls") (*dal, ra, mim, fa, sad, lam*). This origin theory was first proposed by Meninski in his *Thesaurus Linguarum Orientalum* (1680) and then by Laborde in his *Essai sur la Musique Ancienne et Moderne* (1780).

Philosophy

Arab philosophers like al-Kindi (Alkindus) and Ibn Rushd (Averroes) and Persian philosophers like Ibn Sina (Avicenna) played a major role in preserving the works of Aristotle, whose ideas came to dominate the non-religious thought of the Christian and Muslim worlds. They would also absorb ideas from China, and India, adding to them tremendous knowledge from their own studies. Three speculative thinkers, al-Kindi, al-Farabi, and Avicenna (Ibn Sina), fused Aristotelianism and Neoplatonism with other ideas introduced through Islam, such as Kalam and Qiyas. This led to Avicenna founding his own Avicennism School of philosophy, which was influential in both Islamic and Christian lands. Avicenna was also a critic of Aristotelian logic and founder of Avicennian logic, and he developed the concepts of empiricism and tabula rasa, and distinguished between essence and existence.

From Spain the Arabic philosophic literature was translated into Hebrew, Latin, and Ladino, contributing to the development of modern European philosophy. The Jewish philosopher Moses Maimonides, Muslim sociologist-historian Ibn Khaldun, Carthage citizen Constantine the

African who translated Greek medical texts, and the Muslim Al-Khwarzimi's collation of mathematical techniques were important figures of the Golden Age. One of the most influential Muslim philosophers in the West was Averroes (Ibn Rushd), founder of the Averroism School of philosophy, whose works and commentaries had an impact on the rise of secular thought in Western Europe. He also developed the concept of "existence precedes essence".

Another influential philosopher who had a significant influence on modern philosophy was Ibn Tufail. His philosophical novel, *Hayy ibn Yaqdhan*, translated into Latin as *Philosophus Autodidactus* in 1671, developed the themes of empiricism, tabula rasa, nature versus nurture, condition of possibility, materialism, and Molyneux's Problem. European scholars and writers influenced by this novel include John Locke, Gottfried Leibniz, Melchisédech Thévenot, John Wallis, Christiaan Huygens, George Keith, Robert Barclay, the Quakers, and Samuel Hartlib.

Al-Ghazali also had an important influence on Jewish thinkers like Maimonides and Christian medieval philosophers such as Thomas Aquinas and René Descartes, who expressed similar ideas to that of al-Ghazali in *Discourse on the Method*. However, al-Ghazali also wrote a devastating critique in his *The Incoherence of the Philosophers* on the speculative theological works of Kindi, Farabi and Ibn Sina. The study of metaphysics declined in the Muslim world due to this critique, though Ibn Rushd (Averroes) responded strongly in his *The Incoherence of the Incoherence* to many of the points Ghazali raised. Nevertheless, Avicennism continued to flourish long after and Islamic philosophers continued making advances in philosophy through to the 17th century, when Mulla Sadra founded his school of Transcendent Theosophy and developed the concept of existentialism.

Other influential Muslim philosophers include al-Jahiz, a pioneer of evolutionary thought and natural selection; Ibn al-Haytham (Alhacen), a pioneer of phenomenology and the philosophy of science and a critic of Aristotelian natural philosophy and Aristotle's concept of place (topos); Biruni, a critic of Aristotelian natural philosophy; Ibn Tufail and Ibn al-Nafis, pioneers of the philosophical novel; Shahab al-Din Suhrawardi, founder of Illuminationist philosophy; Fakhr al-Din al-Razi, a critic of Aristotelian logic and a pioneer of inductive logic; and Ibn Khaldun, a pioneer in the philosophy of history and social philosophy.

END OF THE GOLDEN AGE

Mongolian Invasion

After the Crusades from the West that resulted in the instability of the Islamic world during the 11th century, a new threat came from the East during the 13th century: the Mongol invasions. In 1206, Genghis Khan from Central Asia established a powerful Mongol Empire. A Mongolian ambassador to the Abbasid Caliph in Baghdad is said to have been murdered, which may have been one of the reasons behind Hulagu Khan's sack of Baghdad in 1258. The Mongols conquered most of the Eurasian land mass, including both China in the east and parts of the old Islamic Caliphate and Persian Islamic Khwarezm, as well as Russia and Eastern Europe in the west, and subsequent invasions of the Levant. Later Mongol leaders, such as Timur, though he himself became a Muslim, destroyed many cities, slaughtered thousands of people and did irreparable damage to the ancient irrigation systems of Mesopotamia.

These invasions transformed a civil society to a nomadic one. Traditionalist Muslims at the time, including the polymath Ibn al-Nafis, believed that the Crusades and Mongol invasions were a divine punishment from God against Muslims deviating from the Sunnah. As a result, the falsafa, some of whom held ideas incompatible with the Sunnah, became targets of criticism from many traditionalist Muslims, though other traditionalists such as Ibn al-Nafis made attempts at reconciling reason with revelation and blur the line between the two.

Eventually, the Mongols that settled in parts of Persia, Central Asia and Russia converted to Islam, and as a result, the Ilkhanate, Golden Horde and Chagatai Khanates became Islamic states. In many instances, Mongols assimilated into various Muslim Iranian or Turkic peoples (for instance, one of the greatest Muslim astronomers of the 15th century, Ulugh Beg, was a grandson of Timur). By the time the Ottoman Empire rose from the ashes, the Golden Age is considered to have come to an end.

Causes of Decline

"The achievements of the Arabic speaking peoples between the ninth and twelfth centuries are so great as to baffle our understanding. The decadence of Islam and of Arabic is almost as puzzling in its speed and completeness as their phenomenal rise. Scholars will forever try to explain it as they try to explain the decadence and fall of Rome. Such questions are exceedingly complex and it is impossible to answer them in a simple way." — *George Sarton , The Incubation of Western Culture in the Middle East'*

Islamic civilization, which had at the outset been creative and dynamic in dealing with issues, began to struggle to respond to the challenges and rapid changes it faced from the 12th century onwards, towards the end of the Abbassid rule. Despite a brief respite with the new Ottoman rule, the decline continued until its eventual collapse and subsequent stagnation in the 20th century. Despite a number of attempts by many writers, historical and modern, none seem to agree on the causes of decline. The main views on the causes of decline comprise the following: political mismanagement after the early Caliphs (10th century onwards), closure of the gates of ijtihad (12th century), institutionalisation of taqlid rather than bid'ah (13th century), foreign involvement by invading forces and colonial powers (11th century Crusades,

13th century Mongol Empire, 15th century Reconquista, 19th century European colonial empires), and the disruption to the cycle of equity based on Ibn Khaldun's famous model of Asabiyyah (the rise and fall of civilizations) which points to the decline being mainly due to political and economic factors.

The North Africa's Islamic civilization collapsed after exhausting its resources in internal fighting and suffering devastation from the invasion of the Bedouin tribes of Banu Sulaym and Banu Hilal. The Black Death ravaged much of the Islamic world in the mid-14th century. Plague epidemics kept returning to the Islamic world up to the 19th century. There was an increasing lack of tolerance of intellectual debate and freedom of thought, with some seminaries systematically forbidding speculative philosophy, while polemic debates appear to have been abandoned in the 14th century. A significant intellectual shift in Islamic philosophy is perhaps demonstrated by al-Ghazali's late 11th century polemic work *The Incoherence of the Philosophers*, which lambasted metaphysical philosophy in favor of the primacy of scripture, and was later criticized in *The Incoherence of the Incoherence* by Averroes.

Institutions of science comprising Islamic universities, libraries (including the House of Wisdom), observatories, and hospitals, were later destroyed by foreign invaders like the Crusaders and particularly the Mongols, and were rarely promoted again in the devastated regions. Not only wasn't new publishing equipment accepted but also wide illiteracy overwhelmed the devastated lands, especially in Mesopotamia. Meanwhile in Persia, due to the Mongol invasions and the plague, the average life expectancy of the scholarly class in Persia had declined from 72 years in 1209 to 57 years by 1242. American economist Timur Kuran proposed an answer why economic development in the Middle East lagged that of the West: Islamic partnership law and inheritance law interacted to keep Middle Eastern enterprises small, never allowing the development of corporate forms.

Some scholars have come to question the traditional picture of decline, pointing to continued astronomical activity as a sign of a continuing and creative scientific tradition through to the 15th and 16th centuries, with the works of Ibn al-Shatir, Ulugh Beg, Ali Kuºçu, al-Birjandi and Taqi al-Din considered noteworthy examples. This was also the case for other fields, such as medicine, notably the works of Ibn al-Nafis, Mansur ibn Ilyas and Þerafeddin Sabuncuoðlu; mathematics, notably the works of al-Kashi and al-Qalasadi; philosophy, notably Mulla Sadra's transcendent theosophy; and the social sciences, notably Ibn Khaldun's *Muqaddimah* (1370), which itself points out that though science was declining in Iraq, Al-Andalus and Maghreb, it continued to flourish in Persia, Syria and Egypt during his time.

ISLAMIC ART

"Islamic art" is a label coined in the West in the nineteenth century. Unlike "Christian art" or "Buddhist art," it does not describe art with a particular set of religious imagery. In fact, Islamic art has few exclusively religious symbols comparable to the Christian cross. Instead, the term "Islamic art" designates all art, religious or secular, that was produced in lands under Muslim leadership.

Its makers and its patrons might be Muslim or not. In this packet we look at works that span nearly a thousand years—from shortly after the foundation of Islam in the seventh century to the seventeenth century when the last two great Islamic empires—the Ottoman and the Safavid—had reached their peak. Although the definition of Islamic art usually includes work made in Mughal India, it is beyond the scope of this packet. The works we will look at here come from as far west as Spain and as far east as Afghanistan.

Naturally, within this span of time and space many variations and styles occur. Yet, Islamic art remains somehow "recognizable" throughout. In the West, the word "art" produces mental images of paintings hung on walls or large-scale sculpture, but these (although not unknown) are not the focus of Islamic art. Rather, the most important outlets for artistic expression in the Islamic world were:

- Architecture
- The arts of the book (calligraphy, manuscript illumination, and bookbinding)
- The arts of the object (especially metalwork, ceramics, glass, and textiles)

And each of these was ornamented with a particularly Islamic vocabulary of surface decoration:

- Calligraphy
- Arabesques, scrolling patterns, and floral or plant designs
- Geometric designs.

Calligraphy

Islam developed in a nomadic Arab culture that valued poetry and oral tradition. The faith's fundamental basis is the message of God that was given to and relayed by the Prophet Muhammad, and that is preserved in the Quran. While Christians accept Christ as God's incarnation, Muhammad does not share God's divinity. The priority of the words themselves, rather than the messenger, left Islam with little use for iconic images like those that developed in early Christianity. Instead, the emphasis on the words and the language of God's message elevated the script in which they were recorded. Calligraphy—beautiful writing—became the most revered of all the arts. It was used—on buildings and art of all types—to communicate the words of the Quran or other messages but also for its decorative effect.

Arabesques

Scrolling patterns of plant and floral motifs were part of the visual vocabulary Islamic art inherited from its early Byzantine and Sasanian predecessors. They became so identified with Islamic art that in the West they came to be called "arabesques." Much of the Islamic world is arid and hot, and vegetation is scarce. Although too much can be made of the influence of this environment on art, it is perhaps natural that images of paradise reflect a lush world, full of flowers and fragrance, and well watered by cooling streams—and that these would be considered beautiful as ornament.

Geometric Designs

Repeating geometric patterns express—and embody—unity within diversity and the harmony that governs all things. They satisfy the Islamic principles of *tawhid* (the unity of all things) and *tawhid tawhid mizan* (order and balance)—and in so doing, they reflect the perfection of God's creation. Allah, the Quran says "ordered all things...."

The Question of Images

It is often believed—incorrectly—that the Quran prohibits images of living beings, either human or animal. The Quran *does* condemn the worship of idols: "O ye who believe, wine and games of chance and idols and divining arrows are an abomination of Satan's handiwork..." (5.92).And the accounts and sayings of the Prophet recorded in the *hadith*—some collected much later—suggest his distrust of representation. Such likenesses could be seen as usurping the creative action of God. From the very first, figures were absent in mosques, and then in other religious settings such as schools. Even the items used in religious buildings avoid figural decoration. But Islamic art is rich with figural decoration elsewhere: in the wall paintings and mural tiles within palaces; in manuscript illumination; on textiles; and on metalwork and ceramics not intended for religious purpose.

MUHAMMAD AND THE BEGINNINGS OF ISLAM

Muhammad was born around the year 570 in Mecca, a wealthy commercial and religious center in western Arabia. When he was about forty years old, Muhammad began to experience visions. One day, a voice exhorted him to "recite in the name of the Lord who created you...." Initially, Muhammad fled in confusion and fear, but the voice called after him, "O Muhammad, you are the messenger of God, and I am the angel Gabriel." This was the beginning of God's revelations to Muhammad; they continued for some ten years.

Muhammad's message about the one true God quickly won followers in Mecca. The city was home to the most important religious shrine in Arabia, where many gods were worshiped. Tensions quickly arose with the city's leaders, and in 622 Muhammad fled with his followers to the city of Yathrib. Soon it was being called Medinat al-Nabi—the town of the Prophet—and then simply Medina. In Medina the new religion took on a secular aspect as followers looked to Muhammad for civic guidance. From the very outset, the adjective "Islamic" described not simply a spiritual and moral reality, but also a political one.

The First Caliphs and the Umayyads

When Muhammad died in 632, no successor had been identified— or even whether a successor was possible. Were individual Muslims bound only to God or also to each other in an Islamic polity? Initially, some Arab tribes withdrew from the Muslim state. Abu Bakr assumed Muhammad's temporal authority (no one could replace him as prophet) and for two years battled breakaway tribesmen before his victory ensured that the political community of Islam endured. Abu Bakr and the three men who followed had been companions of the Prophet and early converts. They came to be called the four "rightly guided caliphs" (632"661) —a word that means "successor." Despite rapid expansion of the faith, serious internal conflicts emerged. After the third caliph was assassinated, a struggle for the succession pitted his kinsman, Mu'awiya, and the Prophet's son-in-law Ali. Ali prevailed but was himself assassinated in 661.

After Ali's death, Mu'awiya was recognized as caliph. He soon identified his son as heir and successor, establishing the first Islamic dynasty. The Umayyads (661"750) moved the capital from Medina to Damascus. Its easier access to the wider world of the Middle East and the Mediterranean made it a more effective center for quickly growing administrative, military, and governmental functions. The mode of government also changed, the consensus of old tribal chiefs giving way to a more autocratic style modeled on the neighboring Byzantine and Sasanian empires. By 750 the Islamic empire covered a quarter of the globe, from the Atlantic Ocean to the Indus River, and had acquired unprecedented wealth. However, what had begun as a dispute over the selection of a new caliph was deepening into a religious split. It centered on the nature of a leader's authority.

Who was qualified to govern the Islamic community and ensure a just society? What was the basis of his legitimacy? Three main groups emerged. One held that anyone who had sinned or committed an injustice was unfit to govern, an extreme view that eventually fell outside the mainstream of political life. The Shi'as— literally the "partisans" of Ali—held that the leader of the Islamic community should be a direct descendant of the Prophet. Sunnis— the word is derived from "tradition"—accepted any caliph who the caliph as the political successor of Muhammad but rejected any claim that he was the Prophet's spiritual heir. Armed revolt struck in many regions in the 740s.The last Umayyad caliph fled to Egypt, where he was killed. Only one member of the family survived. 'Abd al-Rahman escaped to North Africa and from there to Spain, where he established a new Umayyad dynasty at Córdoba that lasted until 1031. Other Muslim rulers would continue to govern parts of southern Spain until 1492.

The Abbasid Dynasty

After the Umayyads fled, a descendant of the Prophet was appointed caliph and inaugurated a new dynasty— the Abbasids (750"1258). The second Abbasid caliph, al-Mansur (ruled 754"775), moved the capital once again, shifting the focus farther east. On the site of a small village, at a point where the Tigris and Euphrates rivers run close to each other, he measured out an entirely new, round city. He named it Madinat al-Salam, city of peace, but it soon reverted to its original name—Baghdad. Although Abbasid caliphs lost real control over the whole of the Islamic empire and within about a hundred years and the first three centuries of their rule are often called a "golden age." Their courts and enormous palace-cities, captured in fantastic tales from the Arabian Nights, were the richest in the world, unsurpassed in luxury, sophistication, and culture. Nothing in Europe compared.

As the Abbasid caliphs weakened, independent or semi-independent dynasties assumed power in Egypt, Iran, and other areas. By the tenth century, Abbasid control was effectively limited to Iraq. Baghdad itself had been captured three times by 1055, once by a Shi'ite dynasty from Persia and twice by Seljuk Turks. Although they retained influence and prestige as the protectors of Sunni orthodoxy, politically the Abbasid caliphs became little more than figureheads. Baghdad was again attacked in 1258, this time in a devastating invasion of Mongol armies from Central Asia. Surviving members of the Abbasid dynasty fled to Egypt, now ruled by Mamluk sultans.

EARLY MEDIEVAL DYNASTIES IN THE WEST

Fatimids, Ayyubids

As Abbasid authority weakened, the Shi'ite Fatimid dynasty (909"1171) —claiming descent from Fatima, daughter of the Prophet and wife of Ali—rose to power in North Africa. They expanded into Egypt and Syria, and in 969 founded a new capital at Cairo (the name means "the victorious"). Fatimid control of trade around the Mediterranean brought enormous prosperity, and Cairo became an important cultural center. After the Fatimids sought aid from Syria against invading Crusader armies, a Syrian officer—Salah al-

Din ibn Ayyub (better known in the West as Saladin)—overthrew the Fatimid ruler to establish a new dynasty. The Ayyubids (1171"1250) restored Egypt to Sunni orthodoxy. Salah al-Din expanded Ayyubid territory into Yemen, Syria, and Iraq, and in 1187 he decisively defeated the Crusader states. Ayyubid territory broke into a collection of semiautonomous principalities after his death, but it continued to enjoy peace and prosperity.

EARLY MEDIEVAL DYNASTIES IN THE EAST

Ghaznavids, Seljuks

Large migrations of nomads from the steppes of Central Asia brought Turkish peoples into the Middle East and Asia Minor. A series of Turkish dynasties replaced the mostly Shi'ite Persian governors who had taken effective control from the Abbasid caliphs in the ninth and tenth centuries. The earliest of these Turkish dynasties were the Ghaznavids (977"1186). From their original base in Afghanistan, they moved into Iran, adopting Persian customs and the Persian language. Early in the eleventh century, the Ghaznavids lost most of Iran to a new Turkish dynasty, the Seljuks (1038"1194). In 1055 the Abbasid caliph in Baghdad was forced to grant the Seljuk leader the title "sultan," a word that means power.

Turkish slave-soldiers had served the caliphate for centuries, but now the Seljuk sultans controlled a large empire outright (although they ruled in the name of the caliph). The Seljuks were military elite. Iran, Iraq, Syria, and Turkey all came under their authority. Islam's rulers were once again nomadic people, and their customs were superimposed over Persian and Arab societies. As Sunnis, the Seljuks worked to restore orthodoxy in the east, largely by building religious schools. They vigorously suppressed the Shi'ism of their Persian predecessors. Although their territory would soon become fragmented and governed by different Seljuk branches, the Seljuks' impact on the Islamic world was important—in political, cultural, and artistic terms—and lasted long after the last Seljuk sultan. Most important was their shift toward Iran, away from Arab lands to the west. A fundamental divide between eastern and western Islam has endured ever since.

LATE MEDIEVAL PERIOD

Mongols and Mamluks

In Syria and Egypt, the death of the last Ayyubid ruler was followed by years of chaos. From the turmoil a military leader emerged to establish a new "dynasty." His name meant Lion; his successor was called Cormorant.These new rulers rose from the ranks of military slaves, mamluks, not as sons of sultans. For the next two hundred fifty years, Mamluk sultans (1250"1517) in Cairo ruled Egypt, Syria, western Arabia, and parts of Anatolia. The Mamluks succeeded in routing the Crusaders from the Middle East, and they battled a new threat from the East. From 1219 on, Iran had suffered repeated and devastating invasions by Mongol armies, led first by Chinggis Khan.

By the time Chinggis Khan died in 1227, Mongol conquests extended from the China Sea to Ukraine—they ruled in China as the Yuan dynasty and in Russia as the Golden Horde. After taking Baghdad in 1258, they established a dynasty of Mongol sultans, known as the Il-Khanids (1258"1335).

The name, which means "lesser khans," identified them as subordinates to the Great Khan in China. They governed from Iraq to Afghanistan and were followed by a series of successor states.A new wave of invasions was launched by Timur, known in the West as Tamerlane. The Timurids (1370"1501) ruled Iran, Iraq, and Central Asia. The Mongol invasions form a decisive break between early and later Islam. From then on two rival empires would control most of the Islamic world.

LATE EMPIRES

Ottomans in the West

By the later fourteenth century, the Mamluks were in political decline. Like Europe, Egypt and Syria had been devastated by the Black Death at the end of the 1340s. Famines created economic problems that were greatly exacerbated when Western explorers found new sea routes to the riches of the East, bypassing the Middle East. The Mamluks fell to a new group of raiding Turks, the Ottomans (1281"1924) who had begun to consolidate power in Asia Minor before 1300.

The Ottoman sultans renewed territorial expansion in the west—even into Europe. In 1453 they captured Constantinople (today Istanbul), the still highly prized capital of the now-faded Byzantine empire, and made it their own capital. The Ottoman sultans assumed leadership of Sunni Islam, integrating government and Islamic law. In addition to orthodox schools, they sponsored Sufi orders, whose more mystical approach appealed to popular piety.

Ottoman policies protected the property and political rights of non-Muslim minorities, and they were open to Western technology and innovation. Ottoman administrations were well-organized bureaucracies. Many able soldiers and officials rose through the system of *devshirme,* which removed promising young boys from non-Muslim homes, sponsored their education, and placed them in palace service. The peak of Ottoman culture and influence came in the sixteenth century with the reign of sultan Süleyman the Magnificent (ruled 1520"1566), who extended the empire into Mesopotamia and Eastern Europe. Ottoman armies threatened Vienna in 1529 and again in 1683. After the sixteenth century, however, Ottoman power declined and the society stagnated—eventually Turkey would be called the "Sick Man of Europe"—but the sultanate continued until shortly after World War I.

THE LATE EMPIRES

Safavids in the East

The Safavid shahs (Persian for "kings") traced their descent from the Prophet's son-in-law Ali, and they went about making Iran a Shi'ite state. In so doing, they established the national identity Iran carries to this day. (The name Persia was abandoned in 1935.) The first Safavid shah was a charismatic leader—red-haired and left-handed—who captured Tabriz at the age of fourteen. His great-grandson Shah 'Abbas strengthened the military and administration, and organized the economy, making Iran a power to rival the Ottomans.

He established his capital at Isfahan and undertook an extensive building campaign. Isfahan's great square—more than twenty acres—is possibly the largest public square in the world; it was the site of markets, polo matches, archery contests, military parades, and executions. At night, it was lit by fifty thousand lamps. The shah cultivated European support against his Ottoman rivals and as partners in trade for luxury goods, especially textiles. As much as anything else, it was the decline of this trade that weakened the Safavid dynasty. In 1722 an Afghan tribal leader captured Isfahan.

ISLAM, THE MOSQUE, AND THE QURAN

Islam is a faith shared by more than a billion people in every part of the world. In Arabic "Islam" means "submission" and comes from the word for peace—the peace Muslims receive in submitting to God. In the West we have tended to associate Islam with the Middle East, where it originated, but today Indonesia is home to the largest Muslim population, more than live in Iran, Iraq, Syria, Egypt, and Saudi Arabia combined. The teachings of Islam were revealed to the Prophet Muhammad in the seventh century A.D. It is the youngest of the world's great monotheistic religions. Muslims see Islam as the continuation—and completion—

of Judaism and Christianity, and they honor patriarchs and prophets from Abraham to Jesus as Muhammad's predecessors.

When Muslims pray to Allah, they are praying to the same one true God worshiped by Christians and Jews—Allah is simply his name in Arabic. Islam makes strict distinction between the Creator and all parts of his creation; Muhammad did not share God's divinity. He was God's prophet, his messenger and a model for believers, but fully human. God is awesome and transcendent, and most Muslim prayers are said in praise and glory rather than as calls for divine help. Muslims believe they will be judged on the righteousness of their lives on earth and that the good will be rewarded with eternal life in paradise

The Quran

God's revelations to Muhammad are codified in the Quran, which is the essential basis of Islamic belief. Unlike the Old or New Testaments, it is not a narrative account of the Prophet's life or a retelling of his teachings—it is God's own words as they were spoken by the angel Gabriel. The word Quran means "recitation." Reciting aloud the poetic language of the Quran remains the most profound expression of faith. Because the Quran contains God's actual words, in Arabic, the language itself acquired enormous prestige, becoming the common language in all Islamic lands. Arabic script—also privileged by its use in the Quran—was adopted for other languages, including Turkish and Persian.

The importance of the Quran and its Arabic text elevated the art of calligraphy. Qurans survive in fairly large numbers, even from early periods. Copying the Quran is an act of devotion, and because of their sacred nature, worn or damaged Qurans were not destroyed. Today, even though Qurans are mass-produced, the physical text is still handled with reverence. While the Quran is the ultimate guide for Muslims, they also refer to the hadith, accounts of the Prophet's deeds and sayings, as recorded by his followers.

The Five Pillars of Islam

Without a formal priesthood, Islam makes few liturgical demands. It asks of believers five fundamental requirements, known as the Five Pillars:

- First and most important is the profession of faith, called the shahada: "There is no god but God and Muhammad is the messenger of God." These words—in Arabic La ilaha illa'allah, Muhammadun rasul Allah—are whispered in the ears of the new born and the dying. As part of the call to prayer, they echo daily in Muslim communities across the globe. Profession of the faith before two Muslim witnesses is all that is needed to become a Muslim: accepting the one true God and Muhammad as his prophet.
- Daily prayers, the salah, are made five times: after first light, at noon, in the afternoon, following sunset, and in the evening. Before praying, Muslims wash to prepare the body and mind, removing physical impurities and mental distraction. Prayers, said in a precise order of words and motions, are directed toward Mecca. The prayer ritual includes recitations from the Quran, postures of praise and humility, contemplation, and finally the sharing of peace with other believers—"peace be with you and the mercy of Allah." Prayers can be performed anywhere, but men are expected to gather at the mosque for midday Friday prayers, when a sermon is preached.
- Alms for the poor are collected in the form of a religious tax, the zakat—a word that means purification and signifies the benefit gained by recipient and giver alike. Muslims believe the zakat will be repaid many times over by the rewards of paradise. Individual donations are also made to religious foundations, hospitals, and to fund public works like fountains.
- All adults who are physically able are called to fast during the month of Ramadan. From sunrise to sunset, Muslims

abstain from food, drink, and sexual relations. This sacrifice aids in turning the mind's focus from worldly concerns. Believers must also avoid unjust practices and pay special care to others. The entire Quran is read during the month, in daily segments. The end of Ramadan is marked by the festival of 'Id al-Fitr, a three-day celebration when alms are distributed to the poor and gifts exchanged.

- The pilgrimage to Mecca, the hajj, is made once in his or her life by every Muslim who is physically and financially able to undertake the journey. The hajj is an annual event that brings together Muslims from across the globe (a lesser pilgrimage can be undertaken at any time). Pilgrims wear simple robes to eliminate differences in nationality and status and to emphasize their shared faith and humility before God. The hajj takes place in Mecca and sites nearby over many days during the final month of the Islamic calendar. It culminates in the feast of sacrifice, the 'Id al-Adha, which commemorates the faith of Abraham, whom Muslims, like Christians and Jews, believe made man's original covenant with God.

The Mosque

The prototype for all mosques was the Prophet's own house in Medina, where his followers gathered in an arcaded courtyard for prayer and to hear Muhammad's words. A roofed area protected them from weather and the midday sun. Muhammad, leaning on a spear or staff, preached in front of the wall that was in the direction of Mecca. One feature that became typical of mosques was not found in the Prophet's house—the minaret, the tower from which the faithful are called to prayer by the muezzin. The first muezzin, an Abyssinian slave who was a trusted companion of Muhammad, called followers from the rooftop of the Prophet's house.

The first minarets may not have been associated with mosques at all. Or, they may have been built for another purpose, perhaps to mark the mosque's position within the crooked streets of ancient towns. Minarets have assumed a number of different forms, from a ziggurat spiral at Samarra (opposite) to the spires of Ottoman Turkey. Because they functioned in many ways within the Islamic community—as a place for communal prayer and individual study, and as a center for civic life—mosques grew to encompass many distinct structures. Some became sprawling complexes with madrasas (religious schools), cemeteries, and even markets.

Three Mosques

These slides illustrate three styles of mosque architecture. The Great Mosque in Damascus was built by the Umayyad caliph al-Walid I (ruled 705"715). It was described by the fourteenth- century traveler Ibn Battuta as "the most magnificent mosque in the world, the finest in construction and noblest in beauty, grace and perfection; it is matchless and unequalled." Al-Walid built mosques in Damascus, Medina, and Jerusalem as expressions of Islam's new wealth and political confidence. Today only the Damascus mosque retains most of its original form. When the Umayyads moved their capital from the Arabian Desert to Damascus, they brought evolving Islamic art closer to the orbit of Byzantine, and ultimately classical, influences.

The mosque site had been a Roman temple precinct and included a church (which al- Walid offered to buy). Al-Walid's building incorporates columns and capitals from the temple, and its prayer hall follows the basic design of the three-aisle Christian basilica (turned sideways). Its decoration looked to classical models. Mosaics reminiscent of Roman wall painting, possibly made by Byzantine artisans, and covered the courtyard walls. They present lush landscapes, with abundant trees, running rivers, and a combination of real and fanciful architecture.

Most modern scholars believe that, on some level, the mosaics reflect an image of paradise, a place—unlike the desert home of Islam—that is verdant and well-watered. What is missing is any representation of people or animals: even these early mosque builders made a strict division between religious and secular settings. While the form of the Great Mosque of Damascus, with its arcaded court and dome to emphasize the mihrab, would be reinterpreted many times, its mosaic decoration would be replaced by calligraphy, arabesques, and geometric patterns. Our second mosque type was introduced by the Seljuks in Iran. Among the earliest examples is the Great Mosque at Isfahan, begun in the tenth century.

Today, the huge complex—150 meters on its longest axis and with hundreds of domes—reflects successive building campaigns and the mosque's many functions as center of the community. It even engulfed the city bazaar. The architecture is distinguished by the use of iwans—opens arched rooms—centered in each of the four courtyard walls. The largest iwan, in the qiblah wall, served as the prayer hall; smaller ones were probably used by religious teachers. Their openings are framed by elaborate surrounds, called pishtaqs, decorated with carved stone or brilliantly colored tiles. Built for the son of Süleyman the Magnificent, the third mosque is representative of the type introduced by Ottoman architects. Built on a square plan, the prayer hall is dominated by a central dome, rising massively above a cascade of secondary domes and semidomes.

Exterior buttressing and large windows create a large light-filled interior space. Slender, pointed minarets mark the corners of the prayer hall, helping to make the space "legible" from the outside. We know the names of very few Islamic architects, but the man who designed the Selimiye mosque is an exception. Sinan (1491"1588) was the greatest Ottoman architect and the Selimye mosque, built when he was in his eighties, is considered his greatest work. Probably of Greek origin, Sinan was recruited through the *devshirme* system, rising into the sultan's elite jannisary guard. In 1538 he was made the chief court architect to Süleyman the Magnificent. Probably most of his training—like that of all Islamic architects— was practical, acquired as a military engineer responsible for building defenses, bridges, and other public works.

A Mosque Pulpit

A sermon *(khutba)* is typically part of the service during midday Friday prayers. It is delivered from a minbar, a tall pulpit placed beside the mihrab. The minbar reflects the raised seat from which Muhammad spoke in Medina, but it was more than just a platform for the preacher; because the ruler's name and titles were read during the *khutba*, minbars were also symbols of authority. Early minbars were portable and wheeled into place when needed, but they soon became permanent fixtures and, in fact, are usually the largest furniture in a mosque.

This one stands some twenty feet high. Its form is typical: a towerlike structure with steps approached through a doorway and leading to a canopied platform at the top. The surface is richly decorated. Inscriptions quote verses from the Quran and praise the Mamluk sultan Qa'itbay. His almost thirty- year rule, 1468"1496, was an unusually long one. He founded a number of new religious institutions and restored many older ones in Egypt and Syria. Probably this minbar was made for a mosque in Cairo, although we do not know which one.

A View of Mecca

The first House founded for men was surely that at Mecca for a blessing and guidance to the world. Therein are manifest signs— Abraham's station, and whosoever enters in is safe. There is due to God from man a pilgrimage unto the House, for whosoever can find his way there." This injunction is the fifth pillar of Islam, the *hajj,* or pilgrimage to Mecca. Probably the tile was bought by someone to commemorate his completion of the *hajj.* Below the inscription is a bird's eye view of the Sacred Mosque at Mecca, heart of the pilgrimage. In the center stands the Ka'bah— the draped rectangular shrine that is set with a meteorite called the Black Stone.

The Quran says the Ka'bah was built by the Jewish patriarch Abraham as the first house of God. It had already become the most important shrine in Arabia in pre-Islamic times and was a source of great prestige and wealth for Mecca. Many gods were worshiped there before Muhammad rid the shrine of idols and idolaters, restoring it to the one true God. The Ka'bah defines the *qiblah* or "point of adoration"— the direction toward which Muslims address their prayers. Other monuments shown and labeled on the tile remain part of the *hajj* rites, including the "station of Abraham," where the patriarch stood when he built the Ka'bah, and the well of Zamzam, from which pilgrims drink. A minbar is also depicted.

Quran for Ramadan

Large, beautifully decorated Qurans, like this one possibly made in Shiraz around 1370, were often produced in sets of thirty separately bound sections—one to be read aloud each day during the month of Ramadan. This one is written in the script known as *muhaqqaq,* which was used mostly for Qurans and whose name means "certain." The Quran contains 114 chapters, called suras, arranged from the longest to the shortest. In the earliest Qurans, chapters were separated by decorative bands, but soon chapter headings became elaborately decorated frames, giving the name of the chapter (though Western writers normally refer to them by number) and the number of verses it contains. Eventually they indicated whether Muhammad had received this revelation in Mecca or Medina.

The oldest Quran fragments date from the eighth century, when a group of heavy angular scripts generally labeled as "kufic" (after the town of Kufa in Iraq) became standard for writing the sacred text. Their austere and monumental simplicity was felt appropriate for this exalted use. Most Kufic Qurans are written on parchment in a horizontal format. Cursive scripts replaced Kufic in most Qurans (except those made in the far west) beginning around 1000. And paper, cheaper and easier to work with, replaced parchment. In 751, near Samarkand, Muslim forces defeated a Chinese army. According to legend, two captured soldiers revealed the Chinese secret of paper-making. Islamic scribes quickly adopted it and, in turn, introduced it to the West.

Science and Learning

Between the ninth and the fourteenth centuries, Islamic science outpaced that of any other culture. Scientistphilosophers had wide- ranging interests, most of them working in many disciplines we consider quite distinct today—medicine, mathematics, astronomy, geography, philosophy, optics. Islamic learning is celebrated for having preserved many of the texts of ancient Greece, passing along a classical tradition that might otherwise have been lost. But Islamic scholars did not simply accept these ancient "authorities," in the way that, say, scholastic philosophers did in medieval Europe. Stressing experiment and observation, they questioned and tested those authorities, laying the foundation on which modern science is based.

The Abbasid caliph al-Ma'mun (ruled 813"833) transformed the library in Baghdad into what he called the "House of Wisdom." At once library and school, it also supported an observatory and a staff of copyists, translators, and bookbinders. Delegations were sent to Constantinople and other cities in search of manuscripts to buy. Within seventy-five years, many Greek works had been translated into Arabic, including philosophical and scientific books by Aristotle, Galen's work on medicine, Euclid's on geometry, and Ptolemy's on geography and astronomy. In many cases it was these Arabic versions that were translated into Latin and disseminated to the West. The House of Wisdom also collected and translated works by Persian and Hindu thinkers.

And its scholars produced commentaries and original works of their own. Probably the greatest of the scholars in al-Ma'mun's time was the mathematician and geographer known as al-Khwarizmi (c. 800"c. 847). His book *On Calculation with Hindu Numerals* is primarily responsible for the adoption of what we today call "Arabic numerals." His revolutionary work on quadratic equations was translated into Latin in 1145 and served as a principal mathematics textbook for the next four hundred years. A part of its title—in Arabic *al-Jabr* (the hunt)—introduced the word algebra into *al-Jabr al-Jabr* the languages of Europe.

Al-Khwarizmi's name itself gives us "algorithm." Using al-Khwarizmi's work in geography—he specified the number of miles in one degree of the earth's surface—Islamic scientists improved on previous geographies and were able to determine the circumference of the earth with remarkable accuracy. Their figure was only forty-one meters off modern measurements. Geography and the related science of astronomy were important to rulers with vast empires and to every Muslim, who needed to know the direction of Mecca and times for prayer. Some of the most significant contributions of Islamic science were in medicine.

Islamic physicians enjoyed particular renown—during the Crusades Salah al-Din (Saladin) sent his personal physician to tend the ailing Richard the Lionhearted, king of England. While contemporaries in many parts of the world sought supernatural causes of disease, Islamic medicine drew on the rational approach of ancient Greek writers such as Galen and Hippocrates and that of the Persian medical school at Jundishapur. While bacteria and the germ theory of disease were unknown, Islamic scientists emphasized the importance of hygiene. When the first hospital was built in Baghdad in the ninth century, the site was selected following experiments in which pieces of meat were left in various locations to determine where decay was slowest to set in.

Around the same time, the caliphate began to examine physicians about their knowledge and to license them. Close control was also maintained over the production of medicines. Baghdad pharmacies provided a range of remedies based on plants as well as sophisticated inorganic compounds. Surgeons removed cataracts and tumors, and performed delicate vascular operations. Ophthalmology was a particular specialty of Islamic medicine, beginning with al-Kindi (c. 800"870), who first identified the parts of the eye. Ibn al-Haytham (c. 965"1039) explained how human vision operates and is regarded as the father of optics.

It had long been thought that the eye sent out rays that struck the object seen—much in the way a bat echolocates. Ibn al-Haytham was able to demonstrate that the eye instead only perceives light reflected from the object. He proved his point by making a pin-hole camera. Another Islamic doctor considered the circulation of blood in the heart. His work contradicted the accepted theories of Galen and anticipated the work of English physician William Harvey by 350 years. Al-Razi (865"925) was the first scientist ever to isolate the clinical symptoms of a particular disease, smallpox. He enumerated seven principles for good health, including moderation in food and drink, cleanliness, and good mental and physical habits. The most widely studied work on medicine and disease was produced by Ibn Sina (980"1037), better known in the West as Avicenna.

The *Canon of Medicine,* translated eighty-seven times, remained the most important medical text in Europe until the seventeenth century. Said to have written some 275 books in Arabic and his native Persian, Ibn Sina was called the "prince of philosophers" by his contemporaries, but some of his ideas also drew criticism as contrary to the teachings of Islam. He studied Aristotle in a neo-platonic spirit, believing (like Plato) in the existence of universal concepts. He distinguished the possible from the necessary—and made a proof of the primacy of God's existence. Another Islamic interpreter of Aristotle was Ibn Rushd (1126"1198) from Spain (called Averroës in the West). Like Ibn Sina he was a physician as well as a philosopher.

His philosophical works made their greatest impact in the West. Believing both religion and philosophy to be true, he sought to harmonize them. His ideas would help secularize Western science and philosophy, separating them from theology and the limits of church dogma. Islamic scholars came from all parts of the Islamic world, and not all of them were Muslim. The *Guide for the Perplexed* and *or the Perplexed or the Perplexed Mishna Torah* by the Jewish philosopher Maimonides (1135"1204) was translated into Hebrew from the Judeo-Arabic in which they had been written. Maimonides, known in Arabic as Ibn Maymun, was born to a family of Jewish intellectuals in Islamic Córdoba, in Spain.

He served as court physician to Salah al-Din and produced books on medicine and astronomy in addition to theological and philosophical works. Ibn Khaldun (1332"1406), born in Tunis, is considered Islam's greatest historical philosopher and the creator of social science— his histories sought not only to present an accounting of events but to explain the social, economic, geographic, and cultural factors that influence them. His researches led him to a cyclical view of history and a belief in the rise and fall of empires. Islamic science had begun to lose its brilliance before the Mongol invasions of the thirteenth century. Many reasons are attested; perhaps most important was that the caliphate had become fragmented and the unified culture it had supported no longer existed.

A Mathematical Jewel

An astrolabe is a mechanical computer that can be used to determine several kinds of astronomical information. It can tell the time of day, even at night, determine latitude, and fix the time of events for casting horoscopes. For Muslims, especially traders and other travelers who needed to know the direction of Mecca and the hour of prayers, the astrolabe was indispensable. They called it the "mathematical jewel." Telling the time for prayer was more complicated than you might imagine. Rather than occurring at specified times on a twenty-four- hour clock, the times for prayer are determined by an older system of time-keeping, whose hours were reckoned from sunrise (the first hour). Noon was the end of the sixth hour and sunset the end of the twelfth. Depending on the season and the latitude, the length of different hours varied in different amounts.

Only as reliable clocks became available in the seventeenth century, did most of the world start to count equal hours of sixty minutes each, irrespective of the "solar" time of day. Astrolabes work by projecting the celestial sphere onto a flat plate—an idea first conceived by the ancient Greeks. Probably Islamic scientists learned of the astrolabe through translations of Greek texts in the eighth and ninth centuries. The oldest surviving Islamic astrolabes date from the tenth century—when one treatise described a thousand uses for it. They remained in popular use in the Islamic world into the nineteenth century, long after other inventions supplanted them in the West. This astrolabe is shown dismantled.

Three separate plates map the celestial projection at specific latitudes. (Others provide a shadow square for solving simple trigonometry problems and give astrological information.) These plates fit into the dished base, marked in degrees around the rim. Over the plates rotates the openwork *rete,* essentially a star map. Its circle marks the elliptic (the projection of the sun's annual path in the sky), its leafy points fixed stars. On the back of the instrument, a rotating sight, the *alidade,* is used to determine the altitude of the sun or a star. This information is used to position the *rete.* Once set, the astrolabe shows the entire sky, both visible and unseen. The back of the astrolabe gives scales for finding the direction of Mecca.

In Case of Spider Bite

Along with works by Greek physicians Galen and Hippocrates, Dioscorides' *Materia medica—the Pharmacy*—was one of the most widely used scientific texts in pre-modern times. Originally written in Greek some time between 40 and 90 A.D., it was translated into Arabic in the mid 800s in Iraq. It was one of the first scientific manuscripts to be translated and among the earliest illustrated (the first illustrated copy was completed in 1083). Later translations were made in Spain and Iran, and scholars added supplements to Dioscorides' original text. Many Latin translations were also made. For more than fifteen hundred years the *Materia medica* remained the primary source of information about drugs made from plants, animals, and minerals—in the Islamic world and in Europe. Dioscorides, a Greek from Cilicia in what is today Turkey, claimed to have first become interested in medicinal plants as a youth.

His travels as a soldier in the Roman army must have allowed him to collect a large number and variety of specimens. He describes about five hundred plants and more than four thousand different remedies, emphasizing that his work differs from earlier herbals because he had observed most of the drugs directly and examined their effects with an empirical approach. Ironically, his work was later accepted as something like medical dogma; only in the mid sixteenth century did European scientists renew his spirit of investigation and experimentation. This leaf is from a copy signed by Abdallah ibn al-Fadl, who was perhaps the painter as well as the calligrapher. Its lively style suggests that it may have been made in Baghdad. Narrative scenes like this one are probably based on illustrations in contemporary literary works.

The physician—seated on a carpet and resting against a fine cushion—instructs his assistant from a book (perhaps it is this same text!) as the younger man blends a poultice. The text, from a chapter about poisons, describes antidotes for the sting of the phalangium spider. Recipes for different poultices are given, one by combining ashes from a fig tree with salt and wine, the other using pounded roots with barley and vinegar. In either case, the wound is to be cleaned first. For several days the patient is to bathe in warm water and drink a medicine made with various plant ingredients.

The World as they found it

Between the seventh and ninth centuries, Islamic trade extended east to China by both land and sea routes; it went south to Zanzibar, and north to Russia. Trade provided both the necessity for and a means of knowing about the earth. The study of geography flourished. The foremost geographer of his day was al-Idrisi. Although he traced his descent to the Prophet, the details of al-Idrisi's life are mostly unknown. He may have been born in Morocco around 1100. He apparently traveled extensively—it was said he had even visited France and England—and studied at the university in Córdoba. He spent fifteen years compiling geography for the Norman king of Sicily, Roger II Guiscard. Al-Idrisi called his work the Book of Roger. It was completed only weeks before his patron's death in 1154 and was accompanied by a map in seventy sections.

This round map reflects a simplified one al-Idrisi prepared to accompany a shorter version of his geography. From our perspective al-Idrisi's maps are upside down: south appears at the top. Sicily, which had earlier been under Muslim control, was then on the edge of the Islamic world. Norman kings, who had established themselves in southern Italy in the eleventh century, welcomed Islamic culture—and Islamic scholars—into the vibrant intellectual life of their courts. Roger actively encouraged all areas of learning but seems to have been especially interested in geography, personally interviewing merchants, sailors, pilgrims, and Crusaders who arrived in his capital at Palermo. Roger asked al-Idrisi to produce a new geographical work, and he made special arrangements for production of new maps.

The geography was to describe the location of the world's cities, their climate, and the distances between them. Teams of "certain intelligent men" accompanied by draftsmen were dispatched abroad to obtain new research. Their first-hand observations were used to expand, correlate, and correct the geographical data. Written in Arabic and Latin, the text begins with a short introduction. Here al-Idrisi accepts the "opinion of philosophers" that the earth is a sphere. He likens its stable suspension in the heavens to that of the yolk inside an egg. His descriptions and maps followed the ancient division of the world into seven climate zones, a system derived from the second-century Greek geographer and astronomer Ptolemy.

Palaces and Poetry

When early Islamic leaders adopted the style of Byzantine and Sasanian emperors, they isolated themselves from their subjects and surrounded themselves with unparalleled luxury. In their palaces, all the senses were engaged: silk rushed smoothly across the skin, gardens delighted the eye with color and the nose with fragrance, water rippling from fountains and pools soothed the ear and spirit, wine warmed the body, poetry the emotions. One Ghaznavid sultan ordered construction of a pavilion made of halva, a sesame sweetmeat. Mongol rulers lived in tent palaces that occupied acres and were furnished with the finest textiles. This display was meant not simply to indulge the court but to awe outsiders with opulence.

A Byzantine ambassador visiting Baghdad in 917 was left to wait two months for an audience with the caliph. Finally he was led through a seemingly endless succession of palaces, gardens, and zoological parks, past elephants and hundreds of lions. In the eleventh century, an Iranian poet and traveler described the Fatimid palace: I saw a series of buildings, terraces, rooms....There was a throne in one of them that took up the entire width of the room. Three of its sides were made of gold on which were hunting scenes depicting riders racing their horses, and other subjects; there were also inscriptions written in beautiful characters. The rugs and hangings were Greek satin and woven precisely to fit the spot where they were to be placed. A balustrade of golden lattice- work surrounded the throne, whose beauty defies description. Behind the throne were steps of silver. I saw a tree that looked like an orange tree, whose branches, leaves, and fruit were made of sugar. A thousand statuettes and figurines also made of sugar were placed there.

Palaces were also administrative centers, whole cities in their own right. The Alhambra (slide 10) probably accommodated some forty thousand people: the ruler, his wives and children; their tutors, attendants, and slaves; senior administrators and judges; and young men who were being trained for the military and bureaucracy. Although palaces encompassed both public and private space, the two were often strictly divided. Ottoman sultans listened to deliberations of officials and the ruling council, which took place on the palace grounds, but they remained invisible inside screened enclosures.

Palace in Spain

Only two Islamic palaces survive from the pre-modern period: the Alhambra, built by the Nasrid rulers of Granada, and the Ottomans' Topkapi palace in Istanbul. The Alhambra was preserved by its Christian conquerors—they captured it in the 1490s—as a symbol of victory, while most other Islamic palaces were allowed to crumble. Built by a relatively minor dynasty, the Alhambra— despite its rich beauty—offers only a hint of the luxury that would have been found in the palaces of greater rulers. The name Alhambra means "red [palace]" and refers to the warm color of its stone against the distant mountains. It was not a single structure but, like other Islamic palaces, a royal complex.

It encompassed five separate palaces and numerous other buildings. The imposing exterior walls and towers give little hint of the luxury within, which was meant to reflect paradise on earth. Inside and outside are ingeniously joined. Gardens unite courtyard and interior. Distances are seen across expansive vistas or in small glimpses that reward a sudden change of direction. Light is used like an artist's medium: shaded walkways give onto bright terraces and dazzling pools; shafts of sun flow into shaded recesses. Flowing water—brought by aqueduct from surrounding hills and piped through an elaborate system of floor channels—brings a soothing sound to rooms inside and out. The Court of the Lions, seen in this slide, is one of two from the medieval Alhambra to survive more or less unchanged. It was used for pleasure rather than official functions.

Tall, slender columns support multilobed arches and vaults elaborated with the faceted shapes of *muqarnas.* In one room, five thousand *muqarnas* in the ceiling fracture entering light into a prismatic display. It was intended to reflect the dome of heaven. As sunlight moved through the room, shifting patterns created an effect like the rotation of stars and planets in the nighttime sky. The room and its effect are described in verse decorating the wall below: And how many arches rise up in its vault supported by columns which at night are embellished by light! You would think that they are the heavenly spheres whose orbits revolve, overshadowing the pillar of dawn when it bravely begins to appear after having passed through the night.

Musicians and Poets

In palace gardens, caliphs and courtiers enjoyed picnics and wine, lyric poetry and music—as the figures do on this ivory box. Inside each roundel, a couple sits under a leafy canopy. The musician on the left plays a horn or flute, the one on the right a lute. Their companions hold wine cups or flasks, and one of them sniffs a bouquet. They are surrounded by luxuriant foliage, birds, and other animals that lend an idyllic feel. Inspired by wine, soothed by music and the fragrance of flowers, these courtiers would be moved to compose extemporaneous verses, a skill expected of them.

We could imagine those singing lines like these from al-Shari al-Taliq, a poet who was a member of Córdoba's ruling family: Just as the sun gives the garden back its breath, so the beloved's brightness restores the lover burnt up with desire. Just as the rose's petals are covered with dew, So my love's cheek is sprinkled with drops of perspiration. It bursts into flower beside a pure yellow narcissus, which I thought was concealing a tender love for the rose... How lovely they are, those stars of the garden that have risen towards the horizon from their flowerbeds.

About thirty ivory caskets like this one are known; inscriptions on some indicate they were made in Córdoba (although this one may have been made in Toledo by craftsmen who emigrated from Córdoba). Under Spain's Umayyad caliphs, between the mid tenth and early eleventh century, Cordoba had flourished to become the greatest city in Europe and a center for the production of luxury goods. Most of the ivories, like this one, are decorated with court scenes. Originally they were painted, and many were studded with small jewels. The blank band running around this box would originally have held an inscription—perhaps a few lyric lines like al-Taliq's above or a panegyric to the caliph likening the well-being of his state to the abundance of a garden. It may have been removed because the casket was made into a Christian reliquary; this is how most of them survived. The silver mounts are later additions.

Objects of Desire

A courtier's eloquence in verse was expected to be matched by physical elegance. Sprawling palace grounds provided ample room for polo matches, archery contests, and other games that gave young men a chance to display their skill and prowess. The handsome polo player on this bowl—almost hidden in the dense garden around him—is an unattainable object of desire. The poet's longing is inscribed in the verses that appear on the rim and around the vessel: O Heart! Do you see any cause for joy? Do you see anything but one whose glances are like scattering jewels? While I live I am content to wish for a moment together. People are all as you see them. It has not been my habit, where lust is concerned, To speak of the pain in my heart to anyone. Despite this, I wish to say one word: I have died for love of you! Respond to my cry for help!

The poet's desire is not simply for the beautiful polo player: it is a yearning to be reunited with God. This neoplatonic idea was a basic component of the Sufi movement. As it would be for Renaissance poets in the West, the unfulfilled pursuit of earthly love was a metaphor for the quest for spiritual union. Through music, poetry, and ecstatic dance, Sufis believed it was possible to regain a state of communion with the Creator.

Compare these lines by the great Persian Sufi poet Jalal al-Din Rumi (1207"1273) about a reed taken from a mattress of straw to become a flute: Hearken to the reed forlorn Breathing, even since 'twas torn from its rushy bed, a strain of impassioned love and pain. The secret of my song, though near, none can see and none can hear. Oh, for a friend to know the sign And mingle all his soul with mine! 'Tis the flame of Love that fired me, 'Tis the wine of Love inspired me, Wouldst thou learn how lovers bleed, Hearken, hearken to the reed.

Tale of Romance

This scene illustrates a moment from Persian poet Nizami's *Khamseh,* one of the two most celebrated—and often painted—works of Persian literature. The other (and earlier) *Shahnama (Book of Kings),* recounts exploits of Iran's heroic past. By contrast the *Khamseh,* literally "quintet," contains a philosophical/mystical tale and four romances. It is often described as a turning point in Persian poetry, the first time dazzling language and images serve love and other human emotions rather than epic action. Nizami traces the love and courtship of the last great Sasanian king, Khusraw II (d. 628), and the beautiful Armenian princess Shirin— her name means "sweet."

They fall in love by seeing each other in portraits, but their face-to-face meeting is long delayed. Before they can marry several obstacles await. In the nighttime episode painted here, Khusraw, still in pajamas, saves Shirin from a lion. Eventually the couple is "united in perfect love," unhappily short-lived: Khusraw is assassinated soon after.

Although the historical Khusraw and Shirin—and Nizami's poem—are much earlier, their lives very much reflect the luxury and refinement of the Safavid court where this illumination was painted: luxurious dwellings, days picnicking and hunting, nights of dance and poetry: How perfect for the lovers were these ecstatic days! The air sparkled; the sky was never so blue, the grass so thick with flowers. And never did Khusraw and Shirin leave one another's sight. In the mornings they would summon their attendants; then Shabdiz and Golgun [their magnificent horses] would be led from the stable and they would ride to the polo field or to the hunt. Chasing after birds and game, Khusraw was astonished at the prowess of Shirin; her skill with the bow and her mastery of her horse's reins matched that of any man. She was a lioness, not a gazelle, and his heart pursued her eagerly. Yet at night when the dancing began, so light was her step that she seemed never to touch the ground. Every night there were sumptuous feasts. Scarcely was one banquet finished than the next began, and each was embellished with music, song and wine, and poetry in praise of love.

Riza' was one of the most renowned illuminators in seventeenth- century Iran. Unlike calligraphers, painters had long remained anonymous. Signatures appear finally in the fourteenth century, but only at the end of the fifteenth century can scholars link individual artists and their work. By the time Riza' came to prominence, painters had begun to assume personalities and the marks of personal style. In part, this was because the market for paintings was changing. Manuscripts had often been dismembered as they became worn and then reassembled into albums. Now a wider audience, less able to afford an entire book, sought single sheets.

In his early career, Riza' had been known for portraits of courtly figures, drawn with a light calligraphic line, delicately fluttering scarves and turbans, and large areas of primary color. In midlife, however, contemporaries reported that he fell in with "lowlifes and wrestlers," and for many years turned away from court subjects. When he returned to them, his line was coarser, his colors darker and earthier. This painting of Khusraw and Shirin is dated 1632, only three years before his death. The 'Abbasi epithet used by Riza' is a title granted him by Iran's Shah 'Abbas I (1587"1629).The shah was an active promoter of all the arts, from manuscript illumination to luxury textiles. He is said to have employed seventy-two painters and even to have kissed the hand of Riza'.

A Carpet Fit for a Shah

In the West, the "Oriental rug" is the most familiar of all the Islamic arts, perhaps not inappropriately since textile production, and especially silk weaving, was so highly regarded in the Islamic world. It is difficult for us—after the Industrial Revolution has made fine patterned cloth an everyday item—to imagine the prestige textiles commanded. They were traded, paid in tribute, and given as diplomatic presents to foreign dignitaries. Whole state economies were based on them; their production has been likened to that of the modern automotive industry. In most periods they were more precious than gold. Although flat-woven textile fragments survive from the earliest Islamic periods, the oldest carpets—rugs with knotted pile— are later.

Perhaps earlier Islamic illuminations illustrate them, but it is difficult to distinguish woven, embroidered or knotted cloth. Pile carpets begin to appear in Italian paintings, and examples from Anatolia survive from the fifteenth century. The oldest whole carpets from Iran—Persian carpets—were made in the early sixteenth century. This is one of the most famous. More than seventeen feet long, it is known as the Chelsea carpet because it was bought in the nineteenth century by the Victoria and Albert Museum from a dealer in London's Chelsea neighborhood. Little is known of its history before that, but it must have been made in Iran in the early sixteenth century. Carpets of this size and quality came from urban court-sponsored workshops.

Nomadic tribes wove carpets on portable looms that could be staked out parallel to the ground wherever their tents were erected. The geometric designs of their rugs reflect the rectangular grid of the vertical warp and horizontal weft threads. Vertical looms in court workshops allowed a finer a much finer set of warp and weft. This freed carpet design from the rigidity of the vertical-horizontal grid. For the first time weavers were able to execute free-flowing patterns, often drawn by the best court artists—medallions, scrolling arabesques, and finely detailed animal and human figures. Carpets could become "painting in a different medium."

Many motifs were adopted from the arts of the book; central medallions, for example, appear to copy tooled leather book covers. In this large carpet the common scheme of a central medallion with quarter medallions in the corners is repeated twice. In the center, the medallion is split and shifted to the edges, opening up the field. The background is filled with flowers and vines inhabited by animals, some grazing, others in combat. The detail is so fine, even the seeds bursting from ripe pomegranates are seen. The presence of animals suggests that the Chelsea carpet was not intended for use in a mosque. More likely, it was made for a palace—whether building or tent.

The sheer size of some carpets hints that they must have been used outdoors. In any setting, they would define and distinguish space, creating a zone of honor. The ruler's seat was normally placed over a carpet's central medallion. Here, where depictions of Chinese-inspired blue-and- white vessels appear in the center, we can imagine actual porcelains placed there. Other elements of Chinese design appear on the Chelsea carpet: cloud bands, dragons, phoenixes, and the fishpond in the very center. Some two thousand carpets survive from the Safavid period.

In part, of course, this reflects their relatively late date, but it is also an indication of increased production in state-sponsored workshops. Safavid rulers took an active interest in textiles and other luxury wares, setting up state industries to produce goods for domestic and foreign markets. Shah Tahmasp, who was said to have designed textiles himself, established works in Kashan, Isfahan, and Kirman—all familiar names to today's carpet lovers.

Arts of the Object in Exchange

Palace culture valued and took pleasure in artistry. Court taste and patronage elevated everyday objects into works of art. We have seen how Islamic learning was transmitted to the West and helped preserve the classical tradition. The arts of the object were a more tangible means for the exchange of artistic culture, and one that operated multidirectionally. Until the sixteenth century, the Middle East was literally the center of the known world, the hub of an almost global trade. People and goods moved through Islamic lands to and from China and Europe, India and Africa, bringing their own artistic cultures and taking some of Islam's away with them. The period when the Mongol dynasties ruled from Iran to China is often called the Pax Mongolica.

People and goods moved with unprecedented ease between the Mediterranean and China, along the various overland routes of the Silk Road. For a millennium or more, luxury textiles were the most important manufactured goods in trade, and the raw materials to make them were quantitatively the largest part of cargoes. Also moving westward were Chinese porcelains and celadon wares. They were highly prized in the Islamic world, inspiring local imitations and innovation. The Chinese art that so impressed Marco Polo reached the West directly through trade, but also through the intermediaries of Islamic interpretations.

In places like southern Italy and Spain, where Islamic states had been established, and in cities like Venice that were busy centers of trade, Islamic objects—glass, textiles, metalwork, ceramics—and the influence of Islamic design were right at hand. But further north, these exotic goods did not arrive until the Crusades. The Crusades exposed western Europeans to the sophistication of Islamic (and Byzantine) cultures: to learning and artistry more advanced than their own. Many Islamic objects were taken home by Crusaders and found their way to church treasuries, where they were preserved as precious objects and often used as reliquaries.

In Renaissance Italy, Islamic goods were highly desirable. As a Florentine writer suggested in 1384, "Really all Christendom could be supplied for a year with the merchandise of Damascus....There are such rich and noble and delicate works of every kind that if you had money in the bone of your leg, without fail you would break it to buy of these things." [quoted in Rosamond E. Mack, *Bazaar to Piazza: Islamic Trade and Italian Art,* 1300–1600.] Medici inventories valued carpets as highly as sculpture by Donatello. Not only were these "noble and delicate works" eagerly sought—they were very influential on Italian design.

An Islamic Castle

The citadel of Aleppo is one of the most outstanding examples of medieval military architecture to survive anywhere. Its appearance today largely reflects the way it looked when the Ayyubid prince al-Malik al-Zahir Ghazi rebuilt it to withstand assault and siege by Crusader armies. As Crusader forces built their own castles, Islamic and Christian castle builders learned from each other. Between 1193 and 1215, Ghazi turned the citadel into a powerful stronghold, surrounded by a deep moat and steep wall (glacis). He restricted entrance to a single portal reached only over a high bridge. The gate was a major fortification in its own right. Five huge iron doors sealed off the route, giving onto a passageway that had five right-angle turns. Invaders were forced to change directions six times—and while this twisting narrow space and near pitch darkness slowed their advance, defenders attacked with arrows or boiling oil from openings in the floor above.

The citadel was much more than a military camp, however. It was the center of government and admini-stration. Inside its strong walls, Ghazi constructed an entire city, with a lavishly decorated palace, bath houses, parade grounds, and a garden. There were two mosques. Granaries, wells, and cisterns ensured supplies of food and water during sieges. Geographer Ibn Shaddad, writing sometime between 1214 and 1228, called the citadel "proverbial for its beauty and strength.... It astonishes he who views it." In 1986 the citadel, in fact all of ancient Aleppo, was designated a UNESCO (United Nations Educational, Scientific, and Cultural Organization) World Heritage Site. In 2000 a major program of restoration began; this work and excavation of the citadel continue. The Great Mosques of Damascus and Isfahan and the Alhambra (slides 1, 2, and 10) are also World Heritage sites.

The "Luck of Edenhall"

The beaker was probably made in Aleppo, Syria, but its fame occurred on English soil, where it had been taken by a returning Crusader. The quality of Syrian glass was renowned; in Europe the technology to make clear glass did not even exist. With its gilded and enameled decoration, the beaker must have seemed just short of miraculous when it arrived in Edenhall, a noble house in the far north of

England. It was precious enough to have probably been used as a chalice. A leather case was made for the beaker in the fourteenth century bearing the sacred IHS monogram.

Over the centuries the real history of the glass was forgotten and replaced by legend, like this one reported in an eighteenth-century magazine: A party of Fairies were drinking and making merry round a well near the Hall, called St. Cuthbert's well, but being interrupted by the intrusion of some curious people they were frightened, and made a hasty retreat and left the cup in question: one of them screaming out "If this cup should break or fall Farewell the Luck of Edenhall."

Just such demise was imagined by a German romantic poet, translated by Henry Wadsworth Longfellow: As the goblet ringing flies apart suddenly cracks the vaulted hall and through the rift the wildfires start the guests in dust are scattered all, with the breaking Luck of Edenhall.

Enameled and gilded vessels were the most highly prized type of Islamic glass. Production of it was a specialty in Egypt and Syria, areas controlled by the Ayyubids and Mamluks during the thirteenth and fourteenth centuries. It is an extremely demanding technique. Gold and colored enamels, themselves made of opaque powdered glass, were bound in an oil medium and painted on the surface. Then the glass was refried to fix them. Careful monitoring of kiln temperatures and multiple refining were required because the gold and different enamel colors fuse at different temperatures.

Praise for a Mamluk Sultan

For many centuries, metalwork was a leading art form that influenced decoration in other media. Inlay with gold or silver seems to have become common from the twelfth century, spreading westward from Seljuk Iran. What has been called a "silver famine" beginning about the same time may have prompted craftsmen to adopt inlay as a way to make scarce resources go further. But the popularity of the glittering bronze or brass vessels probably also responded to a pious avoidance of gold and silver, which were eschewed by the Prophet. This elaborate large tray is an excellent example of Mamluk metalwork. It extols the sultan al-Malik al-Mansur.

The reign name—which means "the king made victorious [by God]"—was used by two different men, both of whom ruled in the middle fourteenth century. Against a background of dense arabesques, multiple inscriptions praise the sultan. The shortest, written in large script around the center, reads, "Glory to our master the sultan, the wise, the diligent, the just, the warlike king—may his victory be glorious." Its long strokes radiate like rays of light. The message is repeated and amplified in other inscriptions; even the small roundels offer "Glory to our master the sultan." An increasingly prominent use of inscriptions was a feature of Mamluk art.

It reflects a military society's natural affinity for hierarchy and public display. Compare the lively hunting and battle narratives on an earlier basin, usually dated between 1290 and 1310. Islamic metalware was traded extensively around the Mediterranean, and its scrolling decoration became popular in many parts of Europe. So many inlaid pieces—some signed in Arabic—were found in the region around Venice that scholars initially assumed them to have been made there by Islamic artists. Because non-Christians were denied guild membership, however, it is more likely most of them were produced by Italian craftsmen. (Guild restrictions like this were common in the West but not in Islamic lands.)

An Italian Portrait of Mehmet the Conqueror

Invented in Iraq in the ninth century, the luster technique enjoyed long and wide popularity. Egypt, Syria, Iran, and Islamic-controlled Spain all developed important centers for luster production—and so eventually did Renaissance

Italy. This plate is an interesting illustration of exchange: it was made using an Islamic technique in an Italian workshop, and depicts Ottoman sultan Mehmet II, the Conqueror, who captured Constantinople in 1453. East or West, the technique for making lusterware pottery was a closely guarded secret.

An Italian in 1558 wrote, "Many potters make the luster kilns on the floors of houses which are locked and under close guard, for they look on the manner of making the kiln as an important secret and say that in this consists the whole art." Lusterwares made in Valencia, Spain, began to be imported to Italy in large numbers in the fifteenth century. They brought much higher prices than local pottery and inspired Italian craftsmen to develop their own wares. Because the island of Majorca was one of the trading centers that brought these goods into Italy, lusterware came to be called *maiolica.*

Major centers of Italian maiolica grew up in the towns of Gubbio and Deruta, where this plate was probably made. Chinese ceramics made their way into the Middle East in the eighth century, appearing in the lavishly appointed palaces of the Abbasid court. Quickly growing demand for these fine wares presented Islamic potters with both inspiration and challenge. Lacking access to the materials and techniques required to produce the hard, pure white porcelain that made the Chinese wares so desirable, Islamic potters improvised. Initially they copied the Chinese shapes and learned to mask the color of local clays with an opaque white glaze. In the eleventh or twelfth century, potters in Iran developed frit-ware, a quartz-based body that fired white all the way through, as porcelain did, although it was not as fine. In the meantime, Islamic potters had been introducing styles of their own.

While the perfection of Chinese porcelains resided in the understated refinement of shape and glaze alone, Islamic potters sought ways to add color and texture and pattern— an impulse characteristic in all Islamic art. The glazed surface invited decoration. Plant and geometric motifs, calligraphy, and eventually figures were painted in cobalt blue over the glaze before firing. Although the very phrase "blue-and-white" immediately conjures an image of a Ming vase, it is possible that the first vessels with blue-on-white decoration were made in ninth-century Iraq. (It used to be widely accepted that the earliest blue- and-white wares were Islamic, but new evidence from China has prompted renewed discussion.)

As trade and contacts increased, influences operated in both directions. By the middle of the fourteenth century, Chinese potters had begun to add cobalt decoration under a clear glaze; by the end of the century wares with underglaze blue were being made in Syria, Egypt, and Iran; by the fifteenth century, they had begun to be made in Ottoman Turkey as well. This fritware jar was made in seventeenth-century Iran, when the Safavid capital at Isfahan was a cosmopolitan center. Production of luxury goods was a state enterprise; Shah 'Abbas had gone so far as to "import" Chinese potters and their families. The blue-and-white wares made in Isfahan include some close imitations of Chinese models but also pots whose decoration features Islamic designs.

Velvets, Coming and Going

Although ceramic and metalwork survive in larger numbers, textiles and the materials for their manufacture were more important in international trade. Works for the production of luxury cloth were essential industries in most Islamic countries. Invading Mongol armies were even said to spare the lives of weavers. A Western traveler to Iran in the seventeenth century claimed that more of the country's population was engaged in making fine cloth than any other occupation. In Italy, too, textile production became an important craft, contributing substantially to the wealth of Florence and other Renaissance cities. Beginning in the 1330s, Italian design was revolutionized by what the Italians called "Tartar" cloths coming Central Asia, Iran, and Syria.

Patterns and techniques became internationalized to the

extent that a fourteenth-century inventory from Rome could not say whether a certain red and gold cloth had been made in nearby Lucca or in distant Mongol lands. A bit later, velvets produced in Iran were imitated by weavers in Venice or Florence, whose velvets were imitated in turn by Ottoman weavers in Turkey. Compare the two fabrics above: the one of the left was made in fifteenth-century Italy, the one on the right in Turkey in the sixteenth century.

The two cloths are velvet, which became popular during the reign of Safavid Shah 'Abbas I (1588"1629). It was used for many purposes—from tent decorations to garments. Velvets are produced by pulling extra warp (vertical) threads to the surface of the fabric around thin wires. When the wire is removed the warps stand up in tiny loops, which can be left as tufts or sheared. The entire surface of a cloth or only pattern areas could be treated with this technique.

Social Studies: Investigation

Investigating works of art can help us learn about the culture in which they were made. Students should choose one of the objects from the image CD and print it out on a color printer. First, ask students, using only their powers of observation and deduction, to speculate on the object, using traditional investigation questions like: Who made it? Who was it made for? What is it? What function does it serve? Where was it made? When was it made? Where does it reside now? Why is it important enough to belong in a museum, if it does? How does it help us understand more about the culture in which it was made? Second, direct students to research their objects and addressing the same investigative questions. Some suggested sources of information are listed in this teaching packet. Third, have students present their research to the class.

This can be in the form of a poster, PowerPoint talk, and/or research paper. Students should include at least one visual image/object to accompany their presentations, in addition to their research objects. A visual image could be - a map of the country from which the object came - a photograph of the setting in which the object was used - examples of the materials used to make the object Visual aids help the audience understand and engage with the presentation and will encourage students to make their own concrete connections to the object.

During the presentations, ask students to take notes. Finally, once all presentations are completed, brainstorm ideas or themes were common to many of the presentations. Write them on the board. What are some of things that can now be understood about Islamic art and culture? The works of art in this packet are rich in history and beauty. Some are even mysterious. For example, a glass goblet made in thirteenth-century Syria and now called the "Luck of Edenhall" has inspired fictional stories to explain its history.

Many objects from Islamic culture are decorated with beautiful and intricate patterns of interlocking geometric shapes. Ranging from the simple to the intricate, geometric patterns can be found in all media, including manuscript illuminations, textiles, and wooden, metal, and ceramic objects. Geometric shapes, repetition, and variation reflect a fundamental Islamic belief in the interconnected, harmonious nature of all creation—the coming together of disparate elements into a unified whole. The circle, a symbol of unity and heaven, is the foundation from which many patterns are developed. The various permutations of rotating triangles and squares within the circle form the basis for many geometric designs.

4

Empire of Faith and Obedience

The name of the religion is Islam, which comes from an Arabic root word meaning "peace" and "submission." Islam teaches that one can only find peace in one's life by submitting to Almighty God (Allah) in heart, soul and deed. The same Arabic root word gives us "Salaam alaykum," ("Peace be with you"), the universal Muslim greeting. Who is a Muslim? A person who believes in and consciously follows Islam is called a Muslim, also from the same root word. So, the religion is called "Islam," and a person who believes in and follows it is a "Muslim." Islam is a major world religion, with over 1 billion followers worldwide (1/5 of the world population). It is considered one of the Abrah-amic, monotheistic faiths, along with Judaism and Christi-anity. Although usually associated with the Arabs of the Middle East, less than 10% of Muslims are in fact Arab. Muslims are found all over the world, of every nation, color and race.

Allah is the proper name for Almighty God, and is often translated merely as "God." Allah has other names that are used to describe His characteristics: the Creator, the Sustainer, the Merciful, the Compassionate, etc. Muslims believe that since Allah alone is the Creator, it is He alone that deserves our devout love and worship. Islam holds to a strict monotheism. Any worship and prayers directed at saints, prophets, other human beings or nature is considered idolatry. Islam means obedience to God. And it is a matter of common sense that this obedience cannot ensure in full measure unless man knows certain basic facts of live and reposes firm faith in them. What are those facts? And what are the primary essentials, which a man must know to fashion his life, in accordance with the Divine Way? This we propose to discuss in the present chapter.

First of all, one should have unshakable belief in the existence of God, for unless a man has a firm and unalloyed faith in God's existence, how can he render obedience to Him? Then one must know the attributes of God. It is the knowledge of the attributes of God, which enables man to cultivate in him the nobles of human qualities and to fashion his life in virtue and godliness. If a man does not know that there is one and only one God Who is the Creator, the ruler, and the Sustainer of the universe and there is none else to share with Him even a shred of the Divine power and authority, he may fall a prey to false god's and offer his homage to them solicit their favor. But if he knows the divine attribute of tawhid (oneness of God), there is not the least possibility of his falling a prey to this illusion.

Similarly, if a man knows that God is omnipresent and omniscient and He sees, hears, and knows everything that we do in public or in private-nay, even our unexpressed thoughts!-then how can he afford to be indulgent and disobedient to God? He will feel that he is under eternal vigil and will, therefore, behave in the most appropriate way. But he who is not aware of these attributes of God may be misled, because of his ignorance, into God's disobedience. So is the case with all other attributes of God. The fact is that the qualities and attributes which a man must possess, if he wants to pursue the way of Islam, can be cultivated and developed only out of profound knowledge of the attributes of God. It is the knowledge of God's attributes, which purifies a man's mind and soul, his beliefs, morals, and actions. And a mere cursory acquaintance with or just an academic knowledge of these attributes is not sufficient for the task ahead-there must be an unflinching conviction firmly rooted in the mind and heart of man so that he may remain immune from insidious doubts and perversions.

Moreover, one must know in detail the way of living by following which one can seek the pleasure of God. Unless a man knows the likes and dislikes of God, how can he choose and adopt the one and reject the other? If a man has no knowledge of the Divine Law, how can he follow it? Thus the knowledge of the Divine Law and the Revealed code of Life is also extremely essential in this respect. But here, again, mere knowledge will not suffice. Man must have full confidence and conviction that it is the Divine Law and that his salvation lies in following this code alone. For knowledge without this conviction will fail to spur man to the Right Path and he may be lost in the blind alley of disobedience.

Finally, one must also know the consequence of belief and obedience and those of disbelief and disobedience. He must know what blessings would be showered upon him if he chooses God's way and leads a life of purity, virtue, and obedience. And he must also know what evil and harrowing consequences would follow if he adopts the way of disobedience and revolt. Thus the knowledge of life after death is absolutely essential for this purpose. Man must have an unwavering belief in the fact that death does not mean the end of life; that there will be resurrection and he will be brought to the highest court of justice, to be presided over by God Himself; that on the Day of Judgment complete justice will prevail; and that good deeds will be rewarded and misdeeds punished. Everybody will get his due and there is no escape. This is bound to happen. This sense of responsibility and accountability is quite essential for the full-fledged obedience of the Law of God.

A man who has no knowledge of the world to come may consider obedience and disobedience quite immaterial.

He may think that the obedient and the disobedient will both meet a similar end: for, after death both will be reduced to mere dust. With this attitude of mind, how can he be expected to submit to all the inconveniences and troubles that are inextricably associated with the life of active obedience, and shun those sins the commission of which does not apparently bring to him any moral or material loss in this world? With this mental attitude a man cannot acknowledge and submit to God's Law.

Nor can a man, who lacks firm belief in the life hereafter and in the Divine Court of Judgment, remain firm and steadfast in the turbulent waters of life with its attraction or sin, crime and evil; for doubt and hesitancy rob a man of his will to action. You can remain firm in your behaviour only if you are firm in your beliefs. If you carry a wavering mind you cannot remain firm and steadfast. You can wholeheartedly follow a course only if you are sure of the benefits that will accrue to you by following it and of the losses and grievances that will engulf you if you disobey it. Thus, a profound knowledge of the consequences of belief and disbelief and of the life after death is extremely necessary for canalizing life into God's obedience. These are the essential facts which one must know if one wants to live the life of obedience, i.e. Islam.

FAITH

Faith is what we have described in the foregoing discussion as 'Knowledge and belief'. The Arabic word Imaan, which we have rendered in English as faith, literally means 'to know', 'to believe', and 'to be convinced beyond the least shadow of doubt'. Faith, thus, is firm belief arising out of knowledge and conviction. And the man who knows and reposes unshakable belief in the unity of God, in His Attributes, in His Law and the Revealed Guidance, and in the Divine code of Reward and punishment is called Mo'min (faithful). This faith invariably leads man to a life of obedience and submission to the will of God. And one who lives this life of submission is known as Muslim.

This should clearly bring home the fact that without faith (Imaan) no man can be a true Muslim. It is the indispensable essential; rather, the very starting point, without which no beginning can be made. The relation of Islam to Imaan is the same as of a tree to its seed. As a tree cannot sprout forth without its seed, in the same way it is not possible for a man, who has no belief to start with, to become a 'Muslim'. On the other hand, just as it can happen that, in spite of sowing the seed, the tree may not grow for a multiple of reasons, or if it sprouts, its growth may be impaired or retarded, in the same way, a man may have faith, but due to a number of weaknesses, he may not become a true and staunch Muslim. Thus we find that faith is the starting point and leads man to the life of submission to God, and that a man cannot become a Muslim without faith.

On the contrary, it is possible that a man may have faith but, because of the weakness of his will power, poor training, or bad company, he may not be living the life of a true Muslim. As such, from the viewpoint of Islam and Imaan, all men may be classified into four categories:

1. Those who have firm faith-a faith that makes them absolutely and whole-heartedly submit to God. They follow the way of God and devote themselves heart and soul to seek His pleasure by doing all that He likes and by avoiding all that He dislikes. In their devotion they are even more fervent that is the common man in pursuit of wealth and glory. Such men are true Muslim.
2. Those who do have faith, who believe in God, His Law and the Day of Judgment, but whose faith is not deep and strong enough to make them totally submit to God. They are far below the rank of true Muslims deserve punishment for their defaultations and misdeeds, but still they are Muslim. They are defaulters and wrong-doers but not rebels. They acknowledge the Sovereign

and His Law and, although they are violating the Law, they have not revolted against the Sovereign. They admit its supremacy and their own guilt. Thus they are guilty and deserve punishment, but Muslims they remain.

3. Those who do not possess faith at all. These people refuse to acknowledge the sovereignty of God and are rebels. Even if their conduct is not bad and even if they are not spreading corruption and violence, they remain rebels and their apparent good deeds are of little value. Such men are like the outlaws. And as, even if any action of an outlaws is in consonance with the law of the land, he does not become a loyal and obedient citizen, in the same way the apparent good of those who revolt against God cannot compensate for the gravity of the real wrong, revolt, and disobedience.
4. Those who neither possess faith nor do good deeds. They spread disorder in the world and perpetrate all kinds of violence and oppression. They are the worst of the people; for they are rebels as well as the wrongdoers and criminals.

The above classification of mankind clearly shows that the real success and salvation of man depends on Imaan (faith). The life of obedience (Islam) takes its birth from the seed of Imaan. This Islam of a person may be flawless or defective. But without Imaan there can be no Islam. Where there is no Imaan there is no Islam. Where there is no Islam there is Kufr. Its form and nature may be different, but in any way it would be Kufr and nothing but Kufr. This brings home the importance of Imaan vis-à-vis life of true and total submission to God?

The Knowledge of God

Now the question arises: How to acquire the know ledge and belief in God, His attributes, His Law, and the Day of Judgment? We have already referred to countless manifestations of God around us and in our own selves, which bear witness to the fact that there is one and only one creator and Governor of this universe and it is He Who controls and directs it. These witnesses reflect the divine attributes of the creator: His great wisdom, His all-embracing knowledge, His omnipotence, His mercy, His all-sustaining power, His force major-in short, His attributes can be traced everywhere in His work. But man's intellect and his capacity to attain knowledge have erred in observing and understanding them.

These are all manifest and clear and our eyes are open to read what is writ large on the creation. But here men have erred and some have declared that there are two gods others began to profess belief in trinity, and still others succumbed to polytheism. Some began nature-worship and others divided into multifarious deities: gods of rain, air, fair, death, etc. As such, although the manifestations of God were quite clear, human reason has faltered on various counts and failed to see the reality in its true perspective. It met deception after deception and resulted in nothing but confusion of thought. We hardly need dilate here on these errors of human judgment.

Similarly, with regard to life after death men have put forward many erroneous notions; for instance, that man is reduced to dust after death and will not rise to life again; or that man is subject to a process of continuous regeneration in this very world and is punished or rewarded in the oncoming cycles of life. Even greater difficulty arises when we come to the question of the code of life. To formulate a complete and balanced code of life that should conform to God's pleasure merely with the help of human reason, is an extremely difficult task.

If a man is equipped with the highest faculties of reason and intellect and he possesses matchless wisdom and experience of many years of deliberation, even then the chances of his formulating right views on life and existence are not very promising. And even if, after a lifelong deliberation, he succeeds in that he will still lack in the confidence that he has really discovered the truth and adopted the right path. Although the fullest and fairest test of man's wisdom, reason, and knowledge might have been to leave him to his own resources without any external guidance so that he those who, through their own sagacious siftings and strivings, might have reached truth and righteousness would have won success and salvation, while those not reaching them would have failed. God, however, spared His human creatures such a hard test?

Through His grace and benevolence He raised for mankind men from among themselves to whom He imparted the true knowledge of His attributes, revealed to them His Law and the Right Code of Living, gave them the knowledge of the meaning and purpose of life and of the life after death and thus showed them the way by pursuing which man can achieve success and eternal bliss. These chosen men are the Messengers of God-His prophets. God has communicated knowledge and wisdom to them by means of wahy (revelation), and the book containing the Divine communications is called the Book of God, or the word of God. Now the test of man's Wisdom and intellect lies in this: does he recognize God's Messenger after thoroughly observing his pure and pious life and carefully studying his noble and flawless teachings?

The man who possesses right wisdom and sound common sense would verify truth and accept the instructions given by the Messenger of truth. If he denies the Messenger of God and his teachings, his denial would signify that he was devoid of the capacity to find out truth and righteousness. On account of this denial he would fail in his test. Such a man will never be able to discover the truth about God and His Law and the life after death.

THE PROPHETHOOD

The earlier discussion brings home the following points:

1. The right course for man is to live in obedience to God, and for the observance of such obedience of knowledge

and faith are absolutely essential: knowledge Of God and His attributes, His likes and dislikes, His Chosen way and of the Day of Judgment; and unflinching faith in the truth and veracity of this knowledge: this is Iman

2. Secondly, God has graciously spared man the arduous task of acquiring this knowledge through his Personal effort alone. He has not put man to this difficult trail. Instead, He revealed this knowledge to the Prophets chosen from amongst men, commanding them to convey the Will of God to other human beings and Show them the right path. This has saved man from formidable misfortunes.
3. Lastly, the duty of the common men and women is to recognize a prophet and, after ascertaining that one Is the true prophet of God, to have faith in him and his footsteps. This is the road to salvation. In this chapter we shall discuss the nature, history, and other aspects of prophethood.

Nature and Necessity

You can see that God has most graciously provided man that entire he needs in this universe. Every new-born child arrives in the world endowed with eyes to see, ears to hear, nose to smell and breathe hands to touch, feet to walk, and mind to think and ponder. All those potentialities, powers, and faculties that a man needs or can need are most carefully provided and marvelously set in his tiny body. Every minute requirement is foreseen and provided for. Nothing, which he needs, is left out. Similar is the case with the world he lives in and everything essential for life is provided here in abundance in the form of air, light, heat, etc. The child, on opening his eyes, finds his food in the mother's breast. Parents love him instinctively and in there has been implanted an irresistible urge to look after him, to bring him up and to sacrifice their all for his welfare. Under the sheltering care of his system of sustenance the child grows to maturity and in every stage of his life obtains from nature that entire he needs. All the material conditions of survival and growth are provided for and he finds that the whole universe is at his service and is serving him on every turn and pass.

Furthermore, man is blessed with all those powers, capacities, and faculties-physical, mental, and moral -which he enquires in his struggle for life. Here God has made a wonderful disposition. He has not distributed these gifts to men strictly equally. Their equal distribution would have made men totally independent of each other and marred the possibilities of mutual care and co-operation. Thus although mankind as a whole possesses all that is needed, yet in between men capacities are distributed unequally and sparingly. Some possess physical strength and prowess, others distinguish them selves for their mental talents. Some are born with greater aptitude for arts, poetry, and philosophy, some possess sharpness of tongue, some others military acumen, commercial intelligence, mathematical keenness, scientific curiosity, literary observation, philosophic disposition, etc. These special aptitudes make a man disinters and enable him to grasp even those intricacies which elude the grip of the common man.

These insights, aptitudes and talents are the gifts of God. They are incarnated in the nature of those men whom God has destined to be thus distinguished. They are mostly inborn and cannot be acquired merely be education and training. Careful reflection upon this disposition of God's gifts also reveals that the talents have been distributed amongst men in a marvelous way. Those capacities which are essential for the general maintenance of human culture have been endowed to the average human beings, while those extraordinary talents which are required only to a limited extent are given only to a small number of people. The number of soldiers, peasants, artisans, and workers is large; but military generals, scholars, statesmen, and intellectuals are comparatively fewer. Similar is the case with all professions, with all the arts and crafts of culture.

The general rule seems to be: higher the capacity and greater the genius, the lesser the number of people who possess them. Super geniuses, who leave an indelible mark on human history and whose achievements guide humanity for ages, are few and far between. Their number is still less. Here we are faced with another question: Is the fundamental need of human culture confined to the need of experts and specialists in the fields of law and politics, science and mathematics, engineering and mechanics, finance and economics and the like, or does it also need men who may show man the Right Path-the way to God and salvation? Other experts provide man with the knowledge of all that is in the world and of the ways and means to use that, but there must be someone to tell man the purpose of creation and the meaning of life itself. What man himself is and why has he been created? Who has provided him with all the powers and resources and why?

What are the proper ends of life and how are they to be achieved? What are the proper values of life and how can they be attained? This is the most cardinal need of man and unless he knows this he cannot erect the edifice of culture on sound foundations and cannot succeed in life here and hereafter. And our reason refuses to believe that God Who has provided man with even the most trivial of his requirements would ignore to provide for this greatest, most paramount and most vital need. Nay, it can never be so. And it is not so. While God has produced men of distinction in arts and sciences. He has also raised men with deep vision, pure intuition, and highest faculties to know and understand him. To them, He Himself revealed the way of godliness, piety, and righteousness.

He gave them the knowledge of the ends of life and values of morality and entrusted them with the duty to communicate the Divine Revelation to other human beings and to show them the Right Path. These men are the Prophets and Messengers of God. The prophets distinguish themselves in the human life is not in accordance with his ideal. Neither his word nor his deed is prompted by any self-interest. He suffers for the good of others, and never makes others for his own good. His whole life is an example of truth, nobleness, and purity of nature, high thinking, and the most exalted form of humanity. His character is without any blemish and even the minutest scrutiny fails to reveal any flaw in his life. And all these facts, all these attributes, make it evident that prophet of God and faith must be reposed in him.

When it becomes quite clear that such and such a person is the true prophet of God, the natural dictate of this realization is that his words should be accepted, his Instructions followed, and his orders obeyed. It is quite unreasonable to accept a man as God's true prophet, and yet not to believe in what he says or not to follow what he ordains; for your very acceptance of him as God's prophet means that you have acknowledged that what he says is from God, and that whatever he dose is in accordance with God's Will and pleasure. Now, disobedience to him is the disobedience of God-and disobedience of God leads to nothing but ruin and devastation. Therefore, the very acceptance of the prophet makes it incumbent on you to bow to his instructions and accept them without any demur whatsoever.

You may not be able fully to grasp the wisdom and usefulness of this or that order, but the every fact that an instruction has emanated from the Prophet is sufficient guarantee for its truth, and there can be no room for doubt or suspicion. Your inability to understand it is no reason for its having flawed or defect; for a common man's understanding is not flawless. It has its own limitations and they cannot be ignored altogether. It is evident that one who dos not know some art thoroughly cannot understand it subtleties, but such a person would be a fool to eject what an expert says, merely on the plea that he himself does not fully understand the expert, It is noteworthy that in every important worldly affair an expert is needed for advice, and when you turn to the expert you thereafter trust his advice and entirely depend upon it.

You rather surrender your own right of judgment and inference and follow him carefully. Every ordinary man cannot be a master in all arts and crafts of the world. The proper way for an average human being is to do what he can and, in respect of things he cannot do, to use all his wisdom and shrewdness in finding out the proper man to guide and help him, and after finding out such a man to accept his advice and follow him. When you are sure that a certain person is the best man available for your purpose, you solicit his advice and guidance, and have complete trust in him. To interfere with him at every step and say, "Make me understand it before you proceed any further," is evidently imprudent. When you engage a solicitor in any legal case, you do not interfere with him on every turn and pass. You rather have faith in him and follow his advice.

For your medical treatment you go to the doctor and follow his instructions. You neither poke your nose in medical matters nor test your skill in logic by debating with the doctor. This is the proper attitude in life. So must be done in case of religion. You need the knowledge of God; you require knowing the mode of life according to God's pleasure; and you possess no means for obtaining this knowledge. It is incumbent upon you, therefore, to look for a true prophet of God; and you will have to use utmost care, discernment, and sagacity in your search for him, for if you choose a wrong man for a true prophet, he will put you on the wrong track. If, however, after properly weighing and measuring all considerations, you decide definitely that a certain person is really God's prophet, then you must trust him completely and obey all his instructions faithfully.

Now it is clear that the Right Path for man is that and that alone which the prophet declares to be so and the correct way of life that only which he informs us to be from God. From this one can easily understand that to have faith in the prophet and to obey and follow him is absolutely necessary for all men, and that a man who puts aside the prophet's instructions and himself tries to carve out a way for himself, deviates from the Right Path and surely goes astray. In this matter man guilty of strange errors. There are not men who admit the integrity and truthfulness of the prophet, but do not repose Iman (faith) in him, nor do they follow him in the affairs of their life. Such men are not only Kafirs, but also behave in an imprudent and unnatural way: for not to follow the prophet after admitting him to be true means that one knowingly follows untruth. And what folly can be greater than that!

Some people declare, we do not need a prophet for our guidance and we can ourselves find out the way to truth. This too is a faulty view. You have probably learnt geometry, and you know that between two points there can be only one straight line, and all other lines must be crooked or will fail to touch the in point in view. The same is the case with way to the truth, which, in the Language of Islam, is called sirat-i-mustaqeem (the Straight Path). This path begins from man and goes straight up to God, and this Path can evidently be one only one; all other paths would be aberrations and will lead astray. Now this Straight path has been indicated by the Prophet, and there is and can be no straight oath besides that. The man who ignores that path and seeks other errands is only a dupe of his own imagination. He chooses a way and imagines it to be right, but soon finds himself entangled and is lost in the mazes and meandering created by his own fancy.

What can you think of a person who has lost his way and when a good man shows him the right one, he definitely ignores the guidance, declaring, "I will not take your guidance nor accept the way you have shown to me, but I will myself grope in this unknown region and try to reach the object of my search, in my own way"? This, in the presence of the clear guidance of the prophets, is sheer stupidity. If everybody tries to start UP again from the scratch, it would be gross waste of time and energy. We never do so in the field of sciences and arts; why here? This is a common error, and even a little reflection reveals its flaws and weaknesses. But if you go a little deeper into the matter, you will notice that a person who denies having faith in the true prophet cannot at all find any way straight or otherwise to reach God.

This is so because a man who refuses to believe the advice of a truthful man adopts such a perverse attitude that the vistas of truth become estranged from him and he becomes a victim of his own obstinacy, arrogance, bias, and perversity. Often this refusal is because of false arrogance, or blind conservatism and obstinate adherence to the way of the forefathers, or slavery of the lower desires of the self, whose gratification becomes impossible by submission to the teachings of the prophets.

If a man is engrossed in any of the above conditions, the Path to truth becomes closed to him. He like a jaundiced person cannot look upon things in the encoloured light of reality. Such a man cannot find out any road to salvation. On the other hand, if a man is sincere and truth-loving and if he is not slave to any of the above complexes, the road to reality becomes paved for him, and there is absolutely no ground for him to refuse to believe in the prophet. Nay, he finds in the teachings of the prophet the very echo of his own soul and discovers himself by discovering the prophet. And, above all, God Himself raises the true prophet. It is He who has sent him UP to mankind to convey His message to His people.

It is His Command to repose faith in the prophet and to follow him. Thus, one who refuses to believe in God's Messenger actually refuses to follow God's Commandments and becomes a rebel. There is no denying the fact that one who refuses to acknowledge the authority of the viceroy of a sovereign actually refuses the authority of the sovereign himself. This disobedience turns him into a rebel. God is the Lord of the universe, the true Sovereign, the King of kings, and it is the bounden duty of every man to acknowledge the authority of His Messengers and Apostles and to obey them as His accredited prophets. And one who turns away from the Prophet of God is surely a kafir, be he a believer God or a disbeliever.

HISTORY OF PROPHETHOOD

Now let us cast a cursory glance at the history of prophethood. Let us see how this long chain began, how it gradually unfolded itself and finally culminated in the prophethood of the last of the prophet, Muhammad (peace be upon him). The human race began from one man: Adam. It was from him that the family of man grew and the human race multiplied. All human beings born in this world have descended form that earliest pair: Adam and Eve. History and religion are agreed on this point. Scientific investigations about the origin of man too do not show that originally different man came into being, simultaneously or at different points of time, in different parts of the world. Most of the scientists also conjecture that one man would have been brought into existence first and the entire human race might have descended from the same one man.

Adam, the first man on earth, was also appointed as the first Prophet of God. He revealed His religion-Islam to him and enjoined him to convey and communicate it is him descendants: to teach them that Allah is One, the Creator, the Sustainer of the world that He is the Lord the universe and He alone should be Worshipped and obeyed; that to Him they will have to return one day and to Him alone they should appeal for help; that they should live good, pious, and righteous life in accordance with God's pleasure and that if they did so they would be blessed by God with goodly reward, and if they turned away from Him and disobeyed

Him they would be losers here and in the hereafter and would be severely punished for this disbelief and disobedience.

Those of Adam's descendants who were good trod the right path shown to them by him, but those who were bad abandoned their father's teachings, and gradually drifted away into devious ways. Some began to worship the sun, the moon, and the stars; others took to the worship of trees, animals, and rivers. Some believed that air, water, fire health, and all the blessings and forces of Nature were each under the control of a different god and that each one of them should be propitiated by means of worship. In this way ignorance gave rise to many forms of polytheism and idolatry, and scores of religions were formulated. This was the age when Adam's progeny had spread fairly over the globe, and formed different races and nations.

Every nation had made a different religion for itself, each with formalities and rituals of its own. God the one Lord and Creator of mankind and the universe was altogether forgotten. Not only that; Adam's descendants forgot even the way of life which God had revealed for them and which their great progenitor had taught them. They had followed their own devices. Every kind of evil custom grew, and all sorts of notions of ignorance spread them. They began to err in discerning right from wrong: many evils began to be considered right and many right things not only ignored but dubbed as wrong. At this stage God began to raise prophets among every people, who preached Islam to them.

Each one reminded his people of the lesson they had forgotten. They taught them God-worship, put an end to idol-worship and the practice of *shirk,* i.e. associating other deities with God, did away with all customs of ignorance, taught them the right way of living in accordance with God's pleasure, and gave them life-giving laws to be followed and enforced in society. God's true Prophets were raised in all countries: in every land and people. They all possessed one and the same religion the religion of Islam. No doubt, the methods of teaching and the legal codes of different Prophets were a little different in accordance with the needs and the stage of culture of the people among whom they were raised. The particular teachings of each Prophet were determined by the kind of evils which he faced and endeavored to eradicate.

The methods of reform differed as it suited to fight different notions and ideas. When the people were in the primitive stages of society, civilization and intellectual development, their laws and regulations were simple; they were modified and improved as the society evolved and progressed. These differences were, however, only superficial and apparent. The fundamental teachings of all the religions were the same, i.e. belief in the unity of God, adherence to a life of piety, goodness and peace, and belief in the life after death with its just mechanism for reward and Punishment. Man's attitude to words God's Prophets has been strange. First he maltreated the Prophets and refused to listen and accept their teachings. Some of the Prophets were expelled from their lands; some were assassinated; some, in face of the people in difference, continued preaching the whole of their lives, and hardly won more than a few followers.

In the midst of harassing opposition, derision, and indignity to which they were perpetually subjected, these Apostles of God, however, did not cease to preach. Their patient determination at last succeeded: their teachings did not remain without effect. Large groups of people and nations accepted their message, and were converted to their creed. The erring tendencies of the people, born of centuries of persistence in deviation, ignorance, and malpractice, now took another form. Though during the lives of their Prophets they accepted and practiced their teachings, yet after their death they introduced their old distorted notions in to their religions, and altered the Prophet's teachings. They adopted quite novel methods of worshipping God; some even took to the worship of their Prophets. Some made the Prophets the incarnations of God; some made their Prophets the sons of God; some associated their Prophets with God in His Divinity.

In short, man's varied attitudes in this respect were a travesty of his reason and a mockery of himself; he made idols of those very persons whose holy mission was to smash idols to pieces. By intermixing religion, custom and rituals of ignorance, baseless and false anecdotes and man-made laws, man so changed and Perverted the ideology of the Prophets that after the lapse of centuries it became a hotchpotch of the real and the fictitious and the teachings of the Prophets were lost in a conglomeration of fictions and perversities so much so that it become impossible to distinguish the grain from the chaff. And, not content with this corruption of the Prophet, they further attached fictitious anecdotes and unworthy traditions to the lives of their Prophets and so polluted their life histories that a real and reliable account of their lives becomes impossible to be discerned. Despite these corruption by the followers, in the work of the Prophets has not been altogether in vain.

Among all nations, in spite of all interpolation and alteration, some traces of Truth have survived. The idea of God and of the life after death was definitely assimilated in some form or other. A few principles of goodness, truth goodness and morality were commonly admitted throughout the whole world. The Prophets, thus, prepared the mental attitude of their respective People in such a way that a universal religion could be safely introduced a religion, which is quite in consonance with the nature of man, which embodies all that was good in all other creeds and societies, and which is naturally and commonly acceptable to the entire mankind. As we have said above, in the beginning separate Prophets used to appear among different nations or groups of People, and the teachings of each Prophet were meant specially and specifically for his each people.

The reason was that at that stage of history, nations were situated separately and were so cut off from each other that one was bound up within the geographical limits of its own territories and the facilities for mutual intercourse were just non-existent. In such circumstances it was very difficult to propagate a common World Faith with its accompanying system of the life of this world. Besides, the general conditions of the early nations were widely different from one another. Their ignorance was great, and among the different Peoples it had given different forms to their moral aberration and distortions of Faith. It was, therefore, necessary that different Prophets be raised to preach the Truth to them and win them over to God's ways to gradually eradicate evils and aberrations; to root out the ways and modes of ignorance and teach them to Practice the noblest Principles of simple, Pious, and righteous life, and thus train and bring them up in the arts and crafts of life.

God alone knows how many, and developing him mentally, morally, and spiritually. Anyhow, man continued to make Progress and at last the time came when he grew from his infancy, and entered the age of maturity. With the progress and spread of commerce, industry, and arts, intercourse was established between nations. From China and Japan, as the distant lands of Europe and Africa, regular routes were opened both by sea and land. Many people learnt the art of writing; knowledge spread. Ideas began to be communicated from one country to the other and learning and scholarship began to be exchanged. Great conquerors appeared, extended their conquests far and wide, established vast empires, and knit many different nations under one political system. Thus nations came closer and to one another, and their differences became less and less.

It became possible under these circumstances that one and the same faith, envisaging a comprehensive and all-embracing way of life, catering to the moral, spiritual, social, cultural, political, economic, and all other needs of man and embodying both religious and seculars elements be sent by God for the entire mankind. More than two thousand years ago mankind had attained caliber that it all seemed to crave for a universal religion. Buddhism, though it consisted only of some moral principles and was not a complete system of life, emerged from India, and spread as far as Japan and Mongolia on one side, and to Afghanistan and Bokhara on the other. Its missionaries traveled far and wide in the world. A few centuries later, Christianity appeared.

Although the religion taught by Jesus Christ (peace be upon him) was none but Islam, his followers reduced it into a hotchpotch called Christianity, and even this overt and Israelis religion was spread in the far- off places of Persia and Asia Minor and info the distant climes of Europe and Africa. From these events it is clearly inferred that the conditions of mankind in that age demanded a common religion for the whole human race and they were so prepared for it that when they found no complete and true religion in existence, they began to propagate among the nations the prevalent religions, howsoever defective, incomplete, or unsatisfying they might be. At such a crucial stage of human civilization, when the mind of man was itself craving for a world religion, a Prophet was raised in Arabia for the whole world and for all nations. The religion he was given to propagate was again Islam-but now in the form of a complete and full-fledged system, covering all aspects of individual and material life of man. He was made a Prophet for the entire human race and was deputed to propagate his mission to the whole world. He was Muhammad the Prophet of Islam (Peace be upon him).

THE PROPHETHOOD OF MUHAMMAD

If we cast a glance at the world at the atlas, we find that the other country could have been more suitable for the much needed world religion than Arabia. It is situated right in the middle of Asia and Europe is not far away from it. At the time of Mohammed's appearance the central part of Europe was inhabited by civilized and culturally advanced nations; and thus these people were more or less at about the same distance from Arabia as were the people of India. This fact gave Arabia a central position. And look at the history of that era and you will find that no other people were more suited for the endowment of this prophethood than the Arabs Great nations of the world had been struggling hard for world supremacy, and in this long struggle and incessant strife, they had exhausted all their resources and vitality. The Arabs were a fresh and virile people. The so-called social progress had produced bad habits among the advanced nations, while among the Arabs no such social organization existed, and they were, therefore, free from the inactivity, debasement and indulgences arising out of luxury and sensual satiety.

The pagan Arabs of the fifth century had not been affected by the evil influence of the artificial systems and civilization of the great nations of the world. They processed all the good human qualities, which the people untouched by the 'social progress' of the time, ought to possess. They were brave, fearless, generous, faithful to their promises, lovers of freedom, and were politically independent not subject to the hegemony of the imperial Powers. They lived a very simple life, and were strangers to the life of luxury and indulgence. No doubt, there were certain undesirable aspects of their life as well, as we shall maintain later on, but the reason for the existence of such aspects was that for thousands of years no prophet had risen among them, nor had there appeared a reformer who might have civilized them and purged their moral life of all evil impurities. Centuries of free and independent life in sandy deserts had bred and nourished extreme ignorance among them. Nor had there appeared a reform who might have civilized them and purged their moral life of all evil impurities.

Centuries of free and independent life in sandy deserts had bred and nourished extreme ignorance among them.

They had, therefore, become so hard-hearted and firm in their traditions of ignorance that to make them human was not the task of an ordinary man. At the same time, however, they did possess a capacity that if some person of extraordinary powers were to invite them for reform and gave them a noble ideal and a complete program they would accept his call and readily rise to act effectively for the achievement of such a goal, and spare no strife for or sacrifice in the cause. They would be prepared to face without the least scruple even the hostility of the entire world in the cause of their mission. And verily it was such a young, forceful, and virile people that were needed for disseminating the teachings of the World Prophet: Muhammad (Peace be upon him)

And then look to the Arabic language. If you study that language and fathom deep into its literature, you will be convinced that there is no other language than Arabic which is more suited to give expression to high ideals, to explain the most delicate and subtle problems of Divine knowledge, and to impress the heart of man and mould it into God's submission. Small phrases and brief sentences express a world of ideas, and at the same time they are so forceful that they steal into the heart, their every sound moves man to tears and ecstasy. They are so sweet that it is felt as if honey were being poured into the ears; they are so full of harmony that every fiber of the listener's body is moved by their symphony. It is such a rich and powerful language that was needed for the Quran, the Great Word of God. It was, therefore, the manifestation of God's great wisdom that He chose the land of Arabia for the birth place of the World Prophet. Let us now see how unique and extraordinary was the blessed personality chosen by God for the mission of the World Prophet.

Rational Vindication

If one were to close one's eyes and imagine oneself in the world of 1400 years ago, one would find that it was a world completely different from ours, having not even the least semblance to the rough and tumble that we find around ourselves. How few and far between were the opportunities for the exchange of ideas! How limited and undeveloped were the means of communication! How little and meager was man's knowledge! How narrow was his outlook! How enveloped was he in superstition and wild and sophisticated ideas! Darkness held the sway. There was only a faint glimmer of learning, which could hardly illumine the horizon of human knowledge. There was neither wireless nor telephone, neither television nor cinematography.

Railways and motor cars and airplanes were undreamed of, and printing presses and publishing concerns were unknown. Hand-written books or copyists alone supplied whatever scanty literary material was there to be transmitted from generation. Education was a luxury, meant only for the most fortunate, and educational institution were every few and between. The store of human knowledge was scanty, man's out look was narrow, and his ideas of man things were confined to his limited surroundings. Even a scholar of that age lacked in certain respects the knowledge possessed by a layman of today, and the most cultured person was less refined than our own man in the street. Indeed, humanity was steeped in ignorance and superstition.

Whatever light of learning there seemed to be is fighting a losing battle against the darkness prevailing all around. What are considered to be matters of common knowledge today could hardly be acquired in those days even after years of calculated thought and patient research. People used to undertake hazardous journeys and spent a whole lifetime in acquiring that modest information which is everybody's heritage in the present age of learning. Things, which are classed as 'myth' and 'superstition' today, were the unquestionable truths of that age. Acts, which we now regard as heinous and barbarous, were then the order of the day. Methods whish appear obnoxious to our moral sense today constituted the very soul of morality, and one different way of life also.

Incredulity had assumed such mighty proportions and had become so wide- so read that people refused to consider anything as lofty and sublime unless it the garb of the supernatural, the extraordinary, the uncanny, and even the untenable. They had developed such an inferiority complex that they could never imagine a human being to possess a godly soul and the saint to human.

ARABIA-THE ABYSS OF DARKNESS

In that benighted era, there was a territory where darkness lay heavier and thicker. The neighboring country of Persia, Byzantium and Egypt possessed a glimmer of civilization and a faint light of learning. But Arabia could receive no share from their cultural Influences. It stood isolated, cut off by vast oceans of sand. Arab traders plodding great distances, which took those months, carried their wares to and from these countries, but they could hardly acquire any grain of knowledge on their journeys. In their own country, they did not have a single educational institution or library. None seemed to be interested in the cultivation and advancement of knowledge. The few who were literate were not educated enough to have anything to do with the existing arts and sciences. They did possess a highly developed language capable of expressing the finest shades of human thought in a remarkable manner. They also possessed a literary taste of high order.

But the study of the remnants of their literature reveals how limited was their knowledge, how low was their standard of culture and civilization, how saturated were their minds with superstitions, how barbarous and ferocious were their thoughts and customs, and how uncouth and degraded were their moral standards and conceptions. It was a country without a government; every tribe claimed sovereignty and considered to be an independent unit. There was no lawexcept the law of the jungle. Loot, arson, and murder of innocent and weak people were the order of the day. Life, Property, and honour were constantly at stake. Different tribes were always at daggers drawn with one another. Any trivial incident was enough to cause blaze out in ferocious fury, which sometimes even developed into a countywide conflagration ceaselessly continuing for several decades.

Indeed, a Bedouin could not understand why he should let off a person of another tribe, whom, he thought, he had every right to kill and plunder. What ever nations they had of morals, culture, and civilization, were primitive and uncouth. They could hardly discriminate between pure and impure, lawful and unlawful, civil and uncivil. Their life was wild, their methods were barbaric. They reveled in adultery, gambling and drinking. Loot and plunder was their motto, murder and rapine their very habits. They would stand stark naked before each other without any qualms of conscience. Even their womenfolk would become nude at the ceremony of circumambulating the Ka'ba.

Out of sheer foolish nations of prestige, they would bury their daughters alive lest anyone should become their son-in-law, they would marry their stepmothers after the death of their fathers. They were ignorant of even the rudiments of everyday routine of eating, dressing, and washing. As regards their religious beliefs, they suffered from the same evils, which were playing havoc with the rest of the world. They worshipped stones, trees, idols, stars, and spirits: in short, everything conceivable except God. They did not know anything about the teaching of the Prophets of old. They had an idea that Abraham and Ishmael were their forefathers, but they know next to nothing about their religious preaching and about the God Whom they worshipped.

The stories of Ad and humbed were to be found in their folklore, but they contained no traces of the teachings of Prophets Hud and Sail. The Jews and the Christians had transmitted to them certain legendary folktales relating to the Israelite Prophets. They presented a harrowing picture of those noble souls. Their teachings were adulterated with the figments of their own imagination and their lives were tarred black. Even today, an idea can be had of the religious conceptions of those people by casting a cursory glance at those Israelite traditions which Muslim commentators of the Quran have conveyed to us. Indeed, the picture which has been presented there of the institution of prophethood and of the Israelite Prophets is the very antithesis of all that those noble followers of truth had stood for.

Saviour Born

In such a Dark Age and in such a benighted country a man is born. In his very childhood his parents die and, a few years later, the sad demise of his grandfather also occurs. Consequently, he is deprived even of that scant training and upbringing which an Arab child of his time could get. In his boyhood he tends the flock of sheep and goats in the company of Bedouin boys. When of age, he takes to commerce. All his association and all his dealings are with the Arabs alone condition has just been described. Education has not even touched him; he is completely unlettered and unschooled. He never gets a chance to sit in the company of learned of learned man, for such men were totally non-existent in Arabia.

He does have a few opportunities to go out of his country, but those journeys are confined to Syria and are nothing more than the usual business trips undertaken by Arab trade caravans. If he men there or has the occasion to observe any aspects of culture and civilization, those random meeting and stray observations cannot be given any place in the making of his personality. For such things can never have that profound influence on anyone which may lift him to tally out of his environment transform him completely, and raise him to such heights of originality and glory that there remains no affinity between him and society he is born.

Nor can they be the means of the acquisition of that profound and vast knowledge which may transform an unlettered Bedouin into a leader not only of his own country and age but of the world at large and of all ages to come. Indeed, whatever the measure of the intellectual and cultural influence of those journeys one might suppose, the fact remains that they could in no case impart to him those conception and principles of religion, ethics, culture, and Civilization which were to tally nonexistent in world of those days, and they could in no way create that sublime and perfect pattern of human character which was nowhere to be found in those days.

Diamond in a Heap of Stones

We may now look at the life and work of this noble man in the context not only of the Arabian society but also of the entire world as it stood in that period. He is totally different from the people among whom he is born and with whom he passes his youth and early manhood, attaining finally his full stature. He never tells a lie. His whole nation is unanimous in testifying to his truthfulness. Even his worst enemies never accuse him of telling a lie on any occasion whatsoever during his entire life. He talks politely and does not uses obscene and abusive language. He has a charming personality and winsome manners with him.

In his dealings with the people he always follows the principles of justice and fair play. He remains in trade and commerce for years, but he never enters into any dishonest transaction. Those who deal with him in business have full confidence in his integrity. The entire nation calls him *"Al-Ameen" (the* Truthful and the Trustworthy). Even his enemies deposit their costly belongings with him for safe custody and he scrupulously fulfils their trust. He is the very embodiment of midst of a society which is immodest to the core. Born and bred among a people who regard drunkenness and gambling as virtues, he never touches alcohol and never indulges in gambling. His people are uncouth, uncultured and unclean, but he personifies in himself the highest culture and the most refined aesthetic outlook. Surrounded on all sides by heartless people, he himself has a heart overflowing with the milk of human kindness.

He helps the orphans and widows. He is hospitable to travelers. He harms no one; rather, he goes all out to suffer hardships for others' sake. Living among those for whom war is bread and butter, he is such a lover of peace that his heart melts for them when they take up arms and cut each other's throats. He keeps aloof from the feuds of his tribe, and is foremost in bringing about reconciliation. Bred up in an idolatrous race, he is so clear-minded and possesses such a pure soul that he regards nothing in the heavens and the earth worth worshipping except the One True God. He does not bow before any created thing and dose not partake of the offerings made to idols, even in his childhood. Instinctively he hates all kinds of worship of all creatures and beings besides God. In brief, the towering and radiant personality of this man in the midst of such a benighted and dark environment may be likened to a beacon-light illumining a pitch-dark night or to a diamond shining in a heap of dead stones.

A Revolution Comes

After spending a great part of his life in such a chaste, pure, and civilized manner there come a revolution in his being. He feels fed up with the darkness and ignorance massed around him. He wants to swim clear of the horrible sea of ignorance, corruption, immorality, idolatry and disorder which surround him on all sides. He finds everything around him out of harmony with his soul. He retires to the hills, away from the hum and drum of habitations. He spends days and night in perfect seclusion and meditation. He fasts so that his soul and his heart may become purer and nobler still. He muses and ponders deep.

He is in search of a light which might melt away the encompassing darkness. He wants to get hold of that power with which he might bring about the downfall of the corrupt and disorderly world of his day and lay the foundations of a new and better world.

Lo! A remarkable revolution comes over his person. All of a sudden his heart is illuminated with the Divine light, giving him the power he had yearned for. He comes out of the confinement of his cave, goes to the people, and addresses them in the following strain:

"The idols which you worship are a mere sham. Cease to worship them from now on ward. No mortal being, no star, no tree, no stone, no spirit, is worthy of human worship. Therefore, bow not you heads in worship before them. The entire universe with everything that it contains belongs to God Almighty alone. He alone is the Creator, the Nourisher, the Sustainer, and, consequently, the real Sovereign before Whom all should bow down and to whom all should pray and render obedience. Thus worship Him along and obey only His commands. Loot and plunder, murder and rapine, injustice and cruelty-all the vices in which you indulge are crimes in the eyes of God. Leave your evil ways. He hates them all. Speak the truth. Be just. Do not kill anyone. Do not rob anyone. Take your lawful share and give due to other in a just manner. You are human beings and all human beings are equal in the eyes of God.

None is born with the slur of shame on his face, nor has anyone come into the world with the mantle of honour hung around his neck. He alone is high and honored who is God fearing and pious, true in words and deeds. Distinctions of birth and glory of race are no criteria greatness and honour. One who fears God and does good deeds is the noblest. One who fears God and does good deeds is the noblest of human beings. One who is shorn of love of God and is steeped in bad manners is doomed. There is an appointed day after your death when you shall have to appear before your Lord.

You shall be called to account for all your deeds, good or bad, and you shall not be able then to hide anything. They whole record of life shall be an open book to Him. You fate shall be determined by your good or bad-actions. In the court of the true Judge-the omniscient does not arise.

You shall not be able to bribe Him. No consideration will be given to your pedigree or parentage. True faith and good deeds alone will stand you in good stead at that time. He who will be fully equipped with them shall take his abode in the Heaven of eternal happiness; while one devoid of them shall be cast in the fire of Hell." This is the message with which he comes. The ignorant nation turns against him. Abuses and stones are showered at his august person. Every conceivable torture and cruelty is perpetrated on him. And this continues not for a day or tow but uninterruptedly for thirteen long troublesome years. At last he is exiled. But he is not given respite even there. He is tormented in various ways in his abode of refuge. The whole of Arabia is incited against him. He is persecuted and hounded down continuously for full eight years there. He suffers it all, but doses not budge an inch from the stand he has taken. He is resolute firm and inflexible in his purpose and stand.

One might inquire: how is it that his nation became his sworn enemy? Was there any dispute about gold and silver or other worldly possessions? Was it due to any blood feud? Did he ask for anything from them? No! The whole enmity was based on the fact that he had asked them to worship the One True God and to lead a life of righteousness, pity, and goodness. He had preached against idolatry and the worship of other beings besides God and had denounced their wrong ways of life. He had cut at the roots of priestcraft. He had inveighed against all distinctions of high and low between human beings, and had condemned the prejudices of clan and race as sheer ignorance; and he wanted to change the whole structure of society which had been handed down to them from time immemorial. In their turn, his countryman told him that the principles of his mission were hostile to their ancestral traditions and asked him either to up or to bear the worst consequences.

One might ask: what for did he suffer all those hardships? His nation offered to accept him as their king and to lay all the riches of the land at his feet if only he would leave preaching his religion and spreading his message. But he chose to refuse the tempting offers and to suffer for his cause, instead. Why? Was he to gain in any way if those people became pious and righteous? Why was it that he cared not a jot for riches and luxury, kingship and glory, and ease and plenty? Was he playing for some higher material gains so that these blessings sank into insignificance in comparison with them? Were those so tempting that he could elect to go through fire and sword and bear tortures of the soul and torments of the body with equanimity for years? One has to ponder over it deeply to find an answer.

Can anyone ever imagine a higher example of self-sacrifice, fellow-feeling and kind-heartedness towards his fellow-beings that a man may ruin his own happiness for the good of others, while those very people for whose betterment he is striving his utmost should stone him, no quarter even in his exile, and that, in this all, he should refuse to refrain from striving for their will-being? Can any insincere person undergo so much suffering for a false cause? Can any dishonest speculator and visionary exhibit such firmness and determination for his ideal as to stick to his guns to the very last and remain unruffled and unperturbed in the face of dangers and tortures of every conceivable description when a whole country rises up in arms against him?

This faith, this perseverance, and this resolution, with which he led his movement to ultimate success, is, therefore, an eloquent proof of the supreme truth of his cause. Had there been the slightest touch of doubt and uncertainty in his heart, he could never have been able to brave the storm which continued in all its fury for twenty-one long years. This is one side of the revolution wrought in his being. The other is even more wonderful and remarkable.

For forty years he lived as an Arab among Arabs. In that long period he was not known as a statesman, a preacher, or an orator. None had heard him imparting gems of wisdom and knowledge as he began to do hereafter. He was never seen discoursing upon the principles of metaphysics, ethics, law, politics, economics, and sociology. Not to speak of being a great general, he was not even known as an ordinary soldier. He had uttered no word about God, the Angels, the revealed Book, the early prophets, the bygone nations, the Day of Judgment, the Life after, Death, Hell and Heaven. No doubt he possessed an excellent character and charming manners, and was highly cultured; yet there was nothing so deeply striking and so radically extraordinary in him who could make men expects something great and revolutionary from him in future. He was known among his acquaintances as a sober, calm, gentle, law-abiding citizen of good nature. But when he came out of the cave with a new message he was completely transformed.

When he began preaching his Message the whole of Arabia stood in awe and wonder and was bewitched by his wonderful eloquence and oratory. It was so impressive and captivating that his worst enemies were afraid of hearing it, lest it should penetrate deep into the recesses of their hearts or the very marrow of their beings and carry them off their feet and make them bid goodbye to their old religion and culture. It was so matchless that the whole legion of Arab poets, preachers, and orators of the highest calibre failed to bring forth its equivalent in beauty of language and splendour of diction when he threw the challenge to his opponents to put their heads together and produce even a single line like the one he recited.

His All- Embracing Message

Along with this, he now appeared before his people as

a unique philosopher, a wonderful reformer, a renowned moulder of culture and civilisation, an illustrious politician, a great leader, a judge of the highest eminence and an incomparable general. This unlettered Bedouin, this dweller of the desert, spoke with such learning and wisdom the like of which none had said before and none could say after him. He expounded the intricate problems of metaphysics and theology. He delivered speeches on the principles of the decline and fall of nations and empires, supporting his thesis by the historical data of the past. He reviewed the achievements of the old reformers, passed judgments on the various religions of the world, and gave verdicts on the differences and disputes between nations.

He taught ethical canons and principles of culture. He formulated such laws of social culture, economic organisation, group conduct, and international relations that even eminent thinkers and scholars can grasp their true wisdom only after life-long research and vast experience of men and thing. Their beauties, indeed, unfold themselves progressively as man advances in theoretical knowledge and practical experience.

This silent and peace-loving trader who had never handled a sword before, who had no military training, who had but once participated in a battle and that also just as a spectator, turned suddenly into such a brave soldier that he did not even once retreat in the fiercest battles. He become such a great general that he conquered the whole of Arabia in nine years, at a time when the weapons of war primitive and the means of communication poorest. His military acumen and efficiency developed to such a high pitch and the military spirit which he infused and the military training which he imparted to motley crowd of Arabs (who had no equipment worth the name) wrought such a miracle that within a few years they overthrew the two most formidable military powers of the day and became the masters of the greater part of the then known world.

This reserved and quiet man who, for full forty years, never gave indication of any political Interest or activity, appeared suddenly on the stage of the world as such a great political reformer and statesman that, without, the aid of radio and wireless and press, he brought together the scattered inhabitants of a desert of twelve hundred thousand square miles, a people who were warlike, ignorant, unruly, uncultured, and plunged in internecine tribal warfare-under one banner, one law, one religion, one culture, one civilisation, and one form of government. He changed their modes of thought, their very habits and their morals. He turned into the cultured, the barbarous into the civilised, and the evildoers and bad characters into pious, God-fearing, and righteous persons. Their unruly and stiff-necked natures were transformed into models of obedience and submission to law and order.

A nation which had not produced a single great man worth the name for centuries gave birth, under his influence and guidance, to thousands of noble souls who went forth to far-off corners of the world to preach and teach the principles of religion, morals and civilisation. He accomplished this feat not through any worldly lure, oppression or cruelty, but by his captivating manners, and his convincing manners, and his convincing teaching. With his noble and gentle behaviour he befriended even his enemies. He captured the hearts of the people with his unbounded sympathy and the milk of human kindness. He ruled justly. He did not swerve from truth and righteousness.

He did not oppress even his deadly enemies who were after his life, who had pelted him with stones, who had turned him out of his native place, who had pitched the whole of Arabia against him nay, not even those who had chewed raw the liver of his dead uncle in a frenzy of vengeance. He forgave them all when he triumphed over them. He never took revenge from anyone for his personal grievances or the wrongs perpetrated on his person. In spite of the fact that he became the ruler of his country, he was so selfless and modest that he remained very simple and sparing in his habits. He lived poorly, as before, in his humble thatched mud-cottage. He slept on a mattress, wore coarse clothes, ate the simplest food of the poor, and sometimes went without any food at all. He used to spend whole nights standing in prayer before his Lord. He came to the rescue of the destitute and the penniless. He felt not the least humility in working as a labourer.

Till his last moments there was not the slightest tinge of kingly pomp and show or hauteur of the high and the rich in him. Like an ordinary man he would sit and walk with people and share their joys and sorrows. He would so mix up and mingle with the crowd that a stranger, an outsider, would find it difficult to point out the leader of the people and the ruler of the nation from the rest of the company. Inspite of his greatness, his behaviour with the humblest person was that of an ordinary human being. In the struggles and endeavours of his whole life he did not seek any reward or profit for his own person, not left any property for his heirs. He dedicated his all to *Millat.* He did not ask his adherents to earmark anything for him or his descendants, so much so that he forbade his progeny from receiving the benefit of Zakat (or poor-tax), lest his follower at any future time may dole out the whole share of Zakat to them.

His Contribution to Human Thought

The achievements of this great man do not end here. In order to arrive at a correct appraisal of his true worth one has to view it in the background of the history of the world as a whole. That would reveal that this unlettered dweller of the desert of Arabia, who was born in the 'dark ages' some 1400 years ago, was the real pioneer of the modern age and the true leader of humanity. He is not only the leader of those who accept his leadership but of those also who do not acclaim him as such: even of those who denounce him! The only difference being that the latter are unaware of the fact that his guidance is still imperceptibly influencing their thoughts and their actions and is the governing principle of their lives and the very spirit of the modern times.

It was he who turned the course of human thought from superstition-mongering, love for the unnatural and the inexplicable, and monasticism towards rational approach, love for reality, and a pious, balanced worldly life. It was he who, in a world which regarded only supernatural happenings as miracles and demanded them for the verification of the truth of a religious mission, inspired the urge for rational proof and the faith in them as the criterion of truth. It was he who opened the eyes of those who had been accustomed till then to look for the signs of God in the natural phenomena. It was he who, in place of baseless speculation, led human beings to the path of rational understanding and sound reasoning on the basis of observation, experiment, and research. It was he who clearly defined the limits and functions of senseperception, reason, and intuition.

It was he who brought about a *rapprochement* between the spiritual and the material values. It was he who harmonised Faith with Knowledge and Action. It was he who created the scientific spirit with the power of religion and who evolved true religiosity on the basis of the scientific spirit. It was he who eradicated idolatry, man-worship and polytheism in all forms so thoroughly and created such a firm faith in the Unity of God that even those religions which were based entirely on superstitions and idolatry were compelled to adopt a monotheistic theme. It was he who changed the basic concepts of ethics and spirituality. To those who believed that asceticism and self-annihilation alone formed the standard of moral and spiritual purity –that purity could not be achieved except by running away from worldly life, disregarding all the urges of the flesh and subjecting the body to all types of tortures-it was he who showed the path or spiritual evolution, moral emancipation, and attainment of salvation through active participation in the practical affairs of the world around them.

It was he who brought home to man his true worth and position; those who acknowledged only a God incarnate or a son of God as their moral preceptor or spiritual guide were told that a human being like them having no pretension to Godhead could become the vicegerent of God on earth; those who proclaimed and worshipped powerful personages as their gods were made to understand that their false lords were mere. It was he who stressed the point that no person could claim holiness, authority, and overlordship as birth-right and that none was born with the stigma of untouchability, slavery, or serfdom on his person. It was he and his teaching which inspired the thoughts of the unity of mankind, equality of human beings, true democracy and real freedom in the world.

Leaving aside this realm of thought and moving a bit further one will find countless practical results of the leadership of this unlettered person firmly impressed on the laws and ways of the world. So many principles of good behaviour, culture and civilisation, purity of thought and deed, which are prevalent in the world today, owe their origin to him.

The social laws which he gave have infiltrated deep into the structure of human social life, and this process continues up to this day. The basic principles of economics which he taught have ushered in many a movement in world history and hold out the same promise for the future. The laws of governance which he formulated brought about many an upheaval in the political notions and theories of the world and continue to assert their influence even today.

The fundamental principles of law and justice which bear the stamp of his genius have influenced to a remarkable degree the administration of justice in the courts of nations, and form a perpetual source of guidance for all legists to come. This unlettered Arab was the first person who set on foot for the first time practically the whole framework of international relations, and regulated the laws of war and peace. For no one had previously even the remotest idea that there could be an ethical code of war also and that relation between different nations could be regulated on the ground of common humanity.

The Greatest Revolutionary

In the cavalcade of world history the sublime figure of this wonderful person towers so high above all the great men of all times who are famous as heroes of nations, that they appear to be dwarfs when contrasted with him. None of them possessed a genius capable of making any deep impression on more than one or two aspects of human life. Some are the exponents of theories and ideas but are deficient in practical action. Some others are men of action but suffer from paucity of knowledge. Some are renowned as statesmen only; others are masters of strategy and manoeuvring. Some have concentrated on one aspect of social life in a manner that other aspects have been overlooked. Some others have devoted their energies to ethical and spiritual verities but have ignored economics and politics.

Some other has taken to economics and politics, but neglect morals and the spiritual side of life. In short, one comes across heroes who are adepts and experts in one walk of life only. His is the only example where all the excellences have been blended into one personality. He is a philosopher and a seer and also a living embodiment of his own teachings. He is a great statesman as well as a military genius. He is a legislator and also a teacher of morals. He is a spiritual luminary as well as a religious guide. His vision penetrates every aspect of life and there is nothing which he touches and does not adorn. His orders and commandments cover a vast field from the regulation of international relations down to the habits of everyday life like eating, drinking, and cleanliness of the body.

On the foundations of his theories he established a civilisation and a culture and produced such a fine equilibrium in the conflicting aspects of life that there is to be found not even the slightest trace of any flaw, deficiency, or incompleteness. Can anyone out any other example of such a perfect and all-round personality? Most of the famous personalities of the world are said to be the products of their environment. But his case is unique. His environment seems to have played no part in the making of his personality. It also cannot be proved that historically his birth synchronised with the order of things in Arabia at that time. What one can say at the most is that the circumstances in Arabia cried aloud for the appearance of such a person who could weld together the warring tribes into one nation and lay the foundation of their economic solidarity and well-being by bringing other countries under their sway-in short, a national leader who would have all the traits of an Arab of those days and, through cruelty, oppression, bloodshed, deceit, and hypocrisy, or by any other fair or foul means, could have enriched his own people, and left a kingdom as a heritage for his successors. One cannot prove any other crying need of the history of Arabia of that time.

What one can say at the most in the light of Hegel's philosophy of history or Marx's historical materialism is that the time and environment demanded the emergence of a leader who could create a nation and build up an empire. But the Hegelian or Marxian philosophy cannot explain how such an environment could produce a man whose mission was to teach the best morals, to purify humanity of all dross, and to wipe out prejudices and superstitions of the days of ignorance and darkness, who looked beyond the watertight compartments of race, nation, and country, who laid the foundations of a moral, spiritual, cultural and political superstructure for the good of the world and not for his country alone, who practically, not theoretically, placed business transactions, civics, politics, and international relations on moral grounds and produced such a balanced and temperate synthesis between worldly life and spiritual advancement that even to this day it is considered a masterpiece of wisdom and foresight exactly in the same way as it was considered in his lifetime. Can anyone honestly call such a person as the product of the all-pervading darkness of Arabia?

He does not only appear to be independent of his environment. Rather, when we look at his achievements we are irresistibly drawn to the conclusion that he actually transcends all limitation of time and space. His vision breaks through all temporal and physical barriers, passes beyond centuries and millenniums and comprehends within itself entire human activity and the whole of human history. He is not one of those whom history has cast into oblivion, and he is not praised only because he was just a good leader in his own time. He is that unique and incomparable leader of humanity who marches with the time, who is modern in every age and in every era, as he was in his own age of history. Truly, his teachings are as modern as tomorrow morn.

Those whom people style as makers of history' are only 'creatures of history'. In fact, in the whole history of mankind, he is the unique example of a 'maker of history'. One may scan the lives and circumstances of the great leaders of the world who brought about revolutions and one will find that on each such occasion the forces of revolution were gathering momentum for the destined upheaval, were taking their course in certain directions and were only waiting for propitious moment to burst out. In harnessing these forces in time for action the revolutionary leader played the part of an actor for whom the stage and the role is set beforehand. On the other hand, amidst all 'makers of history' and revolutionary figures of all times, he is the only person who had to find ways and means to bring together the wherewithal of revolution, who had to mould and produce the kind of men he wanted for his purpose because the very spirit of revolution and its requisite paraphernalia were nonexistent in those people among whom his lot was cast.

He made an indelible impression on the hearts of thousands of his disciples by his forceful personality and moulded them according to his liking. By his iron will he prepared the ground for revolution, moulded its shape and features, and directed the currents into a channel as he wished and desired. Can anyone cite another example of a maker of history of such brilliance and splendour?

The Final Testimony

One may ponder over this matter and wonder how, in the dark ages 1400 years back in a benighted region of the earth like Arabia, an unlettered Arab trader and herdsman came to possess such light, such knowledge, such power, such capabilities, and such finely-developed moral virtues? One may say that there is nothing peculiar about his Message. It is the product of his mind. If it is so, then he should have proclaimed himself as God. And if he had made such an assertion at that time, the peoples of the earth who did not hesitate in calling Krishna and Buddha as gods and Jesus as the Son of God, just out of their own fancy, and who could without compunction worship even the forces of nation like fire, water and air would have readily acknowledged such a wonderful person as the Lord God Himself.

But lo! His assertion is just to the contrary. For he proclaimed that: I am a human being like yourselves. I have not brought any thing to you of my own accord. It has all revealed to me by God. Whatever I possess belongs to Him. This message the like of which the whole humanity is not able to produce, of my own mind. Every word of it has been sent down by Him and all glory to Him Whose Message it is. All the wonderful achievements which stand to my credit in your eyes, all the laws which I have given, all the principles which I have enunciated and taught-none of them is from me. I find myself thoroughly incompetent for producing such things out of my sheer personal ability and capabilities. I look to Divine Guidance in all matters. Whatever He wills I do, what He directs I proclaim.

Hearken! What a wonderful and inspiring example of honesty, truth, and honour it is! A liar and a hypocrite generally try to ascribe to him all the credit for the deeds of others also, even when the falsehood of his statement can be easily proved. But this great man does not appropriate the credit of any of these achievements to his own person even when none could contradict him, as there was no method of finding out the source of his inspiration. What more proof of perfect honesty of purpose, uprightness of character, and sublimity of soul can there be! Who else can be a more truthful person than he who received such unique gifts and embellishments through a secret channel and still he outrightly points out the source of all his enlightenment and inspiration? All these factors lead to the irresistible conclusion that such a man was the true Messenger of God.

Such was our Holy Prophet Muhammad (peace be upon him). He was a prodigy of extraordinary merits, a paragon of virtue and goodness, a symbol of truth and veracity, a great apostle of God, His Messenger to the entire world. His life and thought, his truth and straightforwardness, his piety and goodness, his character and morals, his ideology and achievements-all stand as unimpeachable proofs of his prophethood. Any human being who Studies his life and teachings without bias will testify that verily he was the true prophet of God and the Quran-the Book he gave to mankind-the Book of God. No unbiased and serious seeker after truth can escape this conclusion.

Furthermore, this must also be clearly understood that, now, through Muhammad (peace be upon him) alone can we know the straight path of Islam. The Quran and the only reliable sources that is available to mankind to learn God's Will in its totality. Muhammad (peace be upon him) is the Messenger of God for the whole of mankind and the long chain of prophets has come to an end with him. He was the last of the prophets and all the instructions which it was God's will to impart to mankind through direct revelation were sent by Him through Muhammad (peace be upon him) and are enshrined in the Quran and the Sunnah. Now, whoever be a seeker of truth and enxious to become an honest Muslim, a sincere follower of the way of God, it is incumbent upon him to have faith in God's last prophet, accepted his teachings and follow the way he has he pointed out to man. This is the real road to success and salvation.

FINALITY OF PROPHETHOOD

This brings us to the question of the finality of prophethood. Let us now consider this aspect of the prophethood of Muhammad (peace be upon him). We have already discussed the nature of prophethood and this discussion makes it clear that the advent of a prophet is not an everyday occurrence. Nor is the presence in person or the prophet essential for every land, people, and period. The life and teachings of the prophet are the beacon-light to guide a people to the Right path and as long as his teachings and his guidance are alive he is, as it were, himself alive. The real death of a prophet consists not in his physical demise but in the mitigation of his teachings and the interpolation of his guidance. The earlier prophets have died because their followers have adulterated their teachings, interpolated their instructions, and besmirched their life-examples by attaching fictitious events to them.

Not one of the earlier books-*Torah, Zabur* (psalms of David), injeel (Gospel of Jesus), etc-exists to day in its original text and even the followers of these books confess that they do not possess the original book. The life histories of the earlier prophets have been so mixed up with fiction that an accurate and authentic account of their lives has become impossible. Their lives have become tales and legends and no trustworthy record is a available anywhere. Not only that the records have been lost and their life precepts forgotten but even this cannot be said with certainty as to when and when and where a certain prophet was born and bred, how he lived and what code he gave to mankind. In fact, the real death of a prophet consists in the death of his teachings.

Judging the facts on this criterion no one can deny that Muhammad (peace be upon him) and his teachings are alive. His teachings stand uncorrupted and are uncorruptible. The Quran-the book he gave to mankind-exists in its original text, without the slightest alteration of letter, syllable, jot, or title. The entire account of his life-his sayings, instructions and actions-is preserved with complete accuracy, so much so that even after the lapse of thirteen centuries its delineation in history is so clear and complete that it seems as if we are seeing him with the eyes under our brows. The biography of no other human being is so well preserved as that of Muhammad, the prophet of Islam (peace be upon him). In each and every matter of life we can seek the guidance of Muhammad (peace be upon him) and take a lesson from his life-example. That is why there is no need of any other prophet after Muhammad, the last prophet (peace be upon him).

Furthermore, there are three things which necessitate the advent of a new prophet; it not just the replacement of a departed prophet. These may be summed up as follows:

1. That the teachings of the earlier prophets have been interpolated or corrupted or they have died and their revival is needed. In such a case a new prophet is raised so that he may purge the impurities from the lives of the people and restore religion to its pristine form and Purity, or
2. That the teachings of a prophet who has passed away were incomplete and it is necessary to amend them, improve upon them, or add something to them, when a new prophet is sent is sent to effect these improvements or
3. That the earlier prophet was raised particularly for a certain nation or territory and a prophet for another nation, people, or country be required.

These are the three fundamental conditions which necessitate the raising of a new prophet. A careful perusal of the facts shows that none of these conditions exists today. The teachings of the last prophet, Muhammad (peace be upon him), are alive, have been fully preserved, and made immortal. The guidance he has shown unto mankind is complete and flawless, and is enshrined in the Holy Quran. All the sources of Islam are fully intact and each and every instruction or action of the Holy Prophet can be ascertained without the least shadow of doubt. Thus as his teachings are totally intact, there is no need of any of new prophet on this count.

Secondly, God has completed His revealed guidance through Prophet Muhammad (peace be upon him) and Islam is the complete religion for mankind. God has said that, "Today I have perfected your Faith-religion-for you, and have completed My bounty upon you," and a thorough study of Islam as a complete way of life proves the truth of these Quranic words. Islam gives guidance for life in this world and in the hereafter and nothing essential has now been perfected and there is no ground for new prophethood on the plea of imperfection. Lastly, the Message of Muhammad (peace be upon him) was not meant for any particular people, place, or period. He was raised as the world prophet-the messenger of the truth for the entire mankind. The Quran has commanded Muhammad (peace be upon him) to declare: "O mankind, I am God's Messenger to all of you."

He has been described as "a blessing for all (the people of) the worlds" and his approach has been universal and human. That is why after him there remains no need for new prophethood and he has been described by the Quran as *khatam-un-Nabiyyin* (the last of the chain of the true prophets). Now there fore, the only source for the knowledge of God and His Way is Muhammad (peace be upon him). We can know of Islam only through his teachings which are so complete and so comprehensive that world does not need any new prophet; it needs only such people as have full faith in Muhammad (peace be upon him) who become the standard-bearers of his message, propagate it to the world at large, and endeavour to establish the culture which Muhammad (peace be upon him) gave to Man. The World needs such men of character as can translate his teachings into practice and establish a society which is governed by Divine Law, whose supremacy Muhammad peace be Muhammad (peace be upon him) and on its success hinges the success of Man.

Before we proceed further, it would be advisable to recapitulate the former discussions and sum up their substance. We can summaries them as follows:

1. Although Islam consists of submission and obedience to Allah Lord of the universe, yet as the only authentic and reliable source of knowing Him and His Will and Law is the teaching of the true prophet, we may define Islam as that religion which stands for complete faith in the teachings of the prophet and unflinching obedience to his ways of life. Consequently, one who ignores the medium of the prophet and claims to follow God directly is not a 'Muslim'.
2. In the earlier epochs there had been separate prophets for different nations, and the history of prophethood shows that even in one and the same nation several prophets appeared one after the other. In that age Islam was name of that religion which was taught to a nation by its own prophet or prophet. Though the nature and substance of Islam was the same in every age and country, the modes of worship, codes of law, and other detailed rules and regulations of life were a bit different according to the local and particular conditions of every people. It was not, therefore, necessary for any nation to follow another nation's prophet and its responsibility was confined only to following the guidance given by its own prophet.

3. This period of poly-prophetism came to an end with the advent of Muhammad (peace is upon him). The teachings of Islam were made complete through him; one basic law formulated for the whole world and he was made a prophet unto the entire humanity. His prophethood was not meant for any particular nation or country or period; his message is for all peoples and for all ages. The earlier codes were abrogated by the advent of Muhammad (peace be upon him) who gave the world a complete code of life. Now, neither any prophet is to appear in the future nor is any new religious code going to be revealed till the Last Day. Muhammad's (peace be upon him) teachings are meant for all the children of Adam, the entire human race. Now Islam consists in following Muhammad, viz. To acknowledge his prophethood, to believe in all that he has asked to his believe in, to follow him in letter and spirit, and to submit to all his commands and injunction of God. This is Islam.

This automatically brings us to the question: What has Muhammad (peace be upon him) asked us to believe in? What are the articles of Islamic faith? Now we shall try to discuss these articles and see how simple, how true, how lovable and how valuable they are and to what high pinnacle they raise the status of Man in this world and the life to come!

Faith in the Unity of Allah

The most fundamental and the most important teaching of Prophet Muhammad (peace be upon him) is faith in the prophet Muhammad (peace be upon him) is faith in the unity of God. This is expressed in the primary *kalima* of Islam as *La ilaha illallah* "There is no deity but Allah". This beautiful phrase in the bedrock of Islam is foundation and its essence. It is the expression of this belief which differentiates a true Muslim from a *kafir* (unbeliever), a Mushrik (one who associates others with God in His divinity), or a Dahriya (atheist). The acceptance or denial of this phrase produces a world of difference between man and man. The believers in it become one single community and those who do not believe in it form the opposite group. For the believers there is unhampered progress and resounding success in this world and in the hereafter, while failure and ignominy are the ultimate lot of those who refuse to believe in it.

But the difference which occurs between the believers and the unbelievers is not the result of mere chanting of a few words. Evidently the mere utterance of a phrase or two cannot bring about such a mighty difference. The real force lies in the conscious acceptance of this doctrine and its stipulations and complete adherence to it in practical life. Unless you know the real meaning of the phrase "there is no deity but Allah" and the bearing of its acceptance on human life, you cannot realise the real importance of this doctrine. It would never become effective unless these essentials are achieved. Mere repeating of the word 'food' cannot dull the edge of hunger; mere chanting of a medical prescription cannot heal the disease.

In the same way if the Kalima is repeated without any understanding of its meanings and dictates, it cannot work the revolution which its meanings and dictates, it cannot work the revolution which it is meant to bring about. The revolution in thought and life can occur only if a person grasps the full meaning of the doctrine, realises its significance, reposes true belief in it, and accepts and follows it in letter and spirit. Unless this grasp of the Kalima is developed it cannot become fully effective. We avoid fire because we have a realisation that it burns; we keep away from poison because we believe that its use kills a man. Similarly, if the real meanings of *Tawheed* are fully grasped, it should necessarily make us avoid, in belief as well as in action, every form and shade of disbelief, atheism, and polytheism. This is the natural dictate of belief in the Unity of God.

Meaning of the 'Kalima'

In the Arabic language the word ilah means 'one who is

worshipped', i.e. a being which on account of its greatness and power be considered worthy to be worshipped, to be bowed to in humility and submission. Anything or any being possessing power too great to be comprehended by man is also called ilah. The conception of ilah also includes the possession of infinite powers: that may astonish others. It also conveys the sense that others are dependent upon ilah and that he is not dependent upon anyone else. The word ilah also carries a sense of concealment and mystery, that is, ilah would be a being unseen and unperceptible. The word khuda in Persian, deva in Hindi, and god in English bear, more or less, similar signification. Other languages of the world also contain words with a like sense.

The word *Allah*, on the other hand, is the essential personal name of God. *La ilaha illallah* would literally mean "There is no ilah other than the One Great being known by the name "Allah". It means that in the whole of the universe, there is absolutely no being worthy to be worshipped other than Allah, that it is only to Him that heads should bow in submission and adoration, that He is the only Being possessing all powers, that all powers, that all are in need of His favour, and that all are obliged to solicit His help. He is concealed from our senses, and our intellect fails to perceive what He is.

Having known the meanings of these worlds, let us now find out their real significance. From the most ancient known history of man as well as from the oldest relics of antiquity that we have been able to obtain, it appears that in every age man had recognised some deity or deities and had worshipped them. Even in the present age every nation on the face of the earth, from the most primitive to the most civilised, dose believe in and worship some deity. It shows that the idea of having a deity and of worshipping him is ingrained in human nature. There is doing so.

But the question is: What that thing is and why man feels impelled to do to do so? The answer to this question can be discovered if we try to look into the position of man in this huge universe. A perusal of man and his nature from this view-point shows that he is not omnipotent. Neither he is self-sufficient and self-existing nor are his powers without limitations. In fact, he is weak, frail, needy, and destitute. He is dependent upon a multitude of forces and without their assistance he cannot make headway. There are countless things necessary to maintain his existence, but all of them are not essentially and totally within his powers. Sometimes they come to his possession in a simple and natural way, and at times he finds himself deprived of them.

There are many important and valuable things which he endeavors to get, but sometimes he succeeds in getting them, while sometimes he does not, for it is not completely in his own power to obtain them. There are many important and valuable things which he endeavors to get, but sometimes he succeeds in getting them, while sometimes he does not, for it is not completely in his won power to obtain them. There are many things injurious to him; chances bring his hops to a sudden end; disease, worries, and calamities, always threaten him and mar his way to happiness. He attempts to get rid of them, and success and failure both visit him in this quest. There are many things whose greatness and grandeur overawe him mountains and rivers, gigantic animals and ferocious beasts. He experiences earthquakes, storms, and other natural calamities.

He observes clouds over his head and sees them becoming thick and dark, with peals of thunder, flashes of lightning and continuous fall of heavy rain. He sees the sun, the moon, and the stars in their constant motion. He reflects how great, powerful, and grand these bodies are, and, in contrast to them, how frail and insignificant he himself is! The vast phenomena, on the one hand, and the consciousness of his own frailty, on the other, impress him with a deep sense of his own weakness, humbleness, and helplessness. And it is quite natural that the preliminary idea of divinity coincides with this sense. He thinks of those hands which are wielding these great forces. The sense of their powerfulness makes him seek their help. He tries to please them so that they may be beneficent to him, and he dreads them and tries to escape their wrath so that he may not be destroyed by them.

In the most primitive stage of ignorance, man thinks that the great objects of nature whose grandeur and glory are visible, and which appears to be injurious or beneficent to him, hold in them the real power and authority, and therefore, they are diving. Thus he worships trees, and numerous other objects. This is the worst form of ignorance. When his ignorance dissipates to some extent and some glimmers of light and knowledge appear on his intellectual horizon, he comes to know that these great and powerful objects are in themselves quite helpless and dependent and are in no way better placed than man rather they are still more dependent and helpless.

The biggest and the strongest animal dies like a tiny germ, and loses all his power; great rivers rise and fall and become dry; the high mountains are blasted and shattered by man himself; the productiveness of the earth is not under earth's own control-water makes it prosperous and lack of water makes it barren. Even water is not independent. It depends on air which brings the clouds. Air too is powerless and its usefulness depends on other causes. The moon, the sun, and the stares also are bound up by a powerful law outside whose dictates they cannot make the slightest movement. After these considerations his mind turns to the possibility of some great mysterious power of divine nature which controls the objects he sees and which may be the repositories of all authority.

These reflection give rise to belief in mysterious powers behind the natural phenomena, numberless gods are supposed to be governing various parts and aspects of nature such as air, light, water, etc, and some suggestive material forms or symbols are constructed to represent them. And he begins to worship those forms and symbols. This too is a form of ignorance, and reality remains hidden from the human eye even at this stage of intellectual and cultural pilgrimage. As man progresses still further in knowledge and learning, and as he reflects more and more deeply on the fundamental problems of life and existence, he finds an all-powerful law and an all-encompassing control in the universe. What a complete regularity control in the universe. What a complete regularity is observed in sunrise and sunset, in winds and rains, in the motions of stars and the changes of seasons!

How in a wonderfully harmonious way countless different forces are working jointly, and what a highly potent and supremely wise Law it is, according to which all the various causes in the universe are made to work together at an appointed time to produce an appointed event! Observing this uniformity, regularity, and complete obedience to a firm law in all fields of believe that there must be a deity greater than all others, exercising supreme authority. For, if there were separate, independent deities, the whole machinery of the universe would be upset. He calls this greatest deity by different names, such as 'Allah' '*Permeshwar*,' 'God,' *Khuda-I-Khudaigan*,' etc. but as the darkness of ignorance still persists, he continues worshipping minor deities along with the Supreme One. He imagines that the Divine Kingdom of God may not be different form earthly kingdoms.

Just as a ruler has many ministers, trusted associates, governors, and other responsible officers, so the minor are like so many responsible officers, under the Great God who could not be approached without pleasing and propitiating the officers under Him. So they must also be worshipped and appealed to for help, and should in no case be offended can be made to the Great God. The more man increases in knowledge, the greater become his dissatisfaction with the multiplicity of deities. So the number of minor deities begins to decrease. More enlightened men bring each one of them under the searchlight of scrutiny and ultimately find that none of these man-made deities has any divine character; they themselves are creatures like man, rather more helpless.

They are thus dropped out by one until only one God remains. But the concept of one God still contains some remnants of the elements of ignorance. Some people imaging that has a body as man have, and is settled in a particular place. Some believe that God came down to the earth in human form; others think that God after settling the affairs of the universe has retired and is now taking rest. Some believe that it is necessary to approach God through the media of saints and spirits, and nothing can be achieved without their intercession. Some imagine God to have a certain form or image and they regard it necessary to keep that before them for the purposes of worship. Such distorted notions of godhead have persisted and lingered, and many of them are prevalent among different people even in the present age.

Tawheed is the highest conception of godhead, the knowledge of which God has sent to mankind in all ages through His prophets. It was this knowledge with which, in the beginning, Adam had been revealed to Noah, Abraham, Moses and Jesus (God's blessings be upon them all). It was this very knowledge which Muhammad (God's blessings be upon him) brought to mankind. It is The Knowledge, pure and absolute, without the least shade of ignorance. Man because he guilty of shirk, idol-worship and kufr, only because he turned away from the teachings of the prophets and depended upon his own faulty reasoning, false perceptions or biased interpretations. *Tawheed* dispels all the clouds of ignorance and illumines the horizon with the light of reality. Let us see what significant realities this concept of *Tawheed*-this little phrase: *'la ilaha illallah'*-points out: what truth it conveys and what beliefs it fosters. This we can grasp if we ponder over the following points.

First of all we are faced with the question of divinity. We are face to face with a grand, limitless universe. Man's mind fails to discern its beginning and visualise its end. It is moving on in its chartered course from time immemorial and is continuing its journey in the vast vista of the future. Creatures beyond number have appeared in it and go on appearing every day. The phenomena are so bewildering that a thinking mind finds itself aghast and wonderstruck. Man is unable to understand and grasp the reality by his unaided vision. He cannot believe that all this has appeared just by chance or accident. The universe is not a fortuitous mass of matter. It is not a jumble of uncoordinated objects. It is not a conglomeration of thing chaotic and meaningless.

All this cannot be without a Creator, a Designer, a Controller, a Governor. But who con create and control this majestic universe? Only He can do so master of all; who is infinite and eternal; who is all-powerful, all wise, omnipotent, and omniscient; who is all-knowing and all-seeing. He must have supreme authority over all that exists in the universe. He must possess limitless powers, must be the lord of the universe and all that it contains, must be free from every flaw and weakness and none may have the power to interfere with His work. Only such a being can be the Creator, the Controller and the Governor of the universe. Secondly, it is essential that all these divine attributes and powers must vest in one being-it is virtually impossible for two or more personalities having all the powers and attributes equally to co-exist. They are bound to collide.

Therefore there must be one and only one Supreme Being having control over all others. You cannot think of two governors for the same province or two supreme commanders of the same army! Similarly, the distribution of these powers among different deities, for instance, that one of them is all knowledge, the other all providence and still another life-giver-and each having independent domain in his own field-is unthinkable. The universe is an indivisible whole and each one of such deities will be dependent upon others in bound to occur. And if this happens, the world is destined to go to pieces. These attributes are also untransferable.

It is not possible that a certain attribute might be present in a certain deity at one time and at another time it is found in another deity. A divine being who is incapable of remaining alive himself cannot give life to others. The one who cannot protect his own divine power is definitely unsuited to govern the vast limitless universe. Thus the greater you reflect upon the problem, the firmer would be your conviction that all these divine powers and attributes must exist in one end the same being alone. Thus polytheism is a form of ignorance and cannot stand rational scrutiny. It is a practical impossibility. The facts of life and nature do not fit into that explanation. They automatically bring man to Reality, i.e. Tawheed (the Unity of God).

Now keeping in view this correct and perfect conception of God, cast a searching glance at this vast universe. Exert yourself to the utmost and say if you find among all the objects that your see, among all the things that you perceive, among all that you can think, feel, or imagine-all that your knowledge can comprehend-anyone possessing these attributes. The sum, the moon, the stars, animals, birds or fishes, matter, any man or a group of men-does any of them possess these attributes? Certainly none! For everything in the universe is created, is controlled and regulated, is dependent on others, is mortal and transitory, is not elf-acting and self-propelling-its slightest movements are controlled by an inexorable law and it cannot deviate from that law. Their helpless condition proves that the attire of divinity cannot fit their body.

They do not possess the slightest trace of divinity and have absolutely nothing to do with it. They are simply without the godly powers and it is a travesty of truth and a folly of the highest magnitude to attribute to them the divine status. This is the meaning of 'La ilaha,' i.e. there is no god; no human and material object possesses the divine power and authority deserving worship and obedience but this not the end of our quest. We have found that divinity does not vest in any material or human element of the universe and that none of them possess even the slightest trace of it. This very inquiry leads us to the conclusion that there is a Supreme Being, over and above all that our unwary eyes see in the universe, who possesses the Divine attributes who is the Will behind all phenomena, the Creator of this grand universe, the Controller of its superb Law, the Governor of its serene rhythm, the Administrator of all its working: He is Allah, the Lord of Universe and has none as associate in His Divinity. This is what "illallah" (but Allah) means.

This knowledge is superior to all other kinds of know ledge and the greater you exert, the deeper will be your conviction that this is the starting-point of all knowledge. In every filed of inquiry-may it be that of physics chemistry, astronomy, geology, biology, zoology, economics, politics, sociology, or humanities, you will find that the deeper you probe, the clearer become the indications of the truth of *La ilaha illallah,* in every field of knowledge and inquiry. It is this concept which opens up the doors of knowledge with the light of reality. And if you deny or disregard this reality, you will find that at every step you meet disillusionment, for the denial of this primary truth robs everything in the universe of its real meaning and true significance. The universe becomes meaningless and the vistas of progress get blurred and confused.

THE EFFECTS OF TAWHEED ON HUMAN LIFE

Now let us study effects which the belief in *La ilaha illallah* brings forth upon the life of a man and see why he should always be a success in life, here and in the hereafter.

a. A believer in this *Kalima* can never be narrow-minded or shriveled in outlook. He believes in a God who is Creator of the heavens and the earth, the Master of the

East and the West and Sustainer of the entire universe. After this belief he does not regard anything in the world as a stranger to himself. He looks upon everything in the universe as belonging to the same Lord whom he himself belongs to. He is not partisan in his thinking and behaviour. His sympathy, love, and service do not remain confined to any particular sphere or group. His vision is enlarged, his intellectual horizon widens, and his outlook become liberal and as boundless as is the Kingdom of God. How can this width of vision and breadth of mind be achieved by an atheist, a polytheist, or one who believes in a deity supposed to possess limited and defective powers like a man?

b. This belief produces in man the highest degree of self-respect and self-esteem. The believer knows that Allah alone is the possessor of all power, and that none besides Him can benefit or harm a person, or provide for his need, or give and take away life, or wield authority or influence. This conviction makes him indifferent to, and independent and fearless of, all powers other than those of God. He never bows his head in homage to any of God's creatures, nor does he stretch his hand before anyone else. He is not overawed by anybody's greatness. This quality or attitude of mind cannot be produced by any other belief. For it is necessary that those who associate other beings with God, or who deny God, should bow in homage to some creatures, regard them able to benefit or harm them, and repose all their hopes in them.

c. Along with self-respect this belief also generates in man a sense of modesty and humbleness. It makes him unostentatious and unpretending and unpretending. A believer never becomes proud, haughty or arrogant. The boisterous pride of power, wealth and worth can have no room in his heart, because he knows that whatever he possesses has been given to him by God, and can take away just as He can give. In contrast to this, an unbeliever, when he achieves some worldly merit, becomes proud and conceited because he believes that his merit is due to his own worth. In the same way pride and self-concept are a necessary outcome and concomitant of shirk (association of others with God in His divinity), because a mushrik believes that he has a particular relation with the deities which does exist between them and other people.

d. This belief makes man virtuous and upright. He has the conviction that theirs is no other means of success and salvation for him except purity of soul and righteousness of behaviour. He has perfect faith in God who is above all need, is related to none, is absolutely just, and none has any hand or influence in the exercise of His divine powers. This belief creates in him the consciousness that, unless he lives rightly and acts justly, he cannot succeed. No influence or underhand activity can save him from ruin. As against this, the kefirs and the mushriks always live on false hopes. Some of them believe that God's son has atoned for their sins; some think that they are God's favourites, and will not be punished, others believe that their saints will intercede with God on their believe that their deities and believe that by so bribing the deities they have acquired a license for all frivolities and ill-deeds and depending upon their deities, they do not live pure and good lives. As to the atheists, they do not believe that there is any Being having power over them, to whom they would be responsible for their good or bad action; therefore they consider themselves altogether independent to act in whatever way they like in this world. Their own fancies become their gods and they live like slaves of their wishes and desires.

e. The believer does not become despondent and broken-hearted under any circumstances. He has firm faith in God who is the Master of all the treasures of the earth and the heavens, whose grace and bounty have no limit and whose powers are infinite. This faith imparts to his heart extraordinary consolation, fills it with satisfaction and keeps it filled with hope. In this world he might meet with rejection from all doors, nothing herein might serve his ends,. All means amight, one after another, desert him; but faith in and dependence on God never leave him; and upon their strength he goes on struggling. Such a profound confidence can result from no other belief than belief in one God. Mushirks, kafirs, and atheists have small hearts; they depend upon limited powers; therefore in hours of trouble they are soon overwhelmed by despair and, frequently, they commit suicide.

f. This belief produces in man a very strong degree of determination, patient perseverance, and trust in God. When he makes up his mind and devotes his resources to fulfil the Divine Commands in order to secure God's pleasure, he is sure he has the support and backing of the Lord of the universe, this certainty makes him firm and strong like a mountain, and no amount of difficulties, impediments, and hostile opposition can make him give up his resolution. *Shirk, Kufr,* and atheism have no such effect.

g. On account of man's interference and interpolation, many things have been inserted in those books, which are against reality, revolting to reason, and affronting to every instinct of justice. There are thing which are cruel and unjust and vitiate man's beliefs and action. Furthermore, unfortunately, things have been inserted that are obscene, indecent, and potently immoral. The Quran is free from all such rubbish. It contains nothing against reason, and nothing that can be proved wrong. None of its injunctions is unjust; nothing in it is misleading. Of indecency and immorality not a trace can be found in it. From the beginning to the end the whole Book is full of wisdom and truth. It contains the best of philosophy ad the choicest of law for human civilisation. It points out the right path and guides man to success and salvation. It is on account of these special features of the Quran that all the peoples of the world have been direct to have faith in it, to give up all other Books, and to follow it alone, because it contains all that is essential for living in accordance with God's pleasure, and after it there remains absolutely no need for any other divine Book.

The study of the differenced between the Quran and other divine Books makes one easily understand that the nature of faith in the Quran and that of belief in the former Books is not similar. Faith in the former divine Books should be limited to the confirmation that they were all from God, were true, and had been sent down to fulfil, in their time, the same purpose for which the Quran has been sent. On the other hand, belief in the Quran should be of the nature that it is purely and absolutely God's own words, that it is perfectly true, that every word of it is preserved, that everything mentioned therein is right, that it is the bounden duty of man to carry out in his life each and every command of it; and that whatever be against it must be rejected.

5

Faith in Prophets

In the last chapter we discussed that God's Messengers had been raised among every people, and that they all brought essentially that very religion-Islam-which Prophet Muhammad (peace be upon him) propagated. In this respect all the Messengers of God belong to the same category and stand on a stand on a par with each other. If a man confirms and believes in one of them, he must and ought to confirm all. The reason is quite simple. Suppose ten men make one and the same statement; if you admit one of them to be true, you *ipso facto* admit the remaining nine of them as true, and if you belie anyone of them, by implication you belie all of them. It is for this reason that in Islam it is necessary to have implicit in anyone of the prophet would be a *Kafir*, though he might profess faith in all the other Prophets.

It occurs in traditions that the total number of all the prophets sent to different peoples at different times is 124,000. If you consider the life of the world since it was first inhabited and the number of different peoples and nations that have passed on it, this number will not appear too great. We have to believe positively in those of the prophets whose names have been mentioned in the Quran Regarding the rest we are instructed to believe that all Prophets sent by God for the guidance of mankind were true. Thus we believe in all the prophets raised in India, China, Iran, Egypt, Africa, Europe, and other countries of the world, but we are not in a position to be definite about a particular person outside the list of prophets named in the Quran, whether or not he was a Prophet, for we have not been told anything definite about him.

Nor are we permitted to say anything against the holy men of other religions. It is quite possible that some of them might have been God's Prophets that some of them might have been God's Prophets, and their followers corrupted their teachings after their demise, just as the followers of Moses and Jesus (God's blessings be upon them) have done. Therefore, whenever we express any opinion about them, it would be about the tenets and rituals of their religions; as for the founders of those religions, we will remain scrupulously silent, lest we should become guilty of irreverence towards a Prophet.

As for the fact of being Prophets of God and having been deputed by Him for teaching the same straight path of 'Islam,' there is no difference between Muhammad and other Prophets (God's blessings be upon them all), we have been ordered to believe in all of them alike. But in spite of their equality in this respect, there are the following three differences between Muhammad and other Prophets (God's blessings be upon them all):

1. The Prophets of the past had come to certain people for certain periods of time, while Muhammad (God's blessings be upon him) has been sent for the whole world and for all times to come.
2. The teachings of those Prophets have either disappeared altogether from the world, or whatever of them remains is not pure, and is found intermingled with many erroneous and fictitious statements. For this reason even if anyone wishes to follow their teachings, he cannot do so. In contrast to this, the teachings of Muhammad (God's blessings be upon him), his biography, his discoursed, his ways of living, his morals, habits, and virtues, in short, all the details of his life and work, are

preserved. Muhammad (God's blessings be upon him), therefore, is the only one of the whole line of Prophets who is a living personality, and in whose footsteps it is possible. To follow correctly and confidently.

3. The guidance imparted through the Prophets of the past was not complete and all- embracing. Every Prophet was followed by another who effected alterations and additions in the teachings and injunctions of his predecessors and, in this way, the chain of reforms and progress continued. That is why the teachings of the earlier Prophets, after the lapse of a certain period of time, were lost in oblivion. Obviously there was no need of preserving former teachings when amended and improved guidance had taken their place. At last the most perfect code of guidance was imparted to mankind through Muhammad (God's blessings be upon him) and all previous codes were automatically abrogated, for it is futile and imprudent to follow an incomplete code while the complete code exists. He who follows Muhammad (God's blessings be upon him) follows all the Prophet, for whatever was good and eternally workable in their teaching has been embodied in his teachings. Whoever, therefore, rejects and refuses to follow Muhammad's teachings and chooses to follow some other Prophet, only deprives himself of that vast amount of useful and valuable instruction and guidance in Muhammad's teachings, which never existed in the books of the earlier Prophets and which were revealed only through the Last of the Prophets.

That is why it is now incumbent upon each and every human being to have faith in Muhammad (peace be upon him) and follow him alone. To become a true Muslim (a follower of the Prophet's way of life) it is necessary to have complete faith in Muhammad (peace be upon him) and to affirm that:

a. He is a true Prophet of God;

b. His teachings are absolutely perfect, free from any defect or error;
c. He is the Last Prophet of God. After him no Prophet will appear among any people till the Day of Judgment, nor is any such personage going to appear in whom it would be essential for a Muslim to believe

BELIEF IN LIFE AFTER DEATH

The fifth article of Islamic Faith is belief in life after death. Prophet Muhammad (peace is upon him) has directed us to believe in resurrection after death and in the Day of Judgment. The essential ingredients of this belief, as the life of this world and of all that is in it will come to an end on an appointed day. Everything will be annihilated. That day is called *Qayamah,* i.e. the Last Day. That all the human beings who had lived in the world since its inception will then be restored to life and will be presented before God who will sit in court on that day. This is called *Hashr:* Resurrection.

That the entire record of every man and woman of all their doings and misdoings-will be presented before God for final judgment. That God shall finally adjudge the reward of every person. He shall weigh everyone's good and bad deeds. One who excels in goodness will be rewarded a goodly reward; one whose evils and wrongs overweigh his good deeds, will be punished and that the reward and punishment will be administered judiciously. Those who emerge successful in this judgment will go to paradise and the doors of eternal bliss will be opened upon them; those who are condemned and deserve punishment will be sent to Hell- the abode of fire and torture. These are the essential constituents of belief in life after death.

NEED OF THIS BELIEF

Belief in the life after death has always been a part and parcel of the teachings of the Prophets. Every Prophet asked his followers to believe in it, in the same way as the last of the

Prophets, Muhammad (peace be upon him), has asked us to do. This has always been an essential condition of being a Muslim. All Prophets have categorically declared that one who disbelieves in it, or casts doubts on it, is a *Kafir*. This is so, because denial of life after death makes all other beliefs meaningless. This denial also destroys the very sanction for good life and man is driven to a life of ignorance and disbelief. A little reflection would make this quite clear.

In your everyday life, whenever you are asked to do anything, you immediately think: what is the utility of doing it and what harm is involved in doing it? This is the very nature of man. He instinctively regards a useless action as totally unnecessary. You will never be willing to waste your time and energy in useless, wasteful, and unproductive jobs. Similarly, you won't be very eager to avoid a thing that is harmless. And the general rule is that the deeper your conviction about the utility of a thing, the firmer would be your response to it; and the more doubtful you are about its efficacy, the more wavering and shaky would be your attitude. After all, why does a child put his hand in fire? Because he is not sure that fire burns. Why does he evade studying? Because he does not fully grasp the importance and benefits of education and does not believe in what his elders try to impress upon his mind.

Now think of the man who does not believe in the Day of Judgment. Would he not consider belief in God and a life in accordance with His code of no consequence? What value will he attach to a life in pursuit of His pleasure? To him either obedience to God is of any advantage, or disobedience to Him of any harm. How, the injunctions of God, Him Prophet, and His Book? What incentive would remain there for him to undergo trials and sacrifices and to avoid worldly pleasures? And if a man does not follow the code of God and lives according to his own likes and dislikes, or what use is his belief in the existence of God, if any such belief he has?

That is not all. If you reflect still deeper, you will come

to the conclusion that belief in life after death is the greatest deciding factor in the life of a man. Its acceptance or rejection determines the very course of his life and behaviour. A man who has in view the success or failure of this world alone will be concerned with the benefits and harms that accrue to him in this life only. He will not be prepared to undertake any good act if he has no hope of gaining thereby some worldly interest, nor will he be keen to avoid any wrong act if that is not injurious to his interests in this world.

But a man who believes in the next world as well and has a firm conviction of the final consequences of his acts would look upon all world look upon all worldly gains and losses as temporary and transitory and would not stake his eternal bliss for a transitory and would his eternal bliss for a transitory gain. He will look upon things in their wider perspective and will always keep the everlasting benefit or harm in view. He will do the good, however costly it may be to him in terms of worldly gains, or however injurious it may be to his immediate interests; and he will avoid the wrong, however charming it may look. He will judge the things from the viewpoint of their eternal consequences and would not submit to his whims and caprices.

Thus there is a radical difference between the beliefs, approaches, and lives of the two persons. One's idea of a good act is limited to its beneficence in this brief temporary life as a gain in the shape of money, property, public applause and similar other things which give him position, power, reputation, and worldly happiness. Such things become his objectives in life.

Fulfilment of his own wishes and self-aggrandizement become the be-all and end-all of his life. And he does not deter even from cruel and unjust means in their achievement. Similarly, his conception of a wrong act is that which may involve a risk of injury to his interests in this world like loss of property and life, spoiling of health, besmirching of reputation, or some other unpleasant consequence. In contrast to this man, the believer's concept of good and evil would be quite different.

To him all that pleases God is good and all that invokes His displeasure and wrath is evil. A good act, according to him, will remain good even if it brings no benefit to him in this world, or even entails loss of some worldly possession or injury to his personal interests. He will be confident that God will reward him in the eternal life and that would be the real success. Similarly, he will not fall a prey to evil deeds merely for some worldly gain, for he knows that even if he escapes punishment in his short worldly life, in would be the loser and would not be able to escape punishment by the court of God. He does not believe in the relativity of morals but sticks to the absolute standards revealed by God and lives according to them irrespective of gain or injury in this word.

Thus it is the belief or disbelief in life after death which makes man adopt different courses in life. For one who does not believe in the Day of Judgment it is absolutely impossible to fashion his life as suggested by Islam. Islam says: "In the way of God give *zakat* (charity) to the poor." His answer is: "No, *zakat* will diminish my wealth; I will, instead, take interest on my money." And in its collection he would not hesitate to get attached each and everything belonging to the debtors, though they are poor or hunger-stricken. Islam says: "Always speak the truth and shun lying, though you may gain ever so much by lying and lose ever so much by speaking the truth." But his reply would be: " Well, what shall I do with a truth which is of no use to me here, and which instead brings loss to me ; and why should I avoid lying where it can bring benefit to me without any risk, even that of a bad name?"

He visits a lonely place and finds a precious metal lying there; in such a situation Islam says: "This is not your property, do not take it"; but he would say: "This is a thing I have come by without any cost or trouble; why should I not have it? There is no one to see this pick-up, who might report it to the police or give evidence against me in a court of law, to give me a bad name among the people. Why should I not make use of this valuable?" Someone secretly keeps a deposit with this man, and after that that he dies. Islam says: "Be honest with the property deposited with you and give it over to the heirs of the deceased." He says: "Why?

There is no evidence of his property being with me; his children also have no knowledge about it. When I can appropriate it without any difficulty, without any fear of legal claim, or stain on my reputation, why should I not do so?" In short, at every step in life, Islam will direct him to walk in a course of behaviour; but he will take recourse to the opposite direction. For Islam Measures and values everything from the viewpoint of its everlasting consequence; while such a person always has in view only the immediate and earthly outcome. Now, you can understand why a man cannot be a Muslim without belief in the Day of Judgment. To be a Muslim is a very great thing; the fact is that one cannot even become a good man without this belief, for the denial of the Day of Judgment degrades man from humanity to a place even lower than that of the lowest of animals.

RATIONAL VINDICATION

So far we have discussed the need and importance of belief in the Day of Judgment. Now let us consider how far the constituents of the belief are rationally understandable. The fact is that whatever Muhammad (peace be upon him) has told us about lift after death is clearly borne out by reason. Although our belief in the that Day is based upon our implicit in the Messenger of God, rational reflection not only confirms this belief but also reveals that Muhammad's (peace be upon him) teachings in this respect are much more reasonable and understandable than all other the following viewpoints are found in the world.

1. A section of the people says that there is nothing left of man after death, and that after this life-ending event, there is no other life. According to these people, this

belief has no reality. They say that there is no possibility of it and such a belief is quite unscientific. This is the approach and brings in western science in their support.

2. Another section of the people maintains that man, in order to bear the consequences of his deeds, is repeatedly regenerated in this very world. If he lives a bad life, in the next generation he will assume the shape of an animal, like a dog or a cat, etc, or some tree or some lower kind of man. If his acts have been good, he will be reborn as a man into a higher class. This viewpoint is found in some Eastern religions.
3. There is a third viewpoint which calls for belief in the Day of Judgment, the Resurrection, man's presence in the Divine Court, and the administration of reward and punishment. This is the common belief of all the Prophets.

Now let us consider these viewpoints one by one. The first section, which arrogates to itself the authority and support of science, alleges that there is no reality in life after death. They say that they have never seen anybody coming back after his death. There is not a single case of revival. We see that after death a man is reduced to dust. Therefore death is the end of life and there is no life after death: But just think over this reasoning: is this really a scientific argument? Is the claim really founded on reason? If they have not seen any case of revival after death, they can only say that they do not know what will happen after death. But, instead of remaining within this limit, they declare that nothing will happen after death at the same time alleging that they speak out of knowledge!

In fact they merely generalise on ignorance. Science tells us noting negative or positive in this respect and their assertion that life after death has no existence is totally unfounded. Their claim is not dissimilar to the claim of an ignoramus who has not seen an airplane and on that "knowledge" proclaims that airplanes have no existence at all! If anybody has not seen a thing, it does not mean that that thing has no existence. No man, not even the entire humanity, if it has not seen a thing, can claim that such a thing does not, or cannot, exist. This claim is illusionary and is out and out unscientific. No reasonable man can give it any weight. Now look to belief of the second group.

According to them, a human being is a human being because in his previous animal form he had done good deeds; and an animal is an animal because previously as a human being he had behaved badly. In other worlds to be a man or animal is the consequence of one's deeds in one's former form. One may well ask: "Which of them existed first, man or animal?" If they say man preceded animal, then they will have to accept that he must have been an animal before that, and given a human form for its good deeds. If they say it was animal they will have to concede that must have been a man before that who transformed into an animal for his bad deeds. This puts us into a vicious circle and the advocates of this belief cannot settle any from for the first creature, for every generation implies a preceding generation so that the succeeding generation may be considered as the consequence of the former. This is simply absurd.

Now consider the third viewpoint. Its first proposition is: "This world will one day come to an end. God will destroy and annihilate the universe, and in its place will evolve another higher and far superior cosmos." This statement is undeniably true. No doubt can be cast upon its veracity. The more we reflect on the nature of the cosmos, the more clearly it is proved that the existing system is not permanent and everlasting, for all the forces working in it are limited in their nature, and it becomes a certainty that one day they will be completely exhausted. That is why the scientists agree that one day the sun will become cold and will give up all its energy, the stars will collide with one another, and the whole system of the universe will be upset and destroyed.

Moreover, if evolution is true in the case of the constituents of this universe, why it may not be true for the whole of it? To think of the universe becoming totally non-existent is more improbable than that it will pass into another evolutionary stage and another order of things will emerge in a much more improved and ideal order. The second proposition of this belief is that "man will again be given life". Is it impossible? If so, how did the present life of man become possible? It is evident that God Who created man in this world can do so in the next. Not only is it a possibility, it is also a possibility; it is also a positive necessity, as will be show later.

The third proposition is that "the record of all the actions of man in this world is preserved and be presented on the Day of Resurrection". The proof of the truth of this proposition is provided here in these days by science itself. It was first understood that the sounds which we make produce slight waves in the air and die out. Now, it has been discovered that the sound leaves its impression on its surrounding objects and can be reproduced. Gramophone records are made on the same principle. From this it can be understood that the record of every movement of man is being impressed on all things which come into contact with the waves produced by the movements. This shows that the record of our entire deed is completely preserved and can be reproduced.

The fourth proposition is that "on the Day of Resurrection, God will hold His Court and with just judgment, reward or punish man for his good and bad deeds." What is unreasonable about it? Reason itself demands that God should hold His court and pronounces just judgment. We see here that a man does a good deed and thereby gains nothing in this world. We see another man who does a bad deed and does not suffer for it here. Not only this, we see thousands of cases of a good act bringing trouble on the doer, and of a bad deed and not suffer for it here. Not only this have we seen thousands of cases of a good act bringing trouble on the doer and of the guilty person.

When we notice these events happening every day our reason and sense of justice demand that a time must come when the man who dose good must be rewarded and the one who does evil must be punished. The present order of things as you can see yourself is subject to physical law according to which it is quite natural that a man who has got the means to do evil can do so if he chooses and it is not necessary that its evil consequences should react upon him wholly or partly. If you have a tin of petrol and a match-bow you can set fire to the house of your opponent and you can escape every consequence of this deed if the worldly forces are in your favour. Does it mean that such an offence has got no consequence at all? Certainly not! It means only that its physical result has appeared and the moral result is reserved. Do you really think it reasonable that it should never appear? If you say it should the question is where?

Certainly not in this world because in the physical world only physical world only physical consequences of this higher category can appear only if there comes into existence another other of things wherein rational and moral laws reign supreme and occupy the governing poison and where the physical laws are made subject to them. That is the next world which as we have said before is the next evolutionary stage of the universe. It is evolutionary in this sense that it will be governed by moral laws rather than by physical laws. The rational consequences of man's action, which are reserved wholly or partly in this world, will appear therein. Man's status will be determined by his rational and moral worth adjudged in accordance with his conduct in this life of test and trial. There you will not find a worthy man serving under a fool or a morally superior man in a position inferior to a wretch, as is the case in this world.

The last proposition of this is the existence of Paradise and Hell, which is also not impossible. If God can make the sun, the moon the stars and the earth, why should He not be able to make Paradise and Hell? When He holds His Court and pronounces His judgment rewarding the meritorious and punishing the guilty there must be a place where the meritorious might enjoy their reward honour, happiness and gratification of all kinds and another place where the condemned might feel debasement pain and misery. After considering all these questions no reasonable person can escape the conclusion that the belief in life after death is the most acceptable to reason and common senses, and that there is nothing in it which can be said to be unreasonable or impossible.

Moreover, when a true Prophet like Muhammad (peace be upon him) has stated this to be a fact and it involves nothing but what is good for us wisdom lies in believing it implicitly and not in rejecting it without any sound reasons. The above are the five articles of Faith which from the foundation for the superstructure of Islam. Their gist is contained in the short sentence know as *Kalima-e-tayyibah.* When you declare La ilaha illallah (there is no deity but Allah) you give up all false deities and profess that you are a creature of the One God and when you add to these words *Muhammad-ur-Rasulullah,* (Muhammad is Allah's Messenger) you confirm and admit the Prophethood of Muhammad (God's blessings be upon him). With the admission of his Prophethood it becomes obligatory that should believe in the divine nature and attributes of God, in His angels in His Revealed Books, and in life after death and earnestly follow that method of obeying God and worshipping Him which Prophet Muhammad (peace be upon him) has asked us to follow. Herein lays the road to success and salvation.

PRAYER AND WORSHIP

The earlier discussion has made it clear that the Prophet Muhammad (peace be upon him) has enjoined us to believe in five articles of Faith:

1. Belief in one God. Who has absolutely no associate with Him in His divinity?

2. Belief in God's Angels.
3. Belief in God's Books, and in the Holy Quran as His Last Book.
4. Belief in God's Prophet, and in Muhammad (God's blessing be upon him) as His Last and Final Messenger.
5. Belief in life after death.

These five articles make up the bedrock of Islam. One who believes in them enters the Muslim community. But by a mere verbal profession alone, one does not become a complete Muslim. To become a complete Muslim one has to fully carry out in practice the instruction given by Muhammad (peace be upon him) as ordained by God. For belief in God makes practical obedience to Him incumbent; and it is obedience to God which constitutes the religion of alone is your God, and this means that He is your Creator and you are His creature; that He is your Master, and you are His slave that He is your Ruler and you are His subject.

After having acknowledged Him as your Master and Ruler, if you refuse to obey Him you are a rebel on your own admission. Along with faith in God you believe that the Quran is God's Book. This means that you have admitted all the contents of the Quran to be from God. Thus it becomes your bounden duty to accept and obey whatever is contained in it. Along with that you have admitted Muhammad (peace be upon him) to be God's Messenger, which means that you have admitted that each and every one of his orders and prohibitions are from God. After this admission obedience to him becomes your duty. Therefore you will be a full-fledged Muslim only when your practice is consistent with your profession otherwise your Islam will remain incomplete. Now let us see what code of conduct Muhammad (peace be upon him) has taught as ordained by God Al-mighty. The first and foremost things in this respect are the *'Ibadat' the Primary Duties which must be observed by each and every person professing to belong to the Muslim community.*

SPIRIT OF "IBADAT" OR WORSHIP

'Ibadat' is an Arabic word derived from *'Abd'* (a slave) and it means submission. It portrays that Allah is your Master and you are His slave and whatever a slave does in obedience to and for the pleasure of his Master is *'Ibadat*. The Islamic concept of 'Ibadat' is very wide. If you free your speech from filth, falsehood, malice and abuse and speak the truth and talk goodly things and do all these only because God has so ordained to do they constitute 'Ibadat, however secular they may look in semblance. If you obey the law of God in letter and spirit in your commercial and economic affairs and abide by it in your dealings with your parents relatives friend and all those who come in contact with you verily all these activities of yours are 'Ibadat.

If you help the poor and the destitute give food to the hungry and serve the ailing and the afflicted persons and do all this not for any personal gain of yours but only to seek the pleasure of God, they are nothing short of *'Ibadat*. Even your economic activities the activities you undertake to earn your living and to feed your dependants are *'Ibadat* if you remain honest and truthful in them and observe the law of God.

In short all your activities and your entire life are *'Ibadat* if they are in accordance with the law of God and your heart is filled with His fear and your ultimate objective in undertaking all theses activities is to seek the pleasure of God. Thus whenever you do good or avoid evil for fear of God, in whatever sphere of life and field of activity you are discharging your Islamic obligations. This is the true significance of 'Ibadat, viz. Total submission to the pleasure of Allah, the moulding into the patterns of Islam one's entire life, leaving out not even the most insignificant part thereof. To help achieve this aim a set of formal 'Ibadat (worships) has been constituted which serves as a course of training. The more assiduously we follow the training, the better equipped practices. The 'Ibadat are thus the pillars on which the edifice of Islam rests.

Salat

Salat is the most primary and the most important of these obligations. And what is Salat? It is the prescribed daily prayers which consist in repeating and refreshing five times a day the belief in which you repose your faith. You get up early in the morning, cleanse yourself and present yourself before your Lord for prayer. The various poses that you assume during your prayers are the very embodiment of the spirit of submission; the various recitals remind you of your commitments to your God. You seek His guidance and ask Him again and again to enable you to avoid His wrath and follow His Chosen Path. You read out from the Book of the Lord and express witness to the truth of the Prophet and also refresh your belief in the Day of Judgment and enliven in your memory the fact that you have to appear before your Lord and give an account of your entire life.

This is how your day starts. Then after a few hours the Muezzin calls you to prayers and you again submit to your God and renew your covenant with Him. You dissociate yourself form your worldly engagements for a few moments and seek audience with God. This once again brings to the fore of your mind your real role in file. After this rededication you revert to your occupations and again present yourself to the Lord after a few hours. This again acts as a reminder to you and you once more refocus your attention an the attention on the stipulations of your Faith. When the sun sets and the darkness of the night begins to shroud you, you again submit yourself to God in Prayers so that you may not forget your duties and obligation in the midst of the approaching shadows of the night.

And then after a few hours you again appear before your Lord and this is your last prayer of the day. Thus before going to bed you once again renew your Faith and prostrate before your God. And this is how you complete your day. The frequency and timings of the prayers never let the object and mission of life be lost sight of in the maze of worldly activities. It is but easy to understand how the daily prayers strengthen the foundations of your Faith prepare you for the observance of a life of virtue and obedience to God, and refresh that belief from which spring courage, sincerity, purposefulness, purity of heart, advancement of the soul, and enrichment of morals.

Now see how this is achieved. You perform ablution and perform it in the way prescribed by the Holy Prophet (peace be upon him). You also say your prayers according to the instructions of the Prophet. Why do you do so? Simply because you believe in the prophethood of Muhammad (peace be upon him) and deem it our bounden duty to follow him ungrudgingly. Why don't you intentionally miss-recite the Quran? Isn't it so because you regard the Books as the Word of God and deem it a sin to deviate from its letter? In the prayers you recite many a thing quietly and if you do not recite them and make any deviation therefrom there is no one to check you. But you never do co intentionally. Why? Because you believe that God is ever watchful and He listens all that you recite and is aware of thing open and hidden. What makes you say your prayers at places where there is not one to ask you to offer them or even to see you offering them?

Isn't it so because of your belief that God is ever looking at you? What makes you leave your important business and other occupations and rush towards the mosque for prayers? What makes you terminate your sweet sleep in the early hours of the morning to go to the mosque in the heat of the noon and to leave your evening entertainment's for the sake of prayers? Is it anything other than sense of duty-your realisation that you must fulfil your responsibility to the Lord, come what may? And why are you afraid of any mistake in prayer? Because your heart is filled with the fear of God and you know that you have to appear before Him on the

Day of Judgment and give an account of your entire life. Now look can there be a better course of moral and spiritual training than prayers? It is this training which makes a man a perfect Muslim.

It remains him of his covenant with God, refreshes his faith in Him, and keeps the belief in the Day of Judgment alive and ever-present before his mind's eye. It makes him follow the Prophet and trains him in the observance of his duties. This is indeed a strict training for conforming one's practice to one' ideals. Obviously if a man's consciousness of his duties towards his Creator is so acute that he prizes it above all worldly gains and keep it refreshing through prayers he would certainly be in visiting the displeasure of God which he all along striven to avoid. He will abide by the law of God in the entire gamut of life in the same way as he follows it in the five prayers ever day. This man can be relied upon in other fields of activity as well for if the shadows of sin or deceit approach him he will try to avoid them for fear of the Lord which would be ever present in his heart. And if even after such a vital training a man misbehaves himself in other fields of life and disobeys the law of God it can only be because of some intrinsic depravity of his self.

Then again you must say your prayers in congregation and especially so the Friday prayers. This creates among the Muslims a bound of love and mutual understanding. This arouses in them the sense of their collective unity and fosters among them national fraternity. All of them say their prayers in one congregation and this inculcate in them a deep feeling of brotherhood. Prayers are also a symbol of equality for the poor and the rich the low and the high the rulers and the ruled the educated and the unlettered, the black and the white all stand in one row prostrate before their Lord. They also inculcate in them a strong sense of discipline and obedience to the elected leader. In short prayers train them in all those virtues which make possible the development of a rich individual and collective life.

There are a few of the myriads of benefits we can derive from the daily prayers. If we refuse to avail ourselves of them we and only we are the losers. Our shirking the prayers can only mean one of the two things. Either we do not recognise prayers as our duty or we recognise them as our claim to Faith shall be a shameless lie, for if we refuse to take orders we no longer acknowledge the Authority. In the second case if we recognise the Authority and still flout His Commands then we are the most unreliable of the creatures that ever tread the earth. For if we can do this to the highest authority in the universe, what guarantee is there that we shall not do the same in our dealings with other human beings? And if double play overwhelms a society what a hell of discord it is bound to become!

Fasting

What the prayers seek to serve five times a day fasting in the month of Ramadhan (ninth month of the lunar year) does once a year. During this period from dawn to dusk we eat not a grain of food nor drink a drop of water no matter how delicious the dish or how hungry or thirsty we feel. What is it makes us voluntarily undergo such rigours? It is nothing but faith in God and the fear of Him and of the Day of Judgment. Each and every moment during our fast we suppress our passions and desires and proclaim by our doing so the supremacy of the Law of God. This consciousness of duty and the spirit of patience that incessant fasting for full one month inculcates in us help us strengthen our faith. Rigour and discipline during this month bring us face to face with the realities of life and help us make our life during the rest of the year a life of true subservience to His Will.

From yet another point of view fasting has an immense impact on society for all the Muslims irrespective of their status must observe fast during the same month. This brings to prominence the essential equality of men and thus goes a long way towards creating in then sentiments of love and brotherhood. During Ramadhan evil conceals itself while good come to the fore and the whole atmosphere is filled with piety and purity. This discipline has been imposed on us to our own advantage.

Those who do not fulfil this relied upon in the discharge of their duties. But the worst are those who during this holy month do not hesitate to eat or drink in public. They are the people who by their conduct show that they care not a trifle for the commands of Allah in whom they profess their belief as their Creator and Sustainer. Not only this, they also show that they are not loyal members of the Muslim Community rather they have nothing to do with it. It is evident that in so far as obedience to law and regard for a trust reposed in them goes, only the worst could be expected of such hypocrites.

Zakat

The third obligation is *Zakat*. Every Muslim, whose financial conditions are above a certain specified minimum, must pay annually 21/2% of his cash balance to a deserving fellow being, a new covert to Islam, a traveler, or one involved in debts. This is the minimum. The more you pay the greater the reward that Allah shall bestow on you. The money that we pay as *Zakat* is mot something Allah needs or receives. He is above any want and desire. He, in His benign Mercy, promises us rewards manifold if we help our brethren but there in one basic condition for being thus rewarded. And it is this that when we pay in the name of Allah, we shall not expect nor demand any worldly gains from the beneficiaries nor aim at making our names as philanthropists.

Zakat is as basic to Islam as other forms of 'Ibadat salat (prayers) and saum (fasting). Its fundamental importance lies in the fact that it fosters in us the qualities of sacrifice and rids us of selfishness and plutolatry. Islam accepts within its fold only those who are ready to give away in God's way from their hard earned wealth willingly and without any temporal or personal gain. It has nothing to do with misers. A true Muslim shall, when the call comes, sacrifice all his belongings in the way of Allah, for Zakat has already trained him for such sacrifice. The Muslim society has immensely to gain from the institution of Zakat. It is the bounden duty of every well to do Muslim to help his lowly placed poor brethren.

His wealth is not to be spent solely for his own comfort and luxury there are rightful claimants on his wealth, and they are the nation's widows and orphans, the poor and the invalid those who have ability but lack the means by which they could seek useful employment, those who have the faculties and brilliance but not the money with which they could acquire knowledge and become useful members of the community. He who does not recognize the right on his wealth of such members of his own community is indeed cruel. For there could be no greater cruelty than to fill one's own coffers while thousands die of hunger or suffer the agonies of unemployment. Islam is a sworn enemy of such selfishness, greed and acquisitiveness. Disbelievers, devoid of sentiments of universal love, know only to preserve wealth and to add to it by lending it out on interest. Islam's teachings are the very antithesis of this attitude. Here one shares one's wealth with others and helps them stand on their own legs and become productive members of the society.

Hajj or Pilgrimage

Hajj, or the Pilgrimage to Mecca, is fourth basic 'Ibadat. It is obligatory only on those who can afford it and that too only once in a lifetime. Mecca today stands at site of a small house that the Prophet Abraham (God's blessings be upon him) built for the worship of Allah. Allah rewarded him by calling it His own House and by making it the center towards which all must face when saying prayers. He also made it incumbent on those who can afford to visit is not merely to be a courtesy call. Even this pilgrimage has its rites and conditions to be fulfilled which inculcate in us piety and goodness. When we undertake the pilgrimage, we are required to suppress our passions, refrain from bloodshed, and be pure in word and deed. God promises rewards for our sincerity and submissiveness.

The Pilgrimage is, in a way the biggest of all Ibadat. For unless a man really loves God he would never undertake such a long journey all his near and dear ones behind him. Then this pilgrimage is unlike any other journey. Here his thoughts are concentrated on Allah; his very being vibrates with spirit of intense devotion. When he reaches the holy place, he finds the atmosphere laden with piety and godliness; he visits place which bear witness to the glory of Islam, and all this leaves an indelible impression on his mind, which he carries to his last breath. Then there are as in other *'Ibadat* many benefits that the Muslims can enjoy from this pilgrimage. Mecca is the center towards which the Muslims must converge once a year meet and discuss topics of common interest and in general create and refresh in then selves the faith that all Muslims are equal and deserve the love and sympathy of others irrespective of their geographical or cultural origin. Thus the pilgrimage unites the Muslims of the world into one international fraternity.

Defense of Islam

Though the defense of Islam is not a fundamental tenet but its need and importance have been repeatedly emphasised in the Quran and the Hadith. It is in essence a test of our sincerity and truthfulness as believers in Islam. If we do not defend one whom we call our friend against intrigues or assaults from his foes, nor care for his interest and are guided solely by selfishness we are indeed false pretenders of friendship. Similarly if we profess belief in Islam we must jealously guard and uphold the prestige of Islam. Our sole guide in our conduct must be the interest of Muslim at large and the service of Islam in the face of which all our personal considerations must sink low.

Jihad

Jihad is a part of this overall defense of Islam. *Jihad* means struggle to the utmost of one's capacity. A man who exerts himself physically or mentally or spends his wealth in the way of Allah is indeed engaged in Jihad. But in the language of the Shari'ah this word is used particularly for the war that is waged solely in the name of Allah and against those who perpetrate oppression as enemies of Islam. This supreme sacrifice of lives devolves an all Muslims. If however a section of the Muslims offer themselves for participating in the *Jihad* the whole community is absolved of its responsibility.

But if none comes forward everybody is guilty. This concession vanishes for the citizens of an Islamic State when it is attacked by a non-Muslim power. In that case everybody must come forward for the *Jihad*. If the country attacked has not strength enough to fight back then it is the religious duty of the neighbouring Muslim countries to help her if even they fail then the Muslims of the whole world must fight the common enemy. In all these cases *Jihad* is as much a primary duty of the Muslims concerned as are the daily prayers or fasting. One who shirks it is a sinner. He is plainly a hypocrite who fails in the test of sincerity and all his *'Ibadat* and prayers are a sham a worthless hollow show of devotion.

DIN AND SHARI'AH

Up till now we have been dealing with *Din* or *Faith*. We now come to a discussion of the *Shari'ah* of Prophet Muhammad (peace be upon him). But let us first be clear about the difference between Din and Shari'ah.

Distinction between Din and Shari'ah

In the foregoing chapters we have said that all the Prophets who made their appearance from time to time propagated Islam. This is a very basic fact. They propagated Islam that is a faith in God with all His attributes faith in the Day of Judgment faith in the Prophets and the Books and asked people consequently to live a life of obedience and submission to their Lord. This is what constitutes al-Din and it was common to the teaching of all the Prophets. Apart from this Din there is the Shari'ah or the detailed code of conduct or the canons comprising ways and modes of worship standards of morals and life law that allow and prescribe that judge between right and wrong.

Such canon law has been undergoing amendments from time to time and though each Prophet had the same Din he brought with him a different Shari'ah that would suit the conditions of his own people and time. This served the purpose of training different people over all ages for a better civilization and equipping them with better morals. The process ended with the advent of Muhammad the last Prophet (peace be upon him) who brought with him the final code which was to apply to all mankind for all times to come. Din has undergone no change but now the entire previous *Shari'ah* stand abrogated in view of the comprehensive *Shari'ah* that Muhammad (peace be upon him) has brought with him. This is the climax or the final of the great process of training that was started at the dawn of the human era.

Sources of the Shari'ah

We draw upon two major sources in order to acquaint ourselves with the Shari'ah of Muhammad (peace be upon him), viz. the Quran and the Hadith. The Quran is a divine revelation each and every word of the instructions issued or the memoirs of the last Prophet's conduct and behaviour, as preserved by those who were present in his company or those to whom these were handed down by the first witness. These were later sifted and collected by divines and compiled in the form of books among which the collections made by Malik, Bukhari, Muslim, Tirmizi, Abu Dawud, Nasa'i and Ibn Majah are considered to be the most authentic.

Fiqh

Detailed law derived from the Quran and the Ahadith covering the myriads from of problems that arise in the course of man's life have been compiled by some of the leading legists in the past. Thus the Muslim Peoples shall for ever be grateful to those men of leading and vision who devoted their lives to gaining a mastery of the Quran and the Hadith who made it easy for every Muslim to fashion his everyday affairs according to the requirements of the Shari'ah. It is due to them alone that the Muslims all over the world can follow the Shari'ah easily even though their attainments in religion are never such that they could themselves give a correct and authentic interpretation to the Quran or the Ahadith.

Though in the beginning a large number of religious leaders applied themselves to the task but only four major schools of thought remain. They are:

1. *Fiqh-e-Hanafi:* This is the Fiqh compiled by Abu Hanifa Nu'man bin Thabit with the assistance and cooperation of Abu Yusuf, Muhammad, Zufar, and others all of whom had high religious attainments to their credit. This is known as the Hanafi School of Fiqh.
2. *Fiqh-e-Maliki:* This Fiqh was derived by Malik bin Anas Asbahi.
3. *Fiqh-e-Shafi'i:* Founded by Muhammad bin Idress al-Shafi'i.
4. *Fiqh-e-Hanbali:* Founded by Ahmed bin Hanbal.

All of these were given the final form within two hundred years of the time of the Prophet. The differences that appear in the four schools are but the natural outcome of the fact that is many sided. When different persons employ themselves in interpreting a given event, they come out with explanations according to their own lights. What gives these various schools of thought the authenticity that is associated with them is the unimpeachable integrity of their respective founders and the authenticity of the method they adopted.

That's why all Muslims, whatever school they may belong to regard all the four schools of Fiqh goes unchallenged, one can follow only one of them in one's life, though there is the group of Ahl-i-Hadith who believe that those who have the required knowledge and learning should directly approach the Quran and the Hadith for guidance and those who are not bestowed with such knowledge and faculties should follow whomsoever they may choose to in a particular matter.

Tasawwuf

Fiqh deals with the apparent and the observable conduct the fulfilling of a duty in letter. What concerns itself with the spirit of conduct is known as *Tasawwuf*. For example, when we say our prayers Fiqh will judge us only by the fulfilment of the outward requirements such as ablution. Facing towards the Ka'ba, the timing and the number of Rak'ats while *Tasawwuf* judged by our concentration, devotion, purification of our souls and the effect of prayers on our morals and manners. Thus the true Islamic Tasawwuf is the means of our spirit of obedience and sincerity while Fiqh governs our carrying out commands to the last detail. An *'Ibadat* devoid of spirit, though correct in procedure is like a man handsome in appearance but lacking in character and an *'Ibadat* full of spirit but defective in execution is like a man noble in character but deformed in appearance.

The above example makes clear the relation between *Fiqh* and *Tasawwuf*. But it is to the misfortune of the Muslims that as they sank in knowledge and character with the passage of time they also succumbed to the misguided philosophies of nations which were then dominant partook of them and patched Islam with their perverted dogmas. They polluted the pure spring of Islamic *Tasawwuf* with absurdities that could not be justified by any stretch of imagination on the basis of the Quran and the Hadith. Gradually a section of Muslims appeared who thought and proclaimed themselves immune to and above the requirements of the *Shari'ah*.

These people are totally ignorant of Islam for Islam cannot admit of *Tasawwuf* that loosens itself out of the Shari'ah and takes liberties with it. No Sufi has the right to transgress the limits of the Shari'ah or treat the primary obligations (*Fara'iz*) such as *daily prayers fasting zakat* and the *hajj, Tasawwuf*, in the true sense is but an intense love of Allah and Muhammad (peace be upon him) and such love requires a strict obedience to their commands as embodied in the Book of God and the Sunnah of His Prophet. Anyone who deviates from the divine commands makes a false claim of his love for Allah and His Apostle.

Faith in the Unknown

It is an everyday experience that when you do not know a thing, you look for somebody who knows it and you repose faith in his word and follow him. If you get ill and you cannot treat and cure yourself, look for the doctor and accept and follow his instructions without question. Why because he is properly qualified to give medical advice, possesses experience, and has treated and cured a number of patients. You, therefore, stick to his advice, do whatever he asks you to do and avoid whatever he forbids. Similarly, in matters of Law you believe in whatever your legal advisers say and act accordingly.

In educational matters you have faith in your teacher or instructor and you accept his instructions as true. When you want to go to some place and do not happen to know the way to it, you ask somebody who knows it, and follow the way he points out. In short, the reasonable course that you adopt in the whole of your life about matters which you do not or cannot know is that you approach one who knows them, accept his advice and act accordingly. As your own knowledge of that matter or problem is inadequate, you carefully search for One who knows that and then silently accept his word. You take every pain to select the proper person. But After selecting the right man, you accept his advice unquestioningly.

This kind of belief is called 'belief in the unknown'. For here you have relied upon one who knows, in matters you do not know. This exactly is Iman-bil-ghaib. Thus believing or having faith in what was previously unknown to you is called 'faith in the UN-known' (Iman-bil-ghaib). Iman-bil-ghaib, therefore, signifies that you achieve the knowledge of what was not known to you from one who knows. You do not know God and His real attributes. You are not aware that His angels are directing the machinery of the whole universe according to His orders, and that they surround you on all sides. You have not the proper knowledge of the way of life through which you can seek the pleasure of your Creator. And you are in the dark about the life that is to come.

The knowledge of all these matters is given to you by the Prophets, who had direct contact with the Divine Being and had been endowed with the correct knowledge. And they are the persons whose sincerity, integrity, trustworthiness, godliness and the absolute purity of whose lives stand as irrevocable witness to the truth of their claim to knowledge. And above all, the very wisdom and force of their message makes you admit that they speak the truth and their preaching deserves to be believed and followed. This conviction of yours is Iman-bil-ghaib. Such truth discerning and truth-acknowledging attitude (i.e. Iman-bil-ghaib) is essential for obedience to God and for acting in accordance with His pleasure, for you have no other medium than God's Messenger for the achievement of true knowledge, and without accurate and true knowledge you cannot proceed rightly on the path of Islam.

6

Moderate Islam and Faith

Spengler writes in his latest piece that moderate Islam cannot exist because moderate faith is an oxymoron, in discussing the Abdul Rahman case in Afghanistan:

"Where are the moderate Muslims?" sigh the self-appointed Sybils of the Western media. Faith is life. What does it mean to be moderately alive? Find the "moderate Christians" and the "moderate Jews", and you will have the answer......There really is no such thing as a "moderate" Christian; there simply are Christians, and soon-to-be-ex-Christians.

Same goes for Muslims, he says. A moderate Muslim, or Christian, or Jew, is really an unbeliever in the making, if not already one. Faith is absolute, there are no compromises, no ifs and buts, and it's all or nothing. The "all", in terms of Islam, presents a diabolical threat due to Islam's win-or-lose *on earth*, not the hereafter, nature, it's weddedness to the past, it's inability to let go. Islam does not know moderation or extremism: it only knows success or failure. Unlike Christianity, which prevailed only through the improbable project of abandoning its old center [Europe] to create a new land altogether [America], Islam cannot exist outside of traditional society, which by definition knows no doubt. Nowhere else but in the United States has personal conscience rather than religious establishment succeeded as the guiding principle of Christianity. "Moderate Islam" is an empty construct; the Islam of the Afghan courts is the religion with which the West must contend.

The traditional societies which Islam cannot live without are threatened by globalization; hence the rise of Islamic extremism as it battles for the very survival of Islam itself. All or nothing. Broken by the very well-informed agency "AsiaNews" of the Pontifical Institute for Foreign Missions, the news of the arrest in Egypt of citizens guilty only of being ex-Muslim Christians sheds new light on the dangers encountered by those who convert from Islam to another faith.

The dangers are there even in the West, for Muslims who convert. These protect their decision with a thousand precautions. And the Church does the same toward those who convert to the Christian faith. About their preparation for baptism, the Italian bishop's conference published in 2000 a booklet of instructions. The first: "From the initial greeting, it is important to guarantee discretion." Even the total number of baptisms is kept secret. It is known that, in Italy, approximately one half of the converts are Albanian: and these face the least danger, because in Albania Islam is almost exclusively a nominal religion, with very little social command. But for the Maghrebs, or the Syrians, or the Pakistanis, the risk is serious. Both the Muslim community at home and their own family ban them like apostates. It can happen that their very lives hang by a thread.

Muslim Kurds are another island of relative tolerance toward the converts. Daniel Ali embraced Christianity while he was still living in northern Iraq and fighting against Saddam Hussein. He immigrated to the United States in 1993, was baptized in 1995, and in 1998 entered the Catholic Church. Working together with the Jesuit expert in Arabic studies Mitch Pacwa has created a "Christian-Islamic Forum" and travels around the U.S. to preach Christianity to other Muslims. But a clandestine life is the rule almost everywhere in the world. And on the part of the Catholic Church, there is a widespread tendency to respond to this situation simply by refusing to "create the problem"; that is, to proselytize among Muslims.

An Italian director of the Fondazione Migrantes, who asked to remain anonymous, has worked for years with Tunisian Muslims and says: "We decided not to encourage conversion to Christianity in any way, no matter what Cardinal Giacomo Biffi thinks about it." The bellicose cardinal has exactly the opposite conviction: "Preaching and baptizing are statutory duties of the Church for all. Jesus did not command us to preach the gospel to all creatures except for the Muslims, the Jews, and the Dalai Lama." The tendency to conduct dialogue without evangelizing has its own negative repercussions on those who become Christian nonetheless.

The complaint of a Maghreb woman named Nura made its way last September all the way to the Vatican: "We feel abandoned. After our conversion, we have no one to support us. We ask the Church for help: protect us, defend us." Archbishop Michael Fitzgerald, president of the Pontifical Council for Interreligious Dialogue, responded to her with a bunch of hot air - even worse, with mistrust. "One must always ask for the reasons for this change. It often presents itself as the desire to be a real Italian. But on can be Italian and Muslim at the same time. I would be concerned from the beginning, in the sense of the welcome within the Christian community."

A few days later, on September 28, John Paul II published the list of the new cardinals. Fitzgerald, who was thought would surely get the red hat, was not there. A few weeks later, Joseph Cardinal Ratzinger added in an interview, "We must have the courage to help these people," and get rid of a certain "Christian conscience that is unsure of itself." The authoritative periodical "La Civiltà Cattolica," an unofficial organ of the Holy See, refreshed the public memory about the living conditions in Islamic countries, with an unprecedentedly tough article. So there's been a leap forward. Who knows if Nura will feel any less alone? But here is a closer look at what has happened in Egypt in recent weeks, with an Islamic regime generally classified as "moderate." This inquiry was published in "L'espresso" no. 50, for December 5-11, 2003.

Thou shalt have No Other Allah

At 13 years of age, Ibrahim knew the Koran by heart. The imam in his Cairo neighborhood used him as an example for many young people, and foresaw for him a future as a great preacher of the most radical sort of Islam. Ibrahim had become that young preacher: already at 16 years of age, on Fridays, with the exuberance and impetuosity of his youth, he harangued the faithful who came running to the mosque to hear him, the rising star of the jihad, the holy war. "I had imposed the veil on all the women of my family; my grandmother, my mother, my sisters," he recounts. "I could not endure the non-Islamic expressions of our society in daily life. I kept watch and denounced anyone who did not respect the rules and deviated from the right way."

Ibrahim was preaching in the mid-1990s, when, under the pressure of the Islamic movements, many of them connected with the university of Al Azhar, the hadit had been reintroduced to Egypt. The hadit are the sayings of Mohammed on the isba, the principle that allows anyone to begin an inquiry against someone who strays from the teaching of the sharia, the Islamic law, and on the ridda, the accusation of apostasy. One of the first hadit holds that the blood of a Muslim "may be spilled in three cases: homicide, adultery, and apostasy." Thus the pious citizen is authorized to kill the sinner. On the basis of this dogma, many intellectuals condemned for their unorthodox works were assassinated during those years, or seriously injured, like the Nobel-winning writer Naghib Mahfuz.

Two years ago Ibrahim, who was born into the faith in Allah and the Koran, converted to the Catholic faith. He took the name Mikeil, Michael, the archangel most venerated in Egypt. Convents, churches, and chapels are dedicated to Michael all over the country. The remnants of places of worship consecrated in pre-Islamic Egypt are still visible in the Babylon fortress in Old Cairo. But Ibrahim-Mikeil lives his conversion in great secrecy. His family, his friends, and even his wife are unaware of it. He risks being run over by the accusation of apostasy, he says, "on the part of old friends, a relative, which could become a death sentence, or in the best of cases a sentence which would inflict years of imprisonment and certain torture."

Are Ibrahim's fears well-founded? In a formal sense, no. Article 3 of the Egyptian constitution of 1923 proclaims the equality of all Egyptians before the law, without distinction of race, language, or religion. But the reality is different. Since 1971, a constant tendency toward the islamicization of the Egyptian justice system has been in course. President Anwar Al-Sadat, later killed by Islamic fundamentalists, was the one who accepted certain requests from the Muslim Brotherhood aimed at combating the nationalist parties and the left, which opposed his economic policies: he introduced into the constitution an amendment according to which "sharia is one of the principal sources o239239f legislation," which became, in 1980, the "principal source."

"A Muslim from birth can never change religions," affirms Youssef Sidhom, the director of the Christian weekly "Watani": "They will not only seek by every means to dissuade him, but his very life will be in danger. He will be excluded from his inheritance and from the community to which he belongs. But on the contrary, an Egyptian Christian who embraces the Muslim faith is welcomed with many parties, his identity card is quickly changed, he is helped in his job and with his house." The secrecy in which he lives his new faith has permitted Ibrahim-Mikeil, for now, to escape the police roundups that have led to the arrest of 23 Egyptian converts to Christianity, while hundred of others are being sought. This news, completely ignored by the Egyptian media, was broken from Rome by the agency "AsiaNews", which provides information on the critical situation of Christians in the Islamic world.

The only Arabic newspaper to have recounted the arrests has been "Al Quds," which is produced in London and banned in Egypt. It denounces: "The work of the Egyptian police to criminalize ex-Muslim converts to Christianity continues in silence. We are amazed that a matter of such delicacy should be left in the hands of police forces. It is true that sharia does not allow apostasy, but in a state ruled by law this question should certainly not be confronted in conformity with fundamentalist tendencies."

According to a priest who asked to remain anonymous, "the arrests by the police, which have been infiltrated by now, like the magistratures and professional corporations, are due to the rooting of fundamentalism in the Egyptian educational system. As a matter of fact, there are many cases in which students belonging to minority religions have been heavily discriminated against and maltreated. It happens, for example, that Christian girls in elementary schools are forced to wear the veil. The public schools have suffered strong interference from the imams of Al Azhar and the governing authorities, which have long been inclined to satisfy the requests of the fundamentalists in order to maintain their own power. For months one hears nothing of the arrested converts. And in the meantime, they suffer beastly mistreatment.

Then their fate will be asked of a judge, who is not always impartial. Assuming they are not condemned, the only thing they can do is to go into exile in the United States, Canada, or Australia, in order to avoid disdain both within their families and in the communities around them."These aspects are completely overlooked by the Egyptian media, but not by "Watani." "Ours is an independent newspaper," says the director, Sidhom, "without particular relations with the Church, from which it receives no subsidies." In the face of this return to the crude repression of Christians, Coptic Patriarch Shenuda III, accustomed in the past to remarking on the harmony between Christians and Muslims, has changed his stance, bewailing the numerous attacks against his community.

The life of the Christians, among whom the Copts, at 6-7 million, are the great majority, has not been easy in recent years. The persecution of this community hearkens back to the forms of martyrdom used against the first Christians. One's memory turns back to the terrible events in October of 1998, when Egyptian security forces carried out rapes and crucifixions during incursions into the Coptic village of El-Kosheh, near Luxor. The crucifixions were carried out in groups of 50 persons, who were literally nailed or chained to doors, with each person's legs joined to the next's. There were victims beaten and tortured through the application of electric current to their genitals by the police, who accused them of being infidels. Romani Boctor, 11, was strung up with an electric cable in an attic.

But it is the discrimination perpetrated in all aspects of society that makes life difficult for Christians. By constitutional law, the president must be a Muslim. Christians cannot be prime minister, though they have been in the past. Of the 32 ministers, only two of them are Christian: the finance minister and the minister of the environment. The mayor of a city or village cannot be a Christian. The highest posts in the army, the police, and the president's guard are granted only to Muslims. A Christian cannot assume an important role in a tribunal. Even worse, according to the law, two witnesses must be obtained before a sentence can be passed, but if one of the two is a Christian, the judge may disallow his testimony.

A Christian cannot be the rector of a university or dean of a faculty. The government pays the salaries of the imams, but not of the Christian priests. The University of Al Azhar does not accept Christian students, even though it is maintained by taxes taken from both Muslims and Christians. Added to this entire are the insurmountable obstacles to be faced in building a church. These difficulties can be traced back to a 1934 law that dictates ten conditions for the granting of a permit. For example, a church can not be built on farm land; it must not be close to a mosque or a public monument; police authorization must be obtained if it will be constructed near bridges on the Nile, canals, or railway lines. And the president of the republic must give his signature. "In spite of the protests, the state wants to maintain these conditions, and that provokes in all Egyptians a spirit of fanaticism and of division among Christians and Muslims," says Sameh Fawzi, a Christian journalist.

"The culture and life of the Copts have completely disappeared from the Egyptian press. For this reason, we have intensified our interest in the Christian minorities. We want to foster union among Egyptians, both Christians and Muslims, because all are children of the same nation," says Sidhom, warning: "The state's indifference is bringing Christians to the bitter conviction that Egypt considers them second-class citizens that a Christian is a kafir, an infidel, neither knowing the true religion nor possessing the true faith and thus does not deserve to be heard. And that, in this country, and humiliating discrimination on religious grounds has been created."

Ibrahim-Mikeil understands all of the dangers of his conversion, but lives his Catholic conversion with great serenity. "When I opened my eyes to the violence, I began to consider my religion," he recounts. "I wanted God to be very close to me, but in Islam he seemed very far away. There he is the master of all things, but he is not a God who lives among us. This is what tormented me. Then one day I visited the monastery of St. Catherine of Sinai, and there I received the true inspiration." St. Catherine was the young Egyptian princess who converted to Christianity and was ordered to be beheaded by the Roman emperor Maxentius. Ibrahim-Mikeil's dream? "To go to Rome to be able to pray freely at St. Peter's, ideally with my wife."

On the opposite ends of the broad spectrum of anti-Islam views, there are two very general and deep-rooted miscon-ceptions: one that the Holy Quran preaches intolerance, and the other that Islam is a religion of peace alone. Misre-presentations on the part of both Muslims and non-Muslims could go no further. The basic principle of Islam, a faith in all the prophets of the world, is enough to give the lie to the first misconception. The Quran that preaches not only love and respect for the founders of the great religions of the world but much more than that faith in them — could not shrink down to the narrowness of intolerance for those very religions.

Zero tolerance for zulm — injustice and oppression — in Islam negates the second misconception that it is a religion of peace alone. Most importantly, the root word of Islam is "al-silm" which means "submission" or "surrender." It is understood to mean "submission to Allah." In spite of whatever noble intention has caused many a Muslim to claim that Islam is derived primarily from peace, this is not true. To demystify this pair of grand misconceptions, we need to study words and deeds of the present day self proclaimed "moderates" who are exploiting the second misconception in their favour, which indirectly leads to consolidation of the first.

Musharraf's adding "enlightened" to "moderation" gives an impression as if other opportunists are preaching some kind of inferior or benighted moderation. However, his best explanation could hardly tell the difference between the confusion which several others are spreading in the name of moderate Islam for their self-interest. According to Musharraf, the "suffering" of his "brethren in faith" at the "hands of militants, extremists, terrorists have inspired" him to come up with "the strategy of Enlightened Moderation." Here we must note that Musharraf: a) tries to kill two birds in one shot, i.e., to please both Muslims and the enemies of Islam; b) presents 'enlightened moderation' as a strategy not a value or a form of Islam to avoid annoying Muslims; c) confirms Islamophobes perspective that the root of the global turmoil lies with Muslims alone; d) gives legitimacy to the Islamophobes classification of Muslims and Islam e) attempts to show that Islam and secularism are compatible, and f) hides the source of his inspiration — his self interest.

Like other self-proclaimed moderates, Musharraf has no clarification as to why a true Muslim would not be a moderate without following Musharraf's agenda for moderation or the much vaunted enlightenment. Instead, he tries to prove that the world would have been a peaceful place if there were no "plastic explosives, combined with hi-tech, remotely controlled activation means superimposed by a proliferation of suicide bombers." His strategy begins with meaningless appeals that "something has to be done quickly to stop this carnage."

Compare this biased assessment with the ability and atrocities of those who are neck deep in innocent blood: who have stockpiles of nuclear and biological weapons and who bypassed even the UN to occupy two sovereign states, and who killed at least 150,000 people since 9/11 alone on the basis of lies upon lies. What amounts to a carnage? Nearly 3,000 at the hands of unknown perpetrators or 128,000 at the hands of known liars? Is this enlightened moderation to plead guilty to crimes of unknown culprits and turn a blind eye to the acts of known extremists, and appeal victims of their aggression to "quickly stop this carnage"?

For Musharraf and company moderation is "a two-pronged strategy" of a) "shunning militancy, extremism" and b) "adopting the path of socio-economic uplift." This appeal-based strategy does not explains how the so-called "moderate" Islam is different than the Islam as prescribed by the Quran and Sunnah. Why should one follow them and not the source? As far the two prongs are concerned, no one loves to live in perpetual violence and never-ending poverty. The pre-requisite for addressing these problems is not embracing some kind of convoluted form of Islam. The pre-requisite is brining aggression to a halt, leaving the victims of oppression alone; bringing an end to the exploitative political and economic systems and structures, and most importantly making the aggressor pay reparations for the damage done. Is an attractive title to the strategy for effective subservience good enough to fulfill any of these pre-requisites?

Muslims' alleged obsession with their faith has no role in the miserable situation they are facing today. Instead, it is the lack of obsession that keeps Muslims groping in the dark. They don't need any moderation in embracing or practicing Islam. The title, enlightened moderation, is totally deceptive and irrelevant to the proposed strategy. The strategy, in turn, is totally devoid of common sense and the prevailing reality. Blindness of the proposed strategy touches its peak, when Musharraf adds a series of appeals with regard to "the role to be played by the West," saying the US "must aim at resolutely resolving all political disputes with justice," "resolve the political disputes enumerated above with justice" and "justice must be done and seen to be done." Well said.

The excessive stress on justice, however, shows that the label of moderation is deceptive in the first place. What Musharraf is appealing for is exactly what the so-labeled extremists are demanding. Why is it so that when Musharraf begs for it, it is OK? But if someone else just talks about it, it becomes extremism? Besides the apologetic tone, what makes Musharraf a moderate in this case is his hypocrisy of saying one thing and doing exactly the other. Sustaining an unjust order and demanding justice from the same doesn't make any sense. Facilitating the unjust in occupying Muslim countries; handing as many Muslims as possible for filling the modern-day concentration camps and killing as many of his "brethren in faith" as possible to please Washington, and then appealing for justice to the same unjust authority doesn't simply add up.

The hypocrisy is further reflected in Musharraf's statement that the "root cause of extremism and militancy lies in political injustice, denial and deprivation." That is true. However, is he not playing a lead role in perpetuating "political injustice, denial and deprivation"? Who is responsible for what he calls "acute sense of deprivation, hopelessness and powerlessness," Muslim masses or the former colonialists and the stooges they remotely control for ruling the masses with the barrel of a gun since their strategic withdrawal in the name of decolonization?

Let us agree with Musharraf that "a people suffering from a combination of all these lethal ills are easily available cannon fodder for the propagation of militancy and the perpetration of extremist, terrorist acts." The question, however, is: what is the root cause for these ills? When these ills do not originate because of Islam, why then needlessly introduce different versions of Islam, or a strategy with a deceptive title, to address them?

In the same breath, Musharraf admits: "it is not Islam as a religion which preaches or infuses militancy and extremism but the political disputes which led to antagonism in the Muslim masses." Logically, the discussion should end at this point because if Islam doesn't teach militancy and extremism, it is of no use to introduce "moderate" or "liberal," or "progressive" forms of Islam and leaving the dispute to the unjust to resolve. The need is to tackle the causes that lead to reactionary sentiments, but where is the strategy for that? Musharraf equates moderation with "conciliatory approach" and shows that Islam is not in conflict with secularism. Here Musharraf attempts to make his mantra acceptable to the enemies of Islam by making Islam compatible with secularism.

The above discussion is about Musharraf's icing on the cake of "moderation." It brings us to the real issue: the problem of a few Muslim opportunists who are exploiting the morbid dread of Islam in the hearts of Islamophobes in different ways. They promote themselves by presenting views of the enemies of Islam in different words. It leads to the Islamophobes' objective of introducing different forms of Islam and different classes of Muslims. Islamophobes' intention behind introducing "moderate" Islam and Muslims becomes evident when they reject argument from some leading self-proclaimed "moderates" as "reformist apologetic." To the contrary, persons such as Irshad Manji, who are shunned even by the self-proclaimed "moderates," are presented as a "practicing Muslim" and real moderates because they sound more in consonance with the anti-Islam agenda.

The acceptable-to-Islamophobes "moderates," in fact, believe that "an uncritical acceptance of the Quran as the final manifesto of God" is one of the "disturbing cornerstones of Islam." So the real moderation in the eyes of the standard-setters for "moderate" Muslims is to reject the Quran as the final manifesto of Allah. Are Musharraf and his supporters in the deceptive "enlightened moderation" ready for accepting this kind of standards? If not, they are acceptable as long as they can sell something of interest to their masters. There is no limit to moderation in the eyes of their masters, busy in undermining Islam. The acceptable "moderates" — the "practicing Muslims" such as Irashad Manji — now call the rest of the self-proclaimed "moderates" as "so-called moderates" and equate them with "fundamentalists" for sharing a "sense of spiritual supremacy."

To get out of this confusion, we need to understand that the clear commands for Muslims are to be moderate by default. Being moderate is a prerequisite for being a good Muslim. It is not an identity label for a specific kind of Muslims out there to please and appease others. The most perfect moderates are those who most seriously follow the

Quran and Sunnah. Accordingly, Muslims cannot be part time or partial Muslims to be considered as moderate by virtue of rejecting part of the Quran and accepting part of it (Al-Quran 2:85). Islam is a Muslim's identity. It means submission (to Allah) and peace. It embodies the basic elements of moderation — balance, due proportion, tolerance, justice and equity — because abiding each and tranquility is unthinkable in a situation of extremes. In fact, moderation or balance is the core value, the very soul of Islam.

In the light of specific verses — 2:143, 4:171, 25:67, 17:26-27, 20:81, 6:108, 2:178, 17:33, 5:45, 42:40 — and numerous others where fairness, justice and balance are extolled and excess is deplored, we can safely say that those who suggest moderating Islam, only expose their ignorance of the Divine Message. The fact is that Islam enjoins its followers to give lessons in moderation to other people. What the Muslims need today, therefore, is not lectures in the concept of moderation, but to delve into the treasure trove of guidance that Islam has already bequeathed to them.

To confirm demystification of moderation, we need to see who the visible enemies of Islam consider as "extremists" and "Islamists." The standard-setters for "moderate" Muslims believe that strong belief in the totality of the Quran makes Muslims "Islamists," and "extremists." Accordingly, the most partial believers of the Quran become the most perfect "moderates" because promoters of the "moderate" Muslims believe they "are absolutely at war with the vision of life that is prescribed to all Muslims in the Koran," which, in their view, contains 389 specifically intolerant verses.

This shows what Musharraf is presenting might be some kind of intelligent deception to him. But it is, in fact, a foolish self-deception. He titles his adventure as "enlightened moderation," to make it acceptable to the shrewd enemies of Islam. At the same time, he attempts to deceive Muslims by talking about totally irrelevant things to give the common man an impression that "moderation" is all about good feelings for reconciliation, tolerance and poverty alleviation. The well-known criteria of Islamophobes for "moderate" Muslims clearly shows that this is not what is expected of "moderate" Muslims and their moderation.

Besides what is mentioned above, "moderates" are required to totally reject parts of the Quran, such as rejecting the clear commands about inheritance (Al-Quran 4:11-14, 4:33, 4:176), court testimony (Al-Quran 2:282) and even Riba (Al-Quran 2:275-76, 278-79; 3:130; 4:161; 30:39). The overt Islamophobes publicly say that "the fundamentals of Islam are a threat to us." It clearly shows that Islamophobes do not want the "moderates" they support to follow fundamentals of Islam according to the Quran and Sunnah.

Islam tells Muslims on several occasions not to coerce other people. Accordingly, Muslims must present the message to them in the most cogent and clear way, invite them to the truth and do their best in presenting and conveying the Truth, but it is up to people to accept or not to accept. Thus intolerance could not be ascribed to a book which excludes compulsion from the sphere of religion altogether, and which is full of verses that exhort believes to exercise restraint, mercy and kindness. The question is: If Allah gave choice to believe or not to believe, then why did He punish, and in the case of war physically challenged, the people of Prophet Nuh, Lut, and Shu'aib, the 'Ad, the Thamud, and Pharaoh and his followers and why did Prophet Mohammed PBUH go to many wars?

The answer to this question shows to which extent Islam is a religion of peace. Those people were not punished simply because of their disbelief. They were punished because they had become oppressors. They committed aggression against the righteous, and stopped others to come to the way of Allah. There were many in the world, who denied Allah, but Allah did not punish every one, nor did Prophet Mohammed PBUH go out to slaughter all non-Muslims.

The phenomenon of zulm (injustice and oppression) in any form and at any point of time is repeatedly and emphatically condemned in the Quran. There is no tolerance for zulm and no reconciliation with the oppressors as long as they do not renounce their zulm. The condemnation of 'zulm' or 'wrong' by virtue of its repeated emphasis and the centrality of the terms that define it, has immense significance for building a just social and economic order which characterizes the religion of Islam. As Professor Kenneth Cragg of Cambridge University has explained in his book, The Mind of the Quran, that the usage of "the derivatives of the root 'zalama' verbs, nouns and participles are among the most frequent of all Quranic terms... exceeded only by the most central of all words, like Allah, Rabb and Rasul."

Now compare Kenneth Cragg's explanation of the word zulm in the Quran with the words and deeds of those at the hands of whom their own people in general and Muslims in particular suffer today. According to Cragg: "The basic sense of 'zalama' is to do wrong, to treat wrongfully, to deal unjustly, with or without an object. It is the act of falsifying in not according to what is due, whether to things or to people, to truth or to trust. It means distortion and perversity, tyranny and evil will. More frequently 'zulm' denotes wrong against fellow humanity - injustice, deceit, fraud, slander, treachery, calumny, robbery and the rest." If we start with the Bush and Blair's lying for invading Iraq and go back to search the history of colonialism for the past five hundred years, we will come to the conclusion that the root cause of the present turmoil is nothing but pure zulm of the colonialists of the past and the totalitarians of today on the one hand, and perpetuation of colonial legacy by their puppets among Muslims on the other. Their misinformation campaigns deviates Muslims away from what the Quran repeatedly calls "the Straight Path," and their economic tyranny robs them of every possible opportunity to invest in poverty alleviation and other ventures for human development.

In the light of this discussion, the real purpose of fighting for Muslims is to remove injustice and aggression. Muslims are allowed to keep good relations with non-Muslims. Allah says, "Allah does not forbid you that you show kindness and deal justly with those who did not fight you in your religion and did not drive you out from your homes..." The objective of allowing Muslims to fight was to establish religious freedom, to stop all religious persecution, to protect the houses of worship of all religions, mosques among them. Tolerance, moderation and reconciliation are the mechanism used for upholding human rights, pluralism (including cultural pluralism), and the rule of law. Submission to injustice and tyranny is not tolerance.

Islam is moderate between turning your left cheek to him who hits you on the right one, and between paying someone back tenfold. Allah says: "And those who, when an oppressive wrong is inflected on them, help and defend themselves. The recompense for an injury is an injury equal thereto (in degree), but if a person forgives and makes a reconciliation, his reward is due from Allah; surely He loves not those who do wrong" (42:39-40). He, Most Gracious, also says: "And if you punish (your enemies), punish them with the like of that with which you were afflicted. But if you endure patiently, verily, it is better for those who are patient and endure you patiently; your patience is not but from Allah and grieves not over them and is not distressed because of what they plot" (16: 126-127).

The bottom-line is that there is no such thing as moderate and extremist Islam justified with either of the two grand misconceptions discussed above. Islam doesn't need any prefixes or suffixes. Islam's moderation lies in its balanced approach towards living individual and collective life. Any attempt at justifying classification of Islam and Muslims amounts to helping the Western war lords in their war on Islam. The funeral of British suicide bomber Shehzad Tanweer was held in absentia in his family's ancestral village called 477 GB in Sumandri district, near Lahore, Pakistan. Thousands of people attended, as they did again the following day when a qul ceremony was held for Tanweer. During qul the Quran is recited, earning merit which is passed on to the deceased to speed their journey to paradise. In Tanweer's case this was hardly necessary for being a shahid (martyr) he is deemed to have gone straight to paradise. The 22-year old from Leeds, whose bomb at Aldgate station killed seven people, was hailed by the crowd as "a hero of Islam".

Some in Britain cannot conceive that a suicide bomber could be a hero of Islam. Since 7/7 many have made statements to attempt to explain what a contradiction in terms seems to them. Since the violence cannot be denied, their only course is to argue that the connection with Islam is invalid. Deputy Assistant Commissioner of the Metropolitan Police Brian Paddick said that "Islam and terrorists are two words that do not go together." His boss the Commissioner, Sir Ian Blair, asserted that there is nothing wrong with being a fundamentalist Muslim. Many have argued in the same vein after every recent Islamic terrorist atrocity. But surely we should give enough respect to those who voluntarily lay down their lives to accept what they themselves say about their motives. If they say they do it in the name of Islam, we must believe them. Is it not the height of illiberalism and arrogance to deny them the right to define themselves and their actions in this way?

Those who say that we should not link Islam to terrorism because no one spoke of the IRA as "Catholic terrorists" are being illogical. The IRA never claimed to commit their acts of terrorism on behalf of the Catholic Church. Nationalism, not religion, was their driving force. Some of the "condemnations" of 7/7 given by the British Muslim leadership have little value, hedged as they are with provisos and get-out clauses. What good is it to condemn suicide bombings in London and affirm them in the Middle East? What good is it to say that Islam condemns the killing of the innocent without clarifying how Islam defines "innocence"? We need to hear more comments like those of courageous Muslims who have called on their community to report radicals to the police.

Tony Blair was right in saying that this terrorism is not a new problem. It was there before the Iraq war, and it was there before 9/11. It is not confined to attacks on non-Muslim and Western targets. Right across the Muslim world, there is internal conflict, as for example in Iraq, Pakistan and Egypt, with Muslims destroying each other because of theological differences. Indeed the first sectarian conflict within Islam began in 632, as soon as Muhammad had died. By 657 there was a three-way split in the community; one of these three groups was eventually exterminated by another, and the two remaining are the Sunnis and Shi'as who are still fighting each other today. On 8th July the London-based Muslim Weekly unblushingly published a lengthy opinion article by Abid Ullah Jan entitled "Islam, Faith and Power". The gist of the article is that Muslims should strive to gain political and military power over non-Muslims, that warfare is obligatory for all Muslims, and that the Islamic state, Islam and shari'a [Islamic law] should be established throughout the world. All is supported with quotations from the Quran.

His newspaper is widely read and distributed across the UK. What then is the theology behind the phenomenon of Islamic terrorism which Jan faithfully describes in the Muslim Weekly? Contemporary Islam can be what you make of it. By far the majority of Muslims today live out their lives without recourse to violence, for the Quran is like a pick-and-mix selection. If you want peace, you can find peaceable verses. If you want war, you can find bellicose verses. You can find verses which permit only defensive jihad, or you can find verses to justify offensive jihad.

You can even find texts which specifically command terrorism, the classic one being Q8:59-60 which urges Muslims to prepare themselves to fight non-Muslims: "Against them make ready your strength to the utmost of your power, including steeds of war, to strike terror into (the hearts of) the enemies" (A.Yusuf Ali's translation). Pakistani Brigadier S.K. Malik's book "The Quranic Concept of War" is widely used by the military of various Muslim countries. In it Malik explains Quranic teaching on strategy: "In war our main objective is the opponent's heart or soul, our main weapon of offence against this objective is the strength of our own souls, and to launch such an attack, we have to keep terror away from our own hearts... Terror struck into the hearts of the enemies is not only a means, it is the end itself. Once a condition of terror into the opponent's heart is obtained, hardly anything is left to be achieved. It is the point where the means and the end meet and merge. Terror is not a means of imposing decision on the enemy; it is the decision we wish to impose on him."

If you permit yourself a little judicious cutting, the range of choice in Quranic teaching is even wider. A verse one often hears quoted as part of the "Islam is peace" litany allegedly runs along the lines: "If you kill one soul it is as if you have killed all mankind." But the full and unexpurgated version of Q5:32 states: "If anyone slew a person - unless it be for murder or for spreading mischief in the land - it would be as if he slew the whole people." The very next verse lists a selection of savage punishments for those who fight the Muslims and create "mischief" (or in some translations "corruption") in the land, punishments which include execution, crucifixion and amputation. What kind of "mischief in the land" could merit such a reaction? Could it be interpreted as secularism, democracy and other non-Islamic values in a land? Could the "murder" be the killing of Muslims in Iraq? Just as importantly, do the Muslims who keep quoting this verse realise what a deception they are imposing on their listeners?

It is probably true that in every faith, ordinary people will pick the parts they like best and practise those, while the scholars will work out an official version. In Islam the scholars had a particularly challenging task, given the mass of contradictory texts within the Quran. To meet this challenge they developed the rule of abrogation which states that wherever contradictions are found, the later-dated text abrogates the earlier one. To elucidate further the original intention of Muhammad, they referred to traditions (hadith) recording what he himself had said and done. Sadly for the rest of the world, both these methods led Islam away from peace and towards war.

For the peaceable verses of the Quran are almost all earlier, dating from Muhammad's time in Mecca, while those which advocate war and violence are almost all later, dating from after his flight to Medina. Though "jihad" has a variety of meanings including a spiritual struggle against sin, Muhammad's own example shows clearly that he frequently interpreted jihad as literal warfare and he ordered massacre, assassination and torture. From these sources the Islamic scholars developed a detailed theology dividing the world into two parts Dar al-Harb and Dar al-Islam, with Muslims required to change Dar al-Harb into Dar al-Islam either through warfare or by da'wa (mission). So the mantra "Islam is peace" which we hear repeated in the media so often is almost 1400 years out of date. It was only for about thirteen years that Islam was peace and nothing but peace.

From 622 onwards, it became increasingly aggressive, albeit with periods of peaceful co-existence particularly in colonial times, when the theology of war was not dominant. For today's radical Muslims - just as for the medieval jurists who developed classical Islam - it would be truer to say "Islam is war". One of the most radical Islamic groups in Britain, al-Ghurabaa stated in the wake of the two London bombings, "Any Muslim denies that terror is a part of Islam is kafir." A kafir is an unbeliever (i.e. a non-Muslim), a term of gross insult. Many have expressed sympathy for young men whom they feel have been driven to kill themselves - and as many others as possible. Shahid Malik, MP for Dewsbury, West Yorkshire, has said that suicide bombers are motivated by "feelings of isolation and disaffection, the political anger at what they see as the double standards of the west in relation to international Muslim areas of conflict... and the hatred propagated by domestic extremists such as the BNP".

But we should consider why the bombers react so much more violently to these afflictions than other people do. As Agatha Christie's Poirot once explained and as Shakespeare's Iago demonstrated, the ideal way to murder is by using other people to do the killing. It is noticeable that the senior leaders of radical Islamic groups never themselves perform suicide missions. Rather they manipulate vulnerable and expendable youngsters to do so for them. One such leader is Sheikh Yusuf al-Qaradawi who inspires young Palestinians to become suicide bombers but shows no inclination to seek "martyrdom" himself, or to send his sons on suicide missions. Incidentally, he has also issued a fatwa calling for the killing of British forces in Iraq. Ken Livingstone, who not surprisingly condemned the suicide bombings in the city of which he is mayor, rather more surprisingly went on to support an invitation to al-Qaradawi to attend a conference in Manchester.

While many individual Muslims choose to live their personal lives only by the (now abrogated) peaceable verses of the Quran, it is vain to deny the pro-war and pro-terrorism doctrines within their religion. Could it be that the young men who committed suicide were neither on the fringes of Muslim society in Britain, nor following an eccentric and extremist interpretation of their faith, but rather that they came from the very core of the Muslim community motivated by a mainstream interpretation of Islam? In the days of the British Empire, colonialism had a profound effect on Islam. On the one hand it cut Islam adrift from its classical roots by taking from Islam its political and military power.

On the other hand Lugard's policy of indirect rule allowed the continued existence of Islam in terms of its social structure and the continued use of certain aspects of shari'a.

In India this led to the development of communalism, which allowed Indian Muslims to form their own community and rule themselves by shari'a. This doubtless contributed to the creation of Pakistan in 1947, which came into being specifically to provide a homeland for the Muslims of the sub-continent. A process of Islamisation has led Pakistan to become an Islamic republic. The same development can be seen in the British Muslim community, most of whom have their roots in the Indian sub-continent. Muslims who migrated to the UK came initially for economic reasons, seeking employment. But over the last fifty years their communities have evolved away from assimilation with the British majority towards the creation of separate and distinct communities, mimicking the communalism of the British Raj.

As a Pakistani friend of mine who lives in London said recently, "The British gave us all we ever asked for; why should we complain?" British Muslims now have shari'a in areas of finance and mortgages; halal food in schools, hospitals and prisons; faith schools funded by the state; prayer rooms in every police station in London; and much more. This process has been assisted by the British government thought its philosophy of multiculturalism, which has allowed the Muslim community to consolidate and create a parallel society in the UK.

The Muslim community now inhabits principally the urban centres of England as well as some parts of Scotland and Wales. It forms a spine running down the centre of England from Bradford to London, with ribs extending east and west. It is said that within 10-15 years most cities in these areas will have Muslim-majority populations, and will be under local Islamic political control, with the Muslim community living under shari'a. As early as 1980 M. Ali Kettani was advocating a policy with the aim of achieving such a result. Writing instructions for Muslims living as minorities in Western countries, Kettani urged them to live close together and form their own separate institutions.

What happens after this stage depends on which of the two main religious traditions amongst Pakistani-background British Muslims gains the ascendancy.

The Barelwi majority believe in a slow evolution, gradually consolidating their Muslim societies, and finally achieving an Islamic state. The Deobandi minority argue for a quicker process using politics and violence to achieve the same end result. Ultimately both believe in the end result of an Islamic state in Britain where Muslims will govern their own affairs and, as the finishing touch, everyone else's affairs as well. Islamism is now the dominant Islamic voice in contemporary Islam, and has become the seedbed of the radical movements. It is this that Sir Ian Blair has not grasped. For some time now the British government has been quoting a figure of 1.6 million for the Muslim population. Muslims themselves claim around 3 million, and this is likely to be far nearer to the truth. The growth of the Muslim community comes from their high birth rate, primary immigration and asylum-seekers both official and unofficial. There are also conversions to Islam.

The violence which is endemic in Muslim societies such as Pakistan is increasingly present in Britain's Muslim community. Already we have violence by Pakistani Muslims against Kurdish Muslims, by Muslims against non-Muslims living amongst them (Caribbean people in the west Midlands, for example), a rapid growth in honour killings, and now suicide bombings. It is worth noting that many current conflicts around the world are not internal to the Muslim community, but external as Muslims, seek to gain territorial control, for example, in south Thailand, the southern Philippines, Kashmir, Chechnya, and Palestine. Is it possible that a conflict of this nature could occur in Britain? Muslims must stop the self-deception which claims that Islam is 100% peace. They must with honesty recognise the violence that has existed in their history in the same way as Christians have had to do, for Christianity has had at times a very dark past Some Muslims have, with great courage, begun to do this. Mundir Badr Haloum, who lectures at a Syrian university, wrote last year in the Lebanese daily Al-Safir, "Ignominious terrorism exists, and one cannot but acknowledge its being Islamic."

Furthermore they must look at the reinterpretation of their texts, the Quran, hadith and shari'a, and the reformation of their faith. Mundir Badr Haloum has described this as "exorcising" the terrorism from Islam. Such reform - the changing of certain fairly central theological principles - would not be easy to achieve. For one thing, Muslims believe the text of the Quran is unchangeable because it exists eternally in heaven. For another, there is no recognised central head of Sunni Islam to make or endorse such decisions. But some Muslims have already made a start. Mahmud Muhammad Taha argued for a distinction to be drawn between the Meccan and the Medinan sections of the Quran. He advocated a return to peaceable Meccan Islam which he argued is applicable for today, whereas the bellicose Medinan teachings should be consigned to history. For taking this position he was tried for apostasy, found guilty and executed by the Sudanese government in 1985.

Another modernist reformer was the Pakistani Fazlur Rahman who advocated the "double movement" i.e. understanding Quranic verses in their context, their ratio legis, and then using the philosophy of the Quran to interpret that in a modern, social and moral sense. Nasr Hamid Abu-Zayd, an Egyptian professor who argued similarly that the Quran and hadith should be interpreted according to the context in which they originated, was charged with apostasy, found guilty in June 1995 and therefore ordered to separate from his wife.

The US-based Free Muslims Coalition, which was set up after 9/11 to promote a modern and secular version of Islam, has proposed the following:

1. A re-interpretation of Islam for the 21st century where terrorism is not justified under any circumstances

2. Separation of religion and state
3. Democracy as the best form of government
4. Secularism in all forms of political activity
5. Equality for women
6. Religion to be a personal relationship between the individual and his or her God, not to be forced on anyone

The tempting vision of an Islam reformed along such lines is unlikely to be achieved except by a long and painful process of small steps. What might these be and how can we make a start? One step would be, as urged by the Prince of Wales, that every Muslim should "condemn these atrocities and root out those among them who preach and practise such hatred and bitterness". Universal condemnation of suicide bombers instead of acclamation as heroes would indeed be an excellent start.

Mansoor Ijaz has suggested a practical three-point action plan:

1. Forbid radical hate-filled preaching in British mosques. Deport imams who fail to comply.
2. Scrutinise British Islamic charities to identify those that fund terrorism. Prevent them from receiving more than 10% of their income from overseas.
3. Form community watch groups comprised of Muslim citizens to contribute useful information on fanatical Muslims to the authorities.

To this could be added Muslim acceptance of a secular society as being the basis for their religious existence, an oath of allegiance to the crown which will override their allegiance to their co-religionists overseas, and deliberate steps to move out of their ghetto-style existence both physically and psychologically. For the government the time has come to accept Trevor Phillips' statement that multiculturalism is dead. We need to move on to re-discover and affirm a common British identity founded on the historical Judaeo-

Christian heritage of our society. This would impact heavily on the future development of faith schools, which should now be stopped.

Given the fate of some earlier would-be reformers, perhaps King Abdullah of Jordan or a leader of his stature might have the best chance of initiating a process of modernist reform. The day before 7/7 a conference which he had convened of senior scholars from eight schools of Islamic jurisprudence amazingly issued a statement endorsing fatwas forbidding any Muslim from those eight schools to be declared an apostate. So reform is possible.

The only problem with this particular action is that, whilst it protected Muslim leaders from being killed by dissident Muslims, it negated a very helpful fatwa which had been issued in March by the Spanish Islamic scholars declaring Osama bin Laden an apostate. Could not the King re-convene his conference and ask them to issue a fatwa banning violence against non-Muslims also? This would extend the self-preservation of the Muslim community to the whole non-Muslim world. It will be a long, hard road for Islam to get its house in order so that it can coexist peacefully with the rest of society in the 21st century. But change must start now.

Islam began in Mecca, claimed to be the revelation of God (Allah) through the angel Gabriel to a man named Muhammad. Muhammad was born in approximately AD 570-571. He was born to the powerful tribe of the Quraish in Mekkah (Mecca). His father's name was Abdullah. His mother's name was Aminah. Apparently Abdullah was a merchant who made caravan trips. He died on a trading trip soon after his marriage to Aminah, leaving Muhammad fatherless at birth. Aminah, his mother, died when he was only six years old. Muhammad was taken in by his grandfather, only to have him die when Muhammad was eight years old. At this time, his uncle, Abu Talib, one of the leaders of the Quraish tribe took him in and raised him.

Muhammad was taught the family business and apparently quite successful. A wealthy widow named Khadijah arranged for Muhammad to oversee her trading business, and was so impressed with his skill and appearance that she proposed marriage to him. Muhammad was twenty five and Khadijah was forty when they married. They had six children, two boys and four girls. Both of the sons died early in life. The daughters lived to see Muhammad become the founder of Islam.

Having married the wealthy Khadijah, Muhammad now became a gentleman of leisure and somewhat of a philosopher. He would retreat from society, take trips into the desert and mountains. He would spend his hours in meditation, greatly concerned about the condition of the civilization he saw around himself. He had a personal mission to find "truth." One of his frequent places of seclusion was a cave on Mount Nur. It was while in this cave, during the month of the Ramadan, a pagan festival, that he received his first visitation from Gabriel and recited the verses found in Quran 96:1-5.

At first, Muhammad shared his new revelations with only his family and close friends. During the next three years the message of Muhammad quietly spread among the people of Mekkah, especially among the youth. Then Muhammad is believed to have received instructions from Allah to go public with his message and openly condemn the paganism and idolatry of Mekkah. This open condemnation of idolatry became an economic threat to the prosperity of Mekkah, and as a consequence, organized opposition to Muhammad and Islam began. At this point, Islam was politically weak, and many Muslims died for their faith.

Persecutions became so great that many Muslims fled to Abyssinia (Ethiopia) for refuge. When Mekkan delegates tried to extradite them, after hearing the Muslim's defense, the ruler refused their extradition on the basis that his faith was similar to theirs, and he could not allow them to be harmed. Muhammad continued to proclaim his message, and his following slowly grew. At one point, in 621, a group of delegates from Madinah (Medina) responded to his call and made a covenant with Muhammad and declared themselves to be Muslims.

A year later, in 622, some seventy people from Madinah made a similar declaration and pledged to fight to protect Muhammad against any and all odds. This pledge or covenant from some who were leaders of Madinah was a turning point for Islam. It provided Muslims with a secure base of operations and allowed them to expand from it. Muhammad commanded the Muslims in Mekkah to migrate to Madinah. After some struggle, Medina was declared to be wholly a Muslim community. For thirteen years, Muham-mad had preached in Mekkah with minimal success. He had followed a quiet, non-political approach and merely preached. Now, however, his tactics changed.

He established himself as religious, political, and military leader. Under his guidance, the community of believers became more important than family or tribe. Islam began to be spread through intimidation and force. Entire tribes and cities were "converted" under threat of war or by conquest. Success led to greater success. Inthe year 630, eight years after he had been forced to leave Mekkah, Muhammad returned with such an overwhelming force that the Mekkans made no resistance. Muhammad's forces destroyed all the idols of Mekkah, and declared the Kabah to be the place of worship for Allah.

With the subjugation of Mekkah, Islam became the power on the Arabian Peninsula Tribe after tribe, city after city declared allegiance to Islam and its prophet. They were given no choice. Muhammad returned to Madinah and continued to rule his kingdom from there. Muhammad died in 632 at the age of sixty-three. In twenty-three years he established a religion and social order that is still dominant in the Arab world today. With Muhammad's death, Islam continued to flourish under the leadership of Muhammad's companions. The first Caliph (successor to the prophet - Kalifah) was his father in law and long time friend, Abu Bakr. In his two years of leadership, Abu Bakr consolidated Islamic influence over the entire Arabian Peninsula.

The second caliph was Umar. He was in power from 634 to 644. Under Umar, Syria, Mesopotamia, Egypt and Persia were added to the growing list of Islamic subjects. Others followed, continually expanding the borders of Islam. Under the leadership of the Kalifahs, Islam spread into Europe, Africa, and Asia. The caliphate lasted centuries, shifting from one dynasty to another, but always claiming the religious right to lead. Eventually the caliphate evolved into the Ottomon Empire which lasted until the early 20th century. Islam spread as a social system, a political system, and a religious system and it was spread by force of arms. That was its philosophy in the beginning, and it is still the philosophy of Islam today.

Today Islam is one of the world's dominant religions, and claims as much as one fifth of the world's population. Islam claims to be a united religion with no divisions; however, one does not have to be an astute observer to realize that Islam is, in reality, fragmented into many different branches, some of which are militantly hostile to each other. There is no unity among Muslims as they would have us believe. Two prominent groups, the Shiites and Sunnites had their origins around 660 over who was the legitimate caliph. Other sects followed. With the end of the colonial system, Islamic states were given their autonomy again. With the wealth from petro-dollars, Islam as a religion is being successfully spread over the world. Islam is one of the greatest opponents in existence to the gospel of Christ today, and is one of the fastest growing religions in the world.

When people speak of moderate Islam as the solution to radical Islam, they mean that there is a modernizing core within the Muslim community capable of transforming it into a civilized member of the world community. They foresee that the dar al-Islam, the Realm of Islam, will cease to be at war with the dar al-Harb, the Realm of War, and particularly with that part of the Realm of War known as the West. I describe these ideas as the "ecumenist" school of Western-Islamic relations, because to believe in the existence of moderate Islam is to believe that the two civilizations can erase their mutual divisions and get along as friends—even mingle together, as, in a single, shared civilization.

Yet its proponents still feel a deep need to go on believing in it, since the only alternative they can envision is unending civilizational warfare. It would be a war waged not only between the Western and Islamic parts of the globe, but—because of the huge Muslim immigrant populations already sojourning in Europe and North America—within the West itself. The prospect seems so horrible that the ecumenists cling to the faith in a moderate Islam no matter how unsupported it may be by the evidence.

Notwithstanding these fears, there is a rational alter-native to the belief in a moderate Islam. I call it the "civilizationist" school, because, in contrast with the ecumenist school, it not only posits irreconcilable differences between the two civilizations, but grapples head-on with their practical implications. Thinkers of the civilizationist school note essential facts about Islam that make any friendship or cooperation with it suicidal in the long run. These include the Koranic command on Muslims to engage in jihad against non-Muslim societies until the whole world is Islamized; the imposition of the totalitarian Sharia law wherever Islam becomes politically dominant; and the permanent subjection of non-Muslims to the miserable oppressed status of dhimmis.

According to the civilizationists, there is and can be no such thing as moderate Islam, and therefore no solution to the Islamic problem that can come from *within* Islam, since Islam itself—not "radical" Islam—is the problem. Moreover, the civilizationists do not say these things, as the ecumenists do, because they *want* Islam to be that way, but because Islam, unfortunately, *is* that way. When ecumenists report various moderating trends within Islam, civilizationists respond with skepticism. They point out that the apparent moderateness of any Muslim community consists of either a temporary abeyance of the militancy that defines Islam (and such periods of non-aggression have been an established part of jihad strategy since the days of Muhammad), or simply the natural quiescence of the masses who lead their lives, pray, and don't involve themselves with activist movements.

Such masses do not constitute any moderate Islam. They are not forming any organized political body or belief system distinct from and opposed to jihadism. Furthermore, regardless of any reforms that may occur from time to time within Islamic society, the center of the faith remains the Koran, which commands jihad, death to apostates, death to Christians and Jews, the stoning of adulteresses and all the rest of it. The fundamental point is that Islam cannot reform itself in any lasting way, because Islam has no source of authority apart from the Koran. In any debate between hard-liners and putative moderates, the hard-liners will have the Koran on their side and will ultimately win the debate.

Therefore no matter how long an Islamic society has been relatively peaceful, moderate, and perhaps even irreligious, an unexpected social or political crisis can bring radical Islam to the fore again—any spark can re-ignite jihad. Iran, a modernizing authoritarian regime for decades under the Shah returned to Sharia and jihad within months of his fall from power in 1979. Turkey, officially secular for eighty years, has recently started returning to Islamic rule.

Egypt, the most important "moderate" Arab country, is teeming with fanatical jihadists, whose rantings are published in state-controlled newspapers. More than one Westerner has reported his shock on seeing a thoroughly westernized Muslim woman suddenly show up in traditional Muslim dress and proudly announce that *this* is who she really is. For all the above reasons, civilizationists do not place their trust in anything arising from within Islam, whether traditional, modern, or "moderate." Their sympathy for moderate Muslim dissidents and victims as human beings does not lead them to drop their guard against Islam itself.

The Cultural "Peace" Process

Yet Daniel Pipes that we must cleave to the hope of a moderate Islam because the alternative is too horrible to contemplate. He thus sidestepped the issue of the truth or falsity of his moderate-Islam theory and made an appeal based on the bad consequences of rejecting it. I think Pipes's remark opens up a useful approach to the issue, if we apply the same analysis to *both* sides. I shall proceed, then, to address these questions: what are the likely consequences of our *accepting* the belief in moderate Islam, and what are the likely consequences of our *rejecting* the belief in moderate Islam?

Let us begin by noting that the practical viability of an idea cannot be separated from its underlying truth. If moderate Islam does not exist, a strategy premised on its existence would be delusional, even suicidal. An example is Israel's decades-long quest for peace with the Arabs, fueled by the repeatedly dashed, repeatedly renewed hope that a "moderate" Arab leadership would somehow emerge that would endorse Israel's right to exist. There are, in fact, striking parallels between Pipes's half-realistic, half-utopian approach toward Islam, and the Labor Zionist movement's approach toward the Arabs, starting from before the founding of Israel and culminating in the disastrous Oslo Accords.

On one hand, the Zionists were tough-minded nationalists who knew they would have to fight and defeat the Arabs in order to secure a Jewish homeland; on the other hand, the Zionists were utopian leftists who hoped (and many of them still hope today, against all the evidence) that once the Arabs had been stopped in their attempt to destroy the Jewish state, they would miraculously turn around and accept Israel's existence, inaugurating a glorious epoch of Arab-Jewish brotherhood. As a result of this way of thinking, each time the Israelis have won a war, instead of pressing home their advantage and achieving real and permanent security for their state, they have launched yet another series of negotiations that has only weakened their position and lost the gains that had been achieved at such cost.

In a parallel fashion, Pipes's respect for Islam, his faith in its essential benignity, and his abiding hope (despite all the evidence) that we can ultimately live in complete harmony with it, contradict and undercut his realistic analysis of its dangers. While the analogy is not perfect (most importantly, the Oslo "peace process" included unrepentant terrorists, while Pipes is firm on the fact that we must have nothing to do with radicals or terrorists), the Oslo process nevertheless demonstrates the kinds of perplexities into which the search for a moderate Islam must lead us.

The Palestinian leadership, corresponding in our analogy to the jihadist core of Islam under its "moderate" clothing, never wanted peace on terms that were compatible with Israel's survival. In order to keep the process alive, the Israelis systematically ignored the Palestinians' radical lack of compliance with their obligations under the Oslo Accords and treated them as though they were civilized men engaged in good-faith discussions. The effect of such conciliation was to liberate Palestinian aggression as never before. Within a few months of the signing of the Oslo agreement, the first suicide bombings of Israeli buses began.

This initiated a pattern that lasted throughout the years of the "peace" process, in which intensified suicide bombings would be followed by Israeli crack-downs on the Palestinians, which in turn would lead to a quieting of terror, until the Israelis would once again get their hopes up and let their guard down, and the suicide mass-murders would recommence. Similarly, if we embrace the idea that moderate Islam is the cure for extremist Islam, we will have to *carry out* a *cultural* peace process, in which we strive to build up the "moderate" Muslims (whether in our own country or in the Mideast) and turn them into leaders of the Islamic community.

The path is filled with punji traps. In light of Pipes's desolating observation that we often *cannot even tell a moderate from a radical*, our efforts to raise the influence of "moderate" Muslims—many of whom will turn out *not* to be moderate—will simply mean giving Muslims *qua* Muslims more caché and power in our society, with their demands and perhaps their threats ever increasing, while we get more and more entangled in the process of instructing, exhorting, bribing, and (maybe) changing them, even as we keep desperately assuring ourselves that moderate Muslim solution will work in the long run. Because the search for moderate Muslims requires us not to see the other side as it really is, we must replace truthful speech with politically correct slogans that demoralize us and encourage our enemies.

For example, almost every time Pipes criticizes radical Muslims, he must—in order to prove that he's not a bigot and that he still believes in an ecumenic resolution—assure his audience that "moderate Islam is the answer." Varieties of this double message, repeated constantly by the government and the intelligentsia, create deep confusion and ambivalence in the public mind. On one hand we're being told that radical Muslims are a remorseless wicked enemy; on the other hand, we're being told that almost all Muslims are moderate and harmless, and that we are bigoted if we think otherwise. The net effect of these two contradictory statements is to establish the unassailable legitimacy of Islam in our country. But, since there *is* no moderate Islam, the Islam that gets legitimized will, inevitably, be radical Islam.

The cultural peace process would distract and weaken us in other ways. Instead of spending our energy building up our own society and culture, which is within our power to do, we would be attempting to build up the *Muslims'* society and culture, which is not within our power to do. We would be gambling our freedom and survival on the chance that we can bring something into existence that has never existed. We would be making our safety contingent on whether the moderate Muslims can be what *we* want them to be. We would keep gazing expectantly at each Muslim as a potential moderate, and averting our eyes when he turned out not to be one—just as the leaders of Israel and the U.S. kept closing their eyes to the real nature of the Palestinians for all those years and are *closing them still.*

We would have to keep refusing to acknowledge failure, because that would wreck our fantasy of an ecumenic and peaceful world. Regardless of all disappointments, we will still keep telling ourselves that some wonderful "moderates" are just around the corner and that we have to reach out to them. In the end, our refusal to face the truth about Muslims, our flattery of non-moderate Moslems as "moderates," will convince them that we are saps lacking the wit and will to defend ourselves, which will increase their aggression against us. Like the Marxist dream with its 150 years on the road to nowhere, our dream of a moderate Islam will inevitably collapse one day, and the price might be nearly as high.

If the Universalist dream fails, the alternative could be slaughter. If, on our ecumenist road to peace, we refuse even to consider the possibility that Muslims as a whole might be our permanent enemies, if we decide that even to think such a thought is evil, then we are preventing ourselves from acknowledging something that may, in fact, be true. What then happens if it actually is true?

Mark Goldblatt writing at *FrontPage Magazine* provides a terrifying glimpse of where the demand for a universal peace can lead. Arguing that jihadism can only be defeated if the Muslim populations rise up and defeat them, he continues:

- There are ... only two conceivable scenarios by which the requisite pan-Islamic upheaval will happen. The more humane scenario is the one being pursued by the Bush Administration—that is, establishes a democratic Iraq in the heart of Islam and hope that it inspires moderate Muslims to reject the radical elements among them. ...
- But what if democracy in Iraq fails outright? Or what if it survives but fails to inspire the overwhelming majority of Muslims to reject the radicals? In that case, Islamic terrorism continues unabated. What follows then is the "Hobbesian" scenario [political philosopher Lee] Harris sketches: Sooner or later, the United States will take one hit too many, or one hit too catastrophic, and the American people will set aside their natural aversion to mass bloodshed and demand a disproportionate response. They'll elect a government that promises to end the threat, permanently, whatever the cost—and *the cost will likely be millions of Muslim lives*. [emphasis added.]
- Like the German and Japanese civilians in 1945, Muslim civilians from North Africa through the Persian Gulf and down into Southeast Asia will at last *feel* their absolute defeat. They'll accept that the fundamentalist struggle against the West has been lost. They'll dig out from the ruins of their cities and recognize that they cannot allow the radicals to make martyrs of them all. Then, with our assistance, both military and financial, they'll set out to purge themselves of the terrorist cancer.
- Tragically, the Hobbesian scenario is the more probable of the two.

Goldblatt doesn't consider any options beside the total democratization of the Muslim world on one side and its mass destruction on the other. Scenarios such as the one I suggest below—of forcing and encouraging Western

Muslims to move back to their home countries and isolating them there where they can't harm us—do not occur to him. He more easily envisions the slaughter of millions of Muslims in their native countries than the exclusion of Muslim immigrants from America. He would sooner contemplate genocide than be seen as intolerant.

The attitude is not at all rare today on the political right. For the L-dotters, the moral and practical idea of stopping all Muslim immigration, closing all Wahhabi mosques, and deporting all jihadists and terror supporters is unthinkable and is never spoken of. But the idea of killing millions of human beings *is* thinkable, and has been expressed—with sanguinary enthusiasm—many times.

This is a logical if extreme result of the ecumenist vision. Universalists cannot imagine radically different civilizations residing and flourishing in distinct spheres. They can only imagine a single global system formed by a single set of democratic ideas. A culture permanently hostile to democracy or to America defeats, by its very existence, the Universalist idea. The only way to defend the idea from such a recalcitrant culture would be to annihilate it. By contrast, civilizationists accept the fact of civilizational differences and have no fear of alien civilizations—so long as they stay in their own territory. It follows that we don't need to destroy Islam; we just need to *contain* it within its own sphere so that it can't threaten us.

Results of Rejecting Moderate Islam

To summarize the argument thus far, the consequences of our seeking peace with Islam will be disarray and distraction on our side, surging confidence and aggression on the Muslim side, renewed major terrorist attacks by Islamists against us, and the punitive killing by us of hundreds of thousands or perhaps millions of Muslims—after which, according to Goldblatt, we will become responsible for rebuilding the Muslim world. What are the likely consequences if we reject the quest for peace?

Here again is the Pipes quote that began this whole discussion:

> If one sees Islam as irredeemably evil, what comes next? This approach turns all Muslims—even moderates fleeing the horrors of militant Islam—into eternal enemies. And it leaves one with zero policy options. My approach has the benefit of offering a realistic policy to deal with a major global problem.

Pipes say that the first result of our failing to believe in moderate Islam is that we would see Muslims as our eternal enemies. Yet for the last 1,400 years Muslims have been—as Pipes himself indicates in some of his writings—our very *long-term* enemies. And it was during those same centuries, when Western civilization viewed Islam as its enemy, that it successfully drove back repeated Islamic invasions and saved itself from conquest and extinction. By contrast, it is only in the modern period, when the West stopped viewing Islam as its enemy (which occurred at the same time that the West stopped being publicly Christian), that it dropped its guard and began admitting the Islamic immigrant masses that now threaten the survival of Europe.

So which way is better? To view Muslims as our enemies (which we did for a thousand years and it didn't harm us but *saved* us), or to view Muslims as our friends (which leads promptly to our own defeat, dhimmitude and ultimate extinction)? If a certain party is our enemy, isn't it better to know that he is our enemy, rather than to imagine that he is not? This is especially the case when the appropriate response to the enemy is simply to build solid walls between us and him, rather than to wage a world war in order to force him to become like ourselves.

The Civilizationist Approach

Pipes's second objection to the belief in permanent civilizational conflict is that it leaves us without policy options. In fact, the civilizationist perspective has given birth to a variety of proposals for coping with the Islamic menace, ranging from intellectual confrontation to military confrontation to radical changes in immigration policy. Bat Ye'or, author of *The Decline of Eastern Christianity under Islam* and the soon-to-be published *Eurabia*, has said that our aim as Westerners should not be to save the soul of Islam but to save ourselves, our values, and our civilization.

The approach she urges is primarily intellectual: we must stop closing our eyes to the reality of jihad, stop blaming ourselves for Muslim terrorism, and stop imposing crippling taboos on our own speech. Instead, we must openly discuss the Muslims' jihadist beliefs, both among ourselves and with the Muslims. This would force them to face the truth about themselves, which in turn might bring about a positive alteration in their outlook and demands. An unstated premise of Bat Ye'or's argument is that Muslims *cannot change themselves. We* must help them do it—or rather; we must put them in a position where they will have no choice but to moderate their own attitudes and behavior toward us. Bullies respect strength.

A corollary is that any such positive changes in Muslim attitudes could only be temporary. This is because the changes would not be the result of any organic development arising from *within* the Muslim community, but of pressure and rebuke coming from *without*. As soon as that external pressure and rebuke were withdrawn, as soon as the West reached out a hand of friendship and tolerance, the Muslims would return to their "default" mode, which is jihad. Therefore, as long as Islam exists, the only solution to the problem of Islam is to keep the Islamic world in a powerless condition, as it had been through all of modern times until 1979. Western criticism of and confrontation with Islam must be permanent.

On the military side, Mark Helprin of the *Claremont Review* has proposed a World War II-scale expansion of American military capabilities plus a permanent U.S. base located in an isolated though strategically central spot in the Mideast or Persian Gulf region, giving us the ability to destroy any Muslim regime that becomes dangerous to us. Helprin rejects any notion of occupying and reconstructing a Muslim country after we topple its government. The purpose of his strategy is not to reform or democratize the internal politics of terror-supporting Muslim societies, as President Bush and the neo-conservatives seek to do, but to make militant Muslim leaders realize that they have no hope of harming us and they face the loss of their regimes and their lives if they try.

Once they get this message, they will change their behavior. In Helprin's military plan, as in Bat Ye'or's proposal for intellectual confrontation with Islam, the West does not seek to change the Muslims, but places them in circumstances, not of their choosing, where they will be pushed to change themselves. The demand is not that they become democrats and liberals, but only that they cease being dangerous to us. Angelo Codevilla, also at the *Claremont Review*, goes further than his colleague Mark Helprin, advocates the outright destruction of several terror- and jihad- supporting Muslim regimes, either by killing the members ourselves (about 2,000 in each country) or, better, turning them over to their domestic enemies.

This, he says, is the only way real regime change occurs in the Arab and Muslim world. Like Helprin, Codevilla advises that we have no interest in occupying these countries or building democracies there. The precise borders and political systems of Mideastern Arab societies are not our concern. We're not trying to create a positive, we're only trying to eliminate a negative—the international network of jihadist and Ba'athist terrorists and the regimes that make them possible. Let us also note the remarkable fact that Helprin and Codevilla, who reject the need for universal democracy and accept civilizational differences, talk about killing only the top 2,000 regime members in several hostile countries, while Mark Goldblatt, who sees universal democracy as the only long-range solution, warns that if universal democracy fails we will have to kill millions of innocent Muslims.

Finally, there is the immigration side of the problem. I have proposed at *FrontPage Magazine* a set of policies—the end of mass Muslim immigration, the deportation of all jihad-supporting resident aliens and naturalized citizens, the closing of Wahhabi mosques, and the explicit abandonment of multiculturalism—aimed at achieving a net out-migration of Muslims from this country. If we reduce both the jihadism and the numbers of the U.S. Muslim immigrant community, those who remain will no longer pose a cultural or physical danger to us, simply because they will have become a relatively insignificant group.

Or rather, they will have been *made* insignificant, by *our* decisive actions. As with Bat Ye'or's, Helprin's, and Codevilla's proposals, the aim is not to reform the Muslims, i.e., to "assimilate" them to our way of life, but to confront them and diminished their power. Those policies will have the effect of encouraging the reduced U.S. Muslim population to adapt themselves more to our society, or choose voluntarily to leave. Whatever the specific proposal may be, the basic civilizationist idea is to speak the *truth* about Islam, to *confront* Islam, and to *contain* Islam.

It is to initiate a net out-migration of Muslims from the West and to isolate the Muslim world in its historic lands. It is to restore the Realm of Islam to the powerless and quiescent condition in which it resided during the early modern period. We of the West, along with other non-Muslim peoples, cannot be safe co-existing in this world with Islam, unless Islam has no ability and opportunity to affect us.

Years ago the historian Gertrude Himmelfarb called for the "re-moralization" of society—the reviving of the moral fiber and discipline that had made earlier generations of

Westerners, particularly the Victorians, such strong, disciplined, and self-confident people, whereas we have become unsure, guilt-ridden, and disbelieving in ourselves and our culture. If I may coin a phrase, I would suggest that alongside the re-moralization of our own society, what we need today is the *re-demoralization* of Islamic society.

Of course, Daniel Pipes says: militant Islam is the problem, and moderate Islam is the solution. But I say: *Islam* is the problem. The defeat and *re-demoralization* of Islam, combined with the steady return of Muslims from the West to their own countries, is the solution. Many people will condemn me for saying that Islam is dangerous and must be suppressed. They will say that there are good and deeply rewarding things about Islam, at least from the Muslims' perspective.

But the key point, from *our* perspective, is that Islam can only be "good" *when it has no power*. As soon as Muslims achieve power relative to non-Muslims, or feel that they are *gaining* such power or that they *can* gain such power, then the jihad aspect of Islam automatically kicks in. When we make a cult out of "moderate" Muslims, we are, in the long run, helping Muslims gain power. Their moderateness will revert, sooner or later, to militancy, but they will still have the power—and the moral sanction—that we gave them. The only way to keep Islam's inherent tendency toward jihadism in abeyance is to keep Muslims in a situation where they have no influence over non-Muslims and no chance of achieving it.

To weaken Islam in the manner I'm suggesting is not to deny the Muslims' humanity. Powerlessness or defeat is not what most deeply bothers Muslims, but the loss of honor. As they have demonstrated over and over in their history, they view honorable defeat, even honorable death, as desiderata. Thus Muslims can be powerless, and still keep their honor. It should be the goal of our policy to return the Islamic world to that salutary condition. Once that has happened, Western students and romantics of Islam could still pursue friendships and cultural interchanges with Muslims. Such inter-cultural contacts would no longer be dangerous because they would no longer be premised on the myth that Islam is benevolent to non-Muslims.

If we want the possibility of decent human relations between individual Westerners and Muslims, we must defang the dar al-Islam and keep it that way. Lasting peace—or, rather, the absence of violence—can only be achieved through Western strength and dominance, not through trying to make friends with a non-existent moderate Islam. Under such circumstances a more decent type of Islam may arise. But, as I've said over and over, it will have arisen only because *we* confined the Muslims to narrower quarters on this globe.

Two starkly different paths lie before us. If we pursue the course of ecumenism, we will embark on a decades-long attempt to turn Muslims into moderate Muslims. The endeavor would become the central political project and moral commitment of our society, an obsessive, irrational quest that—like the Oslo "peace" process—we could never permit ourselves to abandon, no matter how many times it had failed. In the process we would empower Islam and lose ourselves.

If we pursue the course of civilizational defense, we will unstring Islam as a global force by decreasing Muslims' presence in the West and containing them within their historic lands. Once the two civilizations are no longer in each other's faces, *our* freedom and safety will no longer depend on our begging, cajoling, and bribing *them* to give up their deepest convictions. Which path is more promising? The path of civilizational realism, in which we recognize Islam as our eternal adversary and act accordingly, or the path of the civilizational peace process, in which we look on a billion Muslims as moderates who have somehow failed so far to realize that they are moderates, but who—we devoutly believe—will somehow discover that they are moderates if *we* keep trying hard enough to convince them of that fact?

John McCain recently reminded Americans that the great strategic challenge facing the West—and, indeed, the civilized world—is extremist Islam. And more important than any martial aspect of that threat, he said, is the ideological struggle between moderate and extremist understandings of Islam.Yet going on seven years after the attacks that brought America's attention to the problem, it is hard to say that we as a nation—a government and a people—have gotten any closer to identifying, much less aiding, those voices of Islamic moderation that we hope will ultimately triumph.

In addition to the widely acknowledged failures of leadership within those U.S. agencies most responsible for public diplomacy and the war of ideas, Americans are far from arriving at any clear or secure sense of what "moderate Islam" or "moderate Muslim" means. And the reason is hardly surprising: Definitions of moderation—itself a hugely problematic word—usually reflects the ideological and political commitments of the definers. In this case, as it turns out, conservatives (or neoconservatives) tend to hold stricter, narrower views of moderation, while liberals often see more shades of acceptability. But nothing is ever quite that simple. Not when there are many on the left (including militant secularists and atheists like Sam Harris and Christopher Hitchens) who see Islam as essentially inimical to moderation or tolerance. To them, the only moderate Muslim is an ex-Muslim.

This range of opinions on what defines moderate Islam is not all bad. By sparking debates, it has sometimes focused public attention on an issue that most Americans would rather simply ignore. If the historian Daniel Pipes and author Robert Spencer tend the boundaries of moderation with Rottweiler ferocity, they often provide a valuable counterpoint to the more flexible (and even squishy) interpretations of scholars like University of Michigan historian Juan Cole or Georgetown University's John Esposito. But the opposing sides often go overboard, the hard-liners seeing nothing but evil intent and the softies seeing nothing but sweetness and light.

The charges and countercharges grow particularly ferocious when it comes to controversial figures like Tariq Ramadan, the Swiss-born Muslim reformist scholar who now lives and teaches in England. The watchdogs say that Ramadan preaches a moderate line while secretly supporting an extremist agenda. More shamefully, they point to a recycled set of unproved charges against the man to make the case that he is a wolf in sheep's clothing. While it is easy to find fault with certain things Ramadan has said or written (and I have done so), it is hard to see how, in the balance, he hasn't had a significantly benign effect in arguing for the compatibility of Islam and liberal values. Yet several years ago, for the most specious of reasons, the U.S. government refused to allow Ramadan to enter the country to teach at Notre Dame—a decision for which the steady tirades of the watchdogs deserve at least some credit.

For their part, the softies tend to give dubious Muslims and Muslim organizations a free pass when scrutiny is called for. When spokespeople for the Council on American Islamic Relations speak harshly of Muslim reformists like Wafa Sultan or Zudhi Jasser, even going so far as to say that these outspoken critics of extremist Islam are not legitimate Muslims, we hear no criticism of CAIR from the likes of the Espositos or the Coles. The fact is, there is a range of moderates, and it is hardly surprisingly that many Muslim moderates disagree even among themselves about who the moderates are. Furthermore, those moderates who are most likely to have any influence among Muslims in the predominantly Muslim world are also the least likely to pass the litmus test of the watchdogs or of those moderate Muslim who live in the West.

While these disagreements are often understandable, many lead to a kind of intellectual dishonesty that is ultimately hurtful to American efforts to identify and support the voices of moderate Islam. His religious legal opinions, or fatwas, have a huge influence on the popular under-standing of the meaning and applications of sharia — the religious principles that underwrite Islamic law. In his teaching, writing, and jurisprudence, Gomaa has made the case that the rich and varied traditions of Islamic law are the best antidote to Islamic extremism, which typically insists upon the most puritanical interpretations of sharia and its meaning. Gomaa, a Sufi Muslim himself, also rejects the efforts of the Islamist to make their religion into an all-encompassing political program and even denounces Islamic political parties on the grounds that they create divisions among Muslims.

And while Gomaa did say that it was un-Islamic for Muslims to own statues or to display them in their homes, he made it very clear that the destruction of antiquities and other statues in the public sphere was unacceptable and indeed criminal. He is also on record deploring the Taliban's destruction of the great Buddhist statuary in Afghanistan. But the watchdogs tend to read selectively and to rely on those sources that support their judgments. Look hard enough and an American reader will doubtless be able to find things in the grand mufti's rulings that don't conform to current standards of enlightened moderation.

For example, he issued a long and complicated fatwa on the issue of wife-beating—a fatwa that acknowledges certain pre-modern cultural and historical contexts in which sharia was used to justify the odious practice. But he also said that since those cultural and historical conditions are not the conditions of modern societies, Muslims today cannot invoke sharia to justify any form of spousal violence. If the reasoning sounds tortured, well, it is. And it would be much more appealing to American ears to hear him simply say that

Islamic law has never sanctioned such practices. But we must recall that Christianity and Judaism have been used—in ways that seemed legitimate at the time—to justify practices and institutions that we now find morally repugnant, including slavery.

The mufti was guilty of being honest about the historically determined interactions between customary practices and religious principles. So how does the watchdog Spencer characterize the man? As the "wife-beatin,' statue-hatin' Mufti Ali Gomaa." Is that accuracy in labeling? The effect of such smear tactics is cumulative and insidious. Particularly in the day of the Internet, where every opinion appears equally authoritative, careless swipes at figures like Egypt's grand mufti create the impression that there are no moderate Muslims with standing in the predominantly Muslim world. Writer Hitchens is no friend of Islam, but what he once wrote about Pipes's dour interpretation of a promising development in Iran accurately describes the default position of many reflexive watchdogs: "To put it bluntly," Hitchens wrote, "I suspect that Pipes is so consumed by dislike that he will not recognize good news from the Islamic world even when it arrives. And this makes him dangerous and unreliable."

Bibliography

Ali, Syed Ameer. *The Spirit of Islam: A History of the Evolution and Ideals of Islam,* with *a Life of the Prophet.* London: Chatto & Windus, 1978.

Bloom, Jonathan and Sheila Blair. *Islam: A Thousand Years of Faith and Power.* New Haven, CT: Yale University Press, 2002.

Booth, E. *Aristotelian Aporetic Ontology in Islamic and Christian Thinkers.* Cambridge, 1983.

Bowker, John. *What Muslims Believe.* Oxford, UK: Onewworld, 1999.

Burrell, D. *Knowing the Unknowable God: Ibn Sina, Maimonides, Aquinas* (Notre Dame: 1986).

Cook, Michael. *The Koran: A Very Short Introduction.* Oxford, UK: Oxford University Press, 2000.

Corbin, H. *History of Islamic Philosophy,* trans. L. Sherrard. London, 1993.

Craig, E. (ed.), *Routledge Encyclopedia of Philosophy.* London, 1998.

Davidson, H.A. *Proofs for Eternity, Creation and the Existence of God in Medieval Islamic and Jewish Philosophy.* Oxford, 1987.

Elias, Jamal J. *Islam.* Upper Saddle River, NJ: Prentice Hall, 1999.

Fakhry, M. *A History of Islamic Philosophy* , 2nd ed. New York, 1983.

Gibb, Hamilton A.R. and J.H. Kramers, eds. *Shorter Encyclopedia of Islam*. Leiden: E.J. Brill, 1997 (reprint ed.).

Hodgson, Marshall G.S. *The Venture of Islam*, 3 Vols. Chicago, IL: University of Chicago Press, 1974.

Keller, Nuh Ha Mim, trans. *Al-Nawawi's Manual of Islam*. Cambridge, UK: The Islamic Texts Society, 1996.

Leaman, O. *An Introduction to Classical Islamic Philosophy*. Cambridge, 2002.

Marmura , M.E. (ed.), *Islamic Theology and Philosophy*. Albany, 1984.

Nasr, Seyyed Hossein. *The Heart of Islam: Enduring Values for Humanity*. San Francisco, CA, Harper San Francisco, 2002.

Newby, Gordon D. *A Concise Encyclopedia of Islam*. Oxford, UK, Oneworld, 2002.

Peters, F.E. *A Reader on Classical Islam*. Princeton, NJ: Princeton University Press, 1994.

Qadir , C.A. *Philosophy and Science in the Islamic World*. London, 1990.

Renard, John, ed. *Windows on the House of Islam: Muslim Sources on Spirituality*. Berkeley, CA: University of California Press, 1998.

Renard, John. *Seven Doors to Islam: Spirituality and the Religious Life of Muslims*. Berkeley, CA: University of California Press, 1996.

Ruthven, Malise. *Islam in the World*. New York: Oxford University Press, 2nd ed., 2000.

Schimmel, Annemarie. *Islam: An Introduction*. Albany, NY: State University of New York Press, 1992.

Schuon, Frithjof. *Islam and the Perennial Philosophy*. London: World of Islam Festival Publ. Co., 1976.

Sharif, M.M. *A History of Muslim Philosophy*, 2 vols. (Wiesbaden: 1963-6).

Stern, S.M. *Medieval Arabic and Hebrew Thought* , ed. F. Zimmermann, London, 1983.

Stern, S.M., Hourani, H. and Brown, V. (eds.), *Islamic Philosophy and the Classical Tradition*. Oxford, 1972.

Waines, David. *An Introduction to Islam.* Cambridge, UK: Cambridge University Press, 1995.

Watt, M.W. Islamic Philosophy and Theology. Edinburgh, 1962, revised ed. 1985.

Watt, William Montgomery. *The Formative Period of Islamic Thought.* Oxford, UK: Oneworld,1998.

Watt, William Montgomery. *What is Islam?* London: Longman, 1970.

Williams, John Alden, ed. *The Word of Islam.* Austin, TX: University of Texas Press, 1994.

Wolfson, H.A. *Studies in the History of Philosophy and Religion* , ed. I. Twersky, G.H. Williams, in 2 vols. Cambridge, MA, 1973, 1977.

Wolfson, H.A. *The Philosophy of the Kalam.* Cambridge, MA, 1976.

Ziai, H. "Islamic Philosophy," in *The Oxford Companion to Philosophy,* ed. T. Honderich. Oxford , 1955.

Index

A

Abbasids, 11, 13, 14, 28, 76, 107.
Age of Discovery, 80.
Agricultural Revolution, 81, 82.
Arabesques, 104, 117, 134, 139.
Arabic Identity, 19.
Architecture, 38, 45, 97, 119, 120, 140.
Astronomy, 88, 89, 96, 120, 121, 123, 201.
Ayyubids, 28, 108, 109, 138.

B

Battle of Badr, 4, 5.
Battle of the Trench, 5.
Battle of Uhud, 5.

C

Calligraphy, 94, 104, 113, 117, 140.
Carpet Fit for a Shah, 133.
Colonial Period, 32.
Conquest of Mecca, 6.

E

Empire of Faith and Obedience, 145.
Ethics, 172, 177, 181.

F

Faith in Prophets, 207.
Faith in the Unknown, 233.
Fall of the Abbasids, 13.
Fasting, 62, 72, 225, 226, 229, 233.
Fatimids, 13, 14, 28, 76, 108.
Finality of Prophethood, 188.

G

Golden Age, 11, 75, 82, 87, 88, 92, 100, 101, 106, 107, 108.

H

Heap of Stones, 172.

I

Industrial Growth, 84.
Islamic Art, 103, 104, 105, 116, 140, 143.

Islamic Castle, 136.
Islamic Science, 86, 121, 123.
Italian Portrait, 139.

J

Jihad, 238, 254, 255, 266, 267, 274, 279, 280, 281, 282.

L

Labour, 82, 84, 85.
Late Empires, 111, 112.
Late Medieval Period, 110.
Life after Death, 147, 148, 151, 152, 162, 163, 215, 216, 217, 218, 221, 224, 225.

M

Market Economy, 82.
Mathematical jewel, 124.
Medieval Dynasties, 108, 109.
Moderate Islam, 235, 243, 264, 265, 266, 267, 268, 269, 270, 273, 277, 278, 279, 281.
Mongolian Invasion, 100.
Mongols and Mamluks, 110.
Mosque Pulpit, 118.
Musicians and Poets, 129.

O

Object in Exchange, 135.

P

Pan-Arabism, 21, 22.
Peer review, 80, 87, 88.
Polymaths, 80.

Q

Quran for Ramadan, 119.

R

Rational Vindication, 167, 214.
Rejecting Moderate Islam, 272.
Revolution Comes, 173.

S

Saviour Born, 171.

T

Tale of Romance, 131.
Tasawwuf, 9, 64, 232, 233.
The Abyss of Darkness, 169.
The Crusades, 80, 100, 121, 136.
The Hijra, 4.
The Mongols, 14, 15, 101, 102.
Three Mosques, 116.

U

Unity of Allah, 192.
Urbanization, 86.

V

Velvets, 141, 142.

Z

Zakat, 180, 226, 227.